PIPE FITTINGS

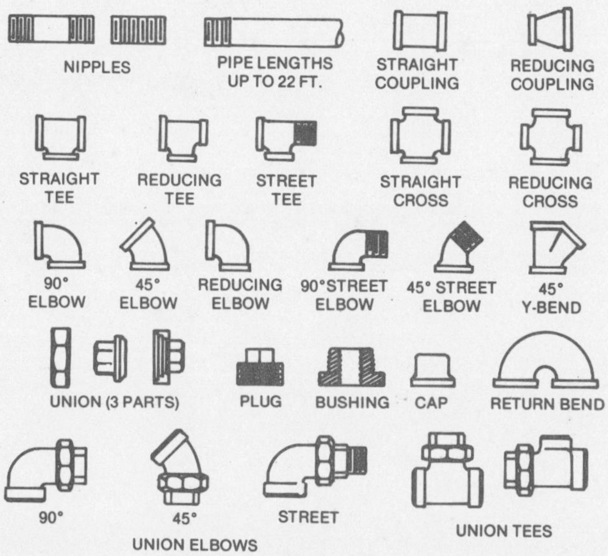

Here are the common steel pipe fittings. Nipples are simply short lengths of pipe threaded on both ends. Reducing fittings join two different sizes of pipe.

Compression fittings of the flared-tube type are the easiest for the novice to handle when working with copper tubing.

STANDARD STEEL PIPE (All Dimensions in Inches)					
Nominal Size	Outside Diameter	Inside Diameter	Nominal Size	Outside Diameter	Inside Diameter
1/8	0.405	0.269	1	1.315	1.049
1/4	0.540	0.364	1 1/4	1.660	1.380
3/8	0.675	0.493	1 1/2	1.900	1.610
1/2	0.840	0.622	2	2.375	2.067
3/4	1.050	0.824	2 1/2	2.875	2.469

SQUARE MEASURE

144 sq in = 1 sq ft
9 sq ft = 1 sq yd
272.25 sq ft = 1 sq rod
160 sq rods = 1 acre

VOLUME MEASURE

1728 cu in = 1 cu ft
27 cu ft = 1 cu yd

MEASURES OF CAPACITY

1 cup = 8 fl oz
2 cups = 1 pint
2 pints = 1 quart
4 quarts = 1 gallon
2 gallons = 1 peck
4 pecks = 1 bushel

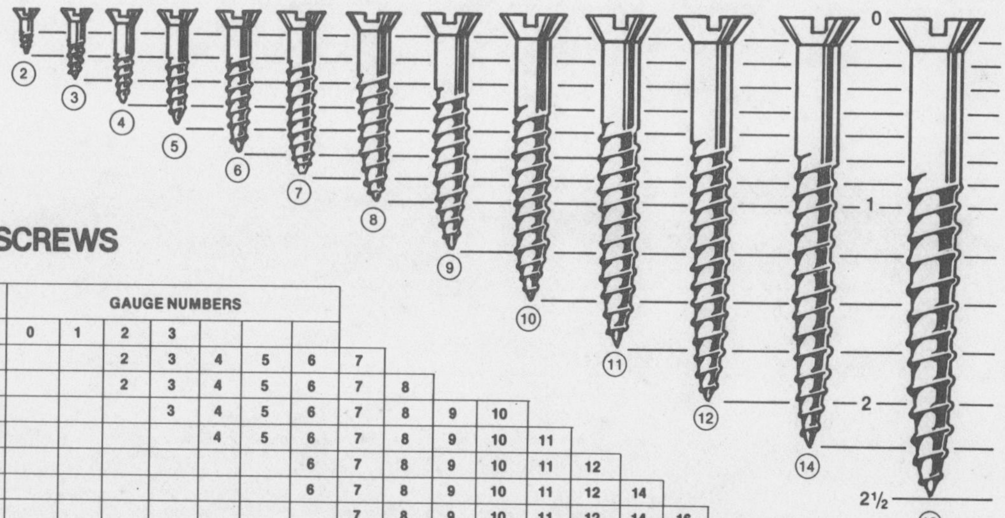

WOOD SCREWS

LENGTH	GAUGE NUMBERS																
1/4 INCH	0	1	2	3													
3/8 INCH			2	3	4	5	6	7									
1/2 INCH			2	3	4	5	6	7	8								
5/8 INCH				3	4	5	6	7	8	9	10						
3/4 INCH					4	5	6	7	8	9	10	11					
7/8 INCH							6	7	8	9	10	11	12				
1 INCH							6	7	8	9	10	11	12	14			
1 1/4 INCH								7	8	9	10	11	12	14	16		
1 1/2 INCH							6	7	8	9	10	11	12	14	16	18	
1 3/4 INCH									8	9	10	11	12	14	16	18	20
2 INCH									8	9	10	11	12	14	16	18	20
2 1/4 INCH										9	10	11	12	14	16	18	20
2 1/2 INCH													12	14	16	18	20
2 3/4 INCH														14	16	18	20
3 INCH															16	18	20
3 1/2 INCH																18	20	24
4 INCH																18	20	24

WHEN YOU BUY SCREWS, SPECIFY (1) LENGTH, (2) GAUGE NUMBER, (3) TYPE OF HEAD—FLAT, ROUND, OR OVAL, (4) MATERIAL—STEEL, BRASS, BRONZE, ETC., (5) FINISH—BRIGHT, STEEL BLUED, CADMIUM, NICKEL, OR CHROMIUM PLATED.

SPECIAL COMPARTMENTS in this catchall closet for sportsmen hold all the gear that doesn't seem at home anywhere else. The tall section even holds skis. For details, see page 2794.

In this volume . . .

HERE'S ANOTHER great storage idea—a train board that slides under the bed. Equipment goes in a cupboard that forms the headboard. See the big section on storage ideas, page 2794.

A DIVING DECK for your pool not only offers a splashing good time, but also a place to store the filter, yard equipment and bicycles. See page 2832. →

THE TWO-SEAT LAWN SWING of yesteryear is making a comeback, and here's a cheerful version that would enhance any lawn. See complete plans on page 2836.

THIS BUILT-IN is truly multipurpose—a room divider, storage wall, hi-fi center and worktable all in one. A counter adds workspace. See the article starting on page 2794.

BUILD THIS HANDSOME COUCH and get a double bed, too! The lower flap door conceals a trundle bed that matches the couch in height. See page 2726.

Popular Mechanics

do-it-yourself encyclopedia

in 20 volumes

a complete how-to guide for the homeowner, the hobbyist—
and anyone who enjoys working with mind and hands!

All about:

home maintenance
home-improvement projects
wall paneling
burglary and fire protection
furniture projects
finishing and refinishing furniture
outdoor living
home remodeling
solutions to home problems
challenging woodworking projects
hobbies and handicrafts
model making
weekend projects
workshop shortcuts and techniques
hand-tool skills
power-tool know-how
shop-made tools
car repairs
car maintenance
appliance repair
boating
hunting
fishing
camping
photography projects
radio, TV and electronics know-how
clever hints and tips
projects just for fun

volume 18

ISBN 0-87851-083-4
Library of Congress Catalog Number 77 84920

MANUFACTURED IN THE UNITED STATES OF AMERICA

contents

VOLUME 18

Clear your drive the easy way

By FRANK M. BUTRICK

PLOW IS attached to the vehicle by chains wrapped around bumper, then hooked over the projecting nailhead.

SEE ALSO
Asphalt driveways . . . Snow-melting systems . . . Snowblowers . . . Tractor lifts

■ WITH EACH PASSING year I've noticed that the snow is getting heavier. So during a recent winter, I did something about my long driveway—which seemed almost endless after a heavy snowfall.

I made a snowplow—at a cost of only $11.93 and four hours' work with hand tools. Since it weighs only 90 lbs., I built it in my basement and then dragged it up the stairs. I don't claim it will do everything that a $300 unit will—you have to get out to lift the blade after each run. And it will ride on top of hard ice or frozen snow, rather than scrape it. But that's small inconvenience for the $288 price difference.

Design yours to suit your vehicle. The one shown fits the rear bumper of a Scout. Or the plow can be scaled down for use on a family car equipped with studded snow tires or chains.

A primary consideration is providing the means for attaching a chain (or mounting): a sturdy luggage rack, trunk opening, trunk

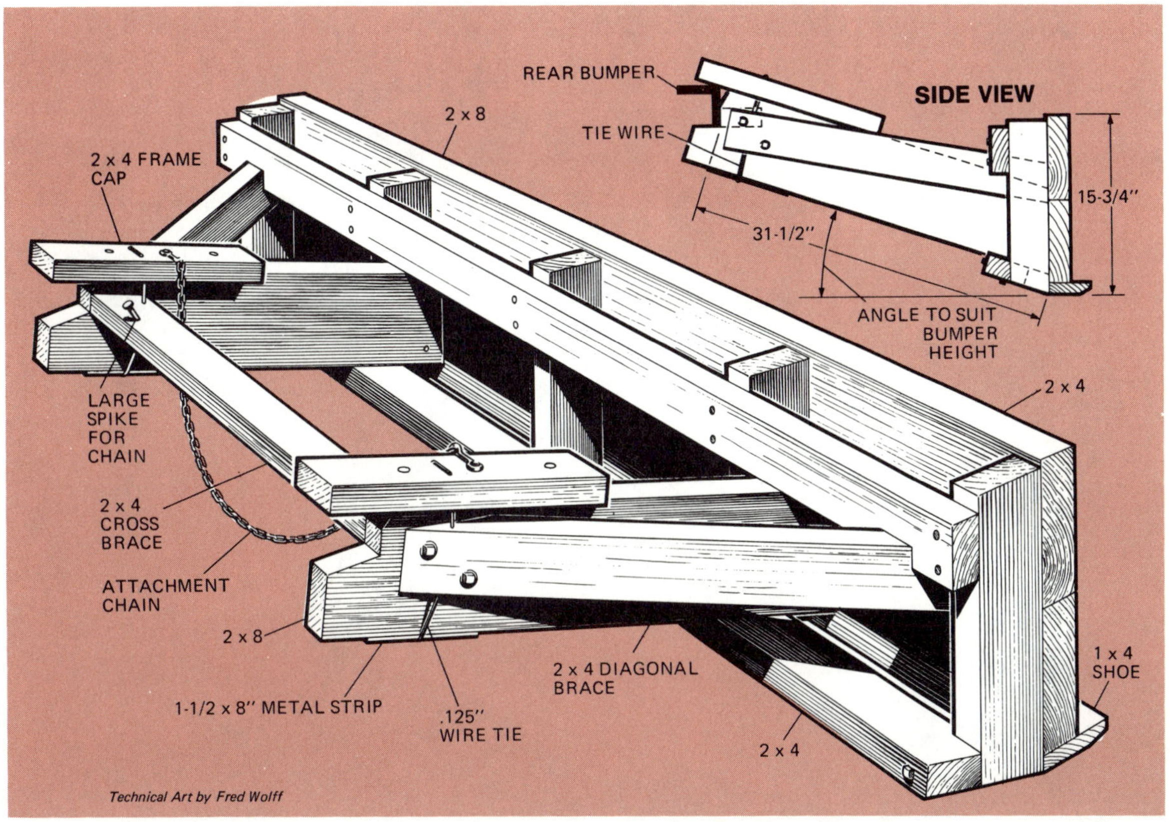

handle, or—on the front end—a loop of heavy wire fastened to the radiator support and arranged to project when the hood is closed. The suspended weight is only 65 lbs., so the selection is more convenience than engineering.

Make a full-sized sketch of the side of the plow, showing your bumper cross section the proper distance from the ground. Lay out the plow face and the angle of the frame and draw the bumper notch, remembering that the plow must have good bearing on your bumper when down, and must not bind when you lift it. Leave heavy stock below the bumper, and use a separate frame cap to support the raised bumper end of the frame.

Lay out the frames and saw them. Space the frames to suit your bumper supports, trailer hitch, or any place that will take the thrust. Nail the vertical ribs to the 2x8s of the plow face, letting the ribs project ⅝ in. below the lower 2x8 to back up the 1x4 shoe. Then nail the frames to the proper ribs, leaving enough space below the frames for the lower stiffener. It is notched to provide good bearing against the ribs to which they are nailed as well as to the frames. A 2x4 is cut to fit between the frames at their bumper end and nailed in place, using two small nails to avoid splitting. Cut and fit the diagonal braces and nail them in place. The upper stiffener rests on the frames and is notched to fit the diagonals.

The joint where the frames, crosspiece, and diagonals meet is nailed sparingly (to prevent splitting the lumber). For reinforcing, force a heavy wire through drilled holes, wedge and twist it tight, and nail down the sharp ends.

Consider the shoe as expendable. In my rough driveway I expect it to last, at the most, one or two seasons. Thus, make it from any inexpensive wood. I used a length of 1x4 furring and beveled it to ride over broken concrete. If your drive has a smooth tie-in with the street, you can probably leave the edge square.

A heavy dog chain provides the attachment and lift chains. Decide where the attaching chain can pass around your bumper and provide some lateral control. The lift chain is 3 ft. long and has a heavy ring at one end and a hook at the other.

Using my plow with the Scout, I have moved hundreds of pounds of loose, broken-up ice and plowed through two-ft.-high snowdrifts.

Build your own sofa-bed

■ THIS GUEST BED that doubles as a sofa is basically a couch built around a purchased high-rise (pop-up) trundle-bed frame.

SEE ALSO

**Armchairs . . . Bed tables . . . Beds . . .
Butcher block furniture . . . Children's furniture . . .
Family rooms . . .Stools . . . Upholstery**

LOWER FLAP DOOR conceals a high-rise trundle bed and lifts for access to it. The lower bed snaps up to the same height as the upper bed.

The inner frame is built first, assembled with 2½-in. No. 10 flathead screws and reinforced with 3-in. corner braces. The crosspiece should be offset about 1-in. from center to allow for carriage bolts that will attach the back of the outer frame.

Web the completed inner frame next and staple No. 40 muslin on top of the webbing.

MATTRESSES butt together at the same level to provide for a full double-bed width. The unit also offers option of being made up and used as two beds.

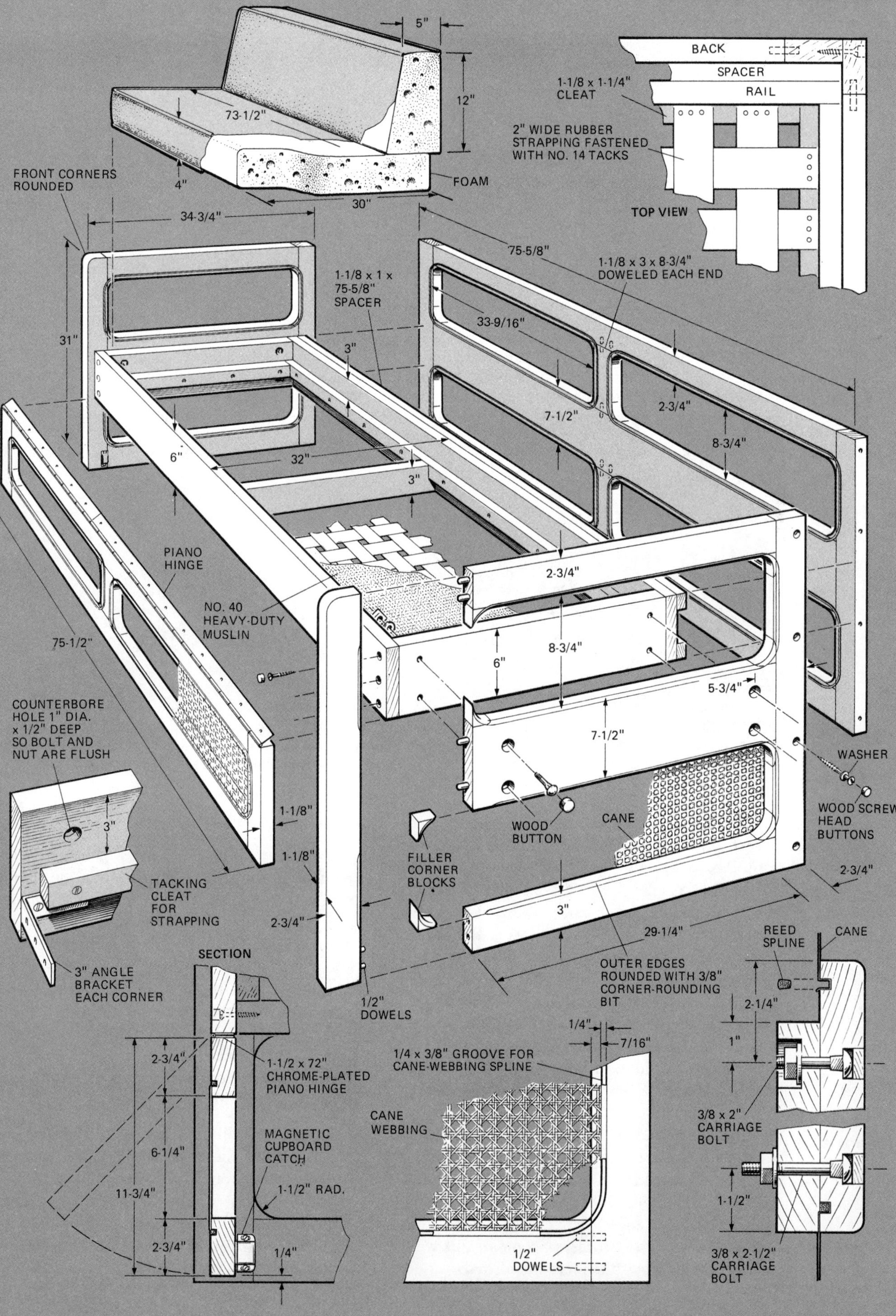
5"
12"
73-1/2"
4"
30"
FOAM
FRONT CORNERS ROUNDED
34-3/4"
BACK
SPACER
RAIL
1-1/8 x 1-1/4" CLEAT
2" WIDE RUBBER STRAPPING FASTENED WITH NO. 14 TACKS
TOP VIEW
75-5/8"
1-1/8 x 3 x 8-3/4" DOWELED EACH END
1-1/8 x 1 x 75-5/8" SPACER
33-9/16"
31"
3"
7-1/2"
2-3/4"
8-3/4"
6"
32"
3"
PIANO HINGE
NO. 40 HEAVY-DUTY MUSLIN
2-3/4"
75-1/2"
6"
8-3/4"
5-3/4"
7-1/2"
COUNTERBORE HOLE 1" DIA. x 1/2" DEEP SO BOLT AND NUT ARE FLUSH
3"
1-1/8"
1-1/8"
WASHER
WOOD SCREW-HEAD BUTTONS
WOOD BUTTON
CANE
FILLER CORNER BLOCKS
TACKING CLEAT FOR STRAPPING
2-3/4"
2-3/4"
3"
29-1/4"
3" ANGLE BRACKET EACH CORNER
SECTION
1/2" DOWELS
OUTER EDGES ROUNDED WITH 3/8" CORNER-ROUNDING BIT
REED SPLINE
CANE
2-1/4"
1"
2-3/4"
1-1/2 x 72" CHROME-PLATED PIANO HINGE
6-1/4"
11-3/4"
MAGNETIC CUPBOARD CATCH
1-1/2" RAD.
2-3/4"
1/4"
1/4"
7/16"
1/4 x 3/8" GROOVE FOR CANE-WEBBING SPLINE
CANE WEBBING
1/2" DOWELS
3/8 x 2" CARRIAGE BOLT
1-1/2"
3/8 x 2-1/2" CARRIAGE BOLT

DRUM SANDER attachment in a drill press or a portable electric drill is used to finish off the inside corner blocks after they're glued in place.

ROUT a continuous ¼x¼-in. groove spaced 7/16 in. from each inside opening. For a good job, use an edge guide that helps you follow inside curves.

DRIVE REED SPLINE into the glued groove with mallet and wedge while cane is wet, taking care to maintain proper alignment of the cane pattern.

TRIM OFF the excess with a razor knife when glue in groove has dried and cane is taut. A liberal allowance of excess cane makes the installation easier.

For the outer frame, cut stiles and rails as shown on the plan, then dowel, glue and clamp all joints to assemble each side of the frame and the back. To make the 40 curved filler blocks for the inside corners, rip a 5/4 board to 4-in. width and draw 10 4-in.-dia. circles just a kerf-width apart on it with a compass. Saw the board apart between the circles, then use a jigsaw or sabre saw to cut out circles. "Waste" around each circle will yield four corner blocks curved to a 2-in. radius. You can cut the circles in half and use these scrap pieces to clamp the glued-in blocks without marring them.

After the frame sides and back have been assembled and sanded, knock down the outward-facing edges of openings with a ⅜-in. rounding-over bit in a router. On opposite sides, rout a ¼x¼-in. continuous groove around each opening, 7/16 in. from its edge. Use an edge guide to follow the curves of the corners—some of this work will be visible when the piece is finished.

installing cane and splines

Paint or varnish the frames. (The cane can be painted or varnished after installation, but varnish will darken it.) When the finish is completely dry, cut pieces of machine-woven (prewoven or "pressed") cane to fit the openings. Soak cane and reed splines in warm water for about two hours to soften them. Dribble a bead of white glue into the groove around the opening, carefully align the wet cane on it, then hammer in the spline with a mallet and a hardwood wedge. Hang flap door on the front of the unit to complete basic assembly.

Sources: You'll need to find a bed retailer willing to sell just the lower frame. An upholsterers' supply shop should carry webbing and muslin (foam, too), but if cane is hard to find locally, write to the Veterans' Caning Shop, 550 West 35th St., New York, NY 10001, for mail-order prices.

Facing vapor barrier

I plan to install wood paneling in a room in my basement; it will go over furring strips attached to a poured concrete wall. There will be insulation between the furring strips, but I have conflicting information on which way to face the vapor barrier—toward the wall or the room?—Dale Edmonson, Des Moines, Iowa.

The vapor barrier should always be on the room side, as it will then tend to prevent formation of condensate on the concrete wall, especially on the lower third of the wall, which is usually at a lower temperature than room air during warmer months. When installing the furring strips, make sure they are correctly spaced and firmly attached to the wall; the best method, I think, is to attach the strips with screws turned into expansive lead anchors.

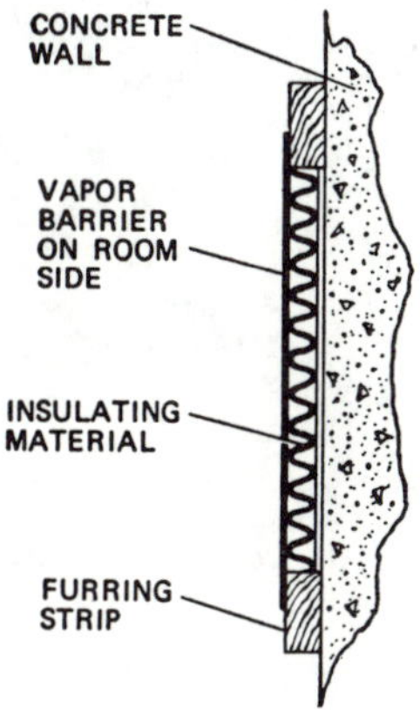

Cracked brickwork

I have a crack in the seven courses of brick above the opening in my fireplace. The crack, which runs vertically through both bricks and joints, is hardly noticeable when the masonry is cold but it opens somewhat when the bricks are warmed by the fire. What can you suggest?—Dale Hurd, Springfield, Mo.

This defect has no simple solution. I'd hesitate to suggest any type of caulking or filler; because of the opening and closing of the crack, the filling is almost certain to break away. You or a mason could repoint the joints with mortar, but you would face the same objectionable possibilities. Opening and closing of the crack is most likely caused by a condition of stress built in at the time of construction.

I hesitate to say this because of cost, but I feel that the only permanent repair is to have the brickwork broken out and replaced by a mason. It's not a do-it-yourself job unless you have had plenty of experience with this kind of work.

Condensation again

In the outside entrance of my basement drops of water are on the concrete-block wall from the floor to 2 feet or more up. Water is also on the entry floor. How do I locate this leak? There seems to be no crack.—Eldred Ames, Terre Haute, Ind.

What you see is condensate forming on the surfaces of the blocks because those near the floor are at a lower temperature than the air that contacts them. If you leave the entryway door open, the condition may correct itself. Otherwise, there is little you can do to prevent it. Actually, it does little harm.

Let them age

I've just had new galvanized gutters and downspouts installed and I'm wondering what paint, or paints, I should use. Can you suggest proper paints and procedures?—John Clement, Tulsa, Okla.

I wouldn't paint those new gutters, either inside or out, for at least six months, preferably a year. It's better to let them "season" for this length of time, letting the weather remove all fingerprints and the acids at soldered joints, and roughen the galvanizing slightly to provide a "tooth" for paint. Then use a metal primer as a first coat; follow with one or two coats of paint matching the house color.

Dingy floor

My oak floors are beginning to show signs of wear. The finish is still there but they look a bit dingy, especially in the more heavily traveled areas. I don't want to refinish them entirely if I can avoid it. How can I brighten them up a bit?—P.R., Colo.

Offhand, it's difficult to say what is *the* one best procedure, except that I would not use a mop or scrub brush. It might be permissible to wipe the floors with a damp cloth well wrung out in water to which a pinch of detergent has been added, but it won't do to wet the floors as you would in mopping or scrubbing. Wiping in this fashion will remove most of the accumulated dirt which probably accounts for most of the discoloration. After wiping in this manner go over the floors with a cloth wrung out in clean water to remove any detergent residues. There also are floor cleaners with a wax base that are quite effective at cleaning and brightening up worn and dingy hardwood floors, *if* the instructions on the container are followed in detail. Other than sanding and refinishing these are about the only steps to be taken and, of course, can be considered only temporary.

A guide to solar energy

You can get collectors, evacuated tubes and concentrators for hot air or water heating. This survey tells what the different solar systems have to offer

By VICTOR D. CHASE

■ IN MANY supposedly primitive societies, homes were built to take maximum advantage of the warmth of sunlight and the coolness of the night. Until recently, this common-sense approach to energy use was all but forgotten in the modern world where fuel seemed abundant and limitless.

But things are changing. As we discover that fuel is not quite as abundant as we supposed or as cheap as we have come to expect, we are also finding good reason to use nature's own thermostat.

The most obvious sign of this increased awareness is the number of solar collectors popping up on the roofs of all types of buildings in all parts of the country. This trend is here to stay and will continue until the sight of solar collectors and photovoltaic cells will be no more unusual than the ever present television antenna.

two solar systems

Today, the state of the art of solar energy breaks down into two broad categories: active and passive. Passive solar systems use energy from the sun much as earlier societies did in their structures—by getting maximum use of the sun as it strikes a building. Passive measures include the positioning of the building on the site, materials used, design, insulation and placement of glazing.

Active solar systems, on the other hand, are the ones we usually think of when we hear the term "solar energy." They use hardware to convert and transport heat. But an active solar system does not work to capacity without support from passive techniques as well. P. Richard Rittelmann, a leading solar architect and a principal in the firm of Burt, Hill & Associates, Butler, Pa., says, "You conserve energy first, and produce energy second."

site selection

Site orientation is important. The long sides of the building should face north and south, with most of the glass toward the south. In most parts of the country, the prevailing winds are from the west, hence a shorter west wall cuts infiltration from those wintry blasts. Even more important is the effect of the sun. The west wall also picks up the greatest heat gain in the summer, so the reduction of this area has benefits the year around.

During the winter, the sun travels from east to west low in the southern sky. Windows facing south tend to act as passive solar collectors picking up a great deal of the sun's heat.

"If the same building is to be air-conditioned," Rittelmann notes, "the summer sun angle is extremely high so you can exclude it from those windows with overhangs." With an active system, a long south wall has the added advantage of presenting a large roof area properly oriented for solar collectors.

active systems

These systems are used to provide domestic hot water and space heating. Given the rapidly rising costs of fossil fuel, solar domestic water and space heating is now cost-effective in many parts of the country. But solar-powered airconditioning is still too expensive to be practical.

Most active solar systems in homes or large-scale commercial buildings have four basic elements:

- They use a collecting device to gather the heat from sunlight.
- They have a storage system to accumulate the heat for nighttime and cloudy-day use.
- They have a delivery system to bring the heat to the spaces to be conditioned.
- They have a backup system for days when there is not enough sunlight or stored heat to do the job.

the solar collector

The purpose of a collector is to gather sunlight (radiant energy) and convert it to heat (thermal energy). Either air or liquid is circulated through a collector to pick up the heat and carry it to its destination.

There are three general types: flat plate, evacuated tube and concentrating collector. The last two are used primarily for high-temperature systems that can include airconditioning. Flat-plate collectors are by far the most common type used, both for residential domestic hot-water and space-heating installations.

The heart of a flat-plate collector is an absorber plate made of metal (copper, aluminum, stainless steel) which has tubing that is either bonded to it or an integral part of it. Heat transfer fluid passes through this tubing. The plate is enclosed in a sealed frame and is painted flat black or covered with a material that retains heat.

SEE ALSO

Boilers . . . Energy, saving . . . Furnaces . . . Heat pumps . . . Heating systems, home . . . Heating systems, solar . . . Solar water heaters . . . Stoves, wood-burning . . . Winterizing, homes

The back of the absorber plate rests against a layer of insulation. An air space over the surface faces the sun, covered by one or two layers of glazing (glass or a type of plastic).

Collectors should be oriented to the south, but the fall-off in performance as you vary from due south is not that great. You can vary the collectors' angle from 20° east to 45° west of due south with only a 6 or 7-percent drop in performance, a feature that opens up many design options.

Although a good flat-plate collector can get up to 200° F. for residential space heating and domestic hot-water systems, there is no reason to go above about 140° F. While it would seem the higher the temperature the better the performance of the solar system, in the case of flat-plate collectors the reverse is true.

keep it cool

"We design a heating system to use the lowest temperature it reasonably can, since flat-plate collectors operate more efficiently at lower temperatures," Rittelmann explains.

The higher the temperature of the collector, the greater the temperature difference between collector and outside air. A big temperature difference means more heat lost to the outside air. Yet the greater the heat loss to the outside air, the slower the transfer fluid must flow through the collector to absorb the same amount of heat.

freeze protection

When liquid is used, it is generally either water or an antifreeze solution. With water, the danger of freeze-ups exists in most parts of the country, and some drain-down technique must be built into the system to prevent freeze damage to the collectors. Many systems are designed to drain automatically when the circulating pump shuts off.

The antifreeze alternative presents its own problems. First a heat exchanger must be incorporated into the system to transfer heat from the antifreeze circulating through the collectors to the large water storage tank most frequently used. Due to the high cost of antifreeze, it is economically prohibitive to fill the storage tank (about 1000 gallons for a residential space-heating system) with this liquid. But a heat exchanger reduces the efficiency of the system because some energy is lost in the transfer process.

Another problem is that many antifreeze solutions are toxic and some parts of the country have codes (for good reason) against using toxic substances on the heat supply side and potable water on the hot water supply side of single solar water systems. Also, be it water or antifreeze, liquid collectors can develop leaks.

a lot of hot air

Air collectors, on the other hand, tend to be simpler and less risky, with a lower initial cost.

On the negative side, air is not as good a heat transfer medium as water. As a result, the collectors are slightly less efficient, and so is the storage. While in most water systems the heat is stored in water, in most air systems rocks are commonly used for heat storage.

Unfortunately, stone has about one-fifth the heat storage capacity per pound as does water. Thus, three to five times more space is needed for air-system heat storage than for liquid. Stones used must be thoroughly cleaned and air going to the collectors must be filtered.

distribution systems

The most basic active solar system is a domestic water heater piped to a set of collectors. But the heater should include a conventional heating mechanism to supplement the solar system.

The next step up the ladder includes solar space heating. The most direct way is to route solar-heated water from a collector array through a coil placed in the return air duct of a conventionally fired furnace. Or, in the case of an air system, warm air can be introduced directly from the collectors into the return air duct. Either way, a standard furnace blower distributes heat throughout the building.

Fan coil units are used in larger buildings where individual room temperature control is desirable. Here, the hot water is piped directly to the rooms to be heated. Each room has a fan which blows air over a set of coils through which hot water passes.

combined systems

In most solar space-heating installations, a domestic water heating device is also included. In some cases, a heat exchanger leading from the conventional domestic hot water tank is immersed in the solar water storage tank. In others, the heat exchanger is immersed directly in the domestic hot water tank.

With air systems, the heat exchanger is placed in the path of the hot air coming off the collectors. Sometimes, the hot-water tank itself is used as a heat exchanger and buried in the rock storage pile to absorb heat directly from it.

Combined systems can reasonably be expected

TWELVE ROWS of collectors totaling 10,000 sq. ft. constitute one of the world's largest liquid-system installations atop an elementary school in Atlanta, GA. The 576 PPG flat-plate units handle more than 60 percent of the heating and cooling load.

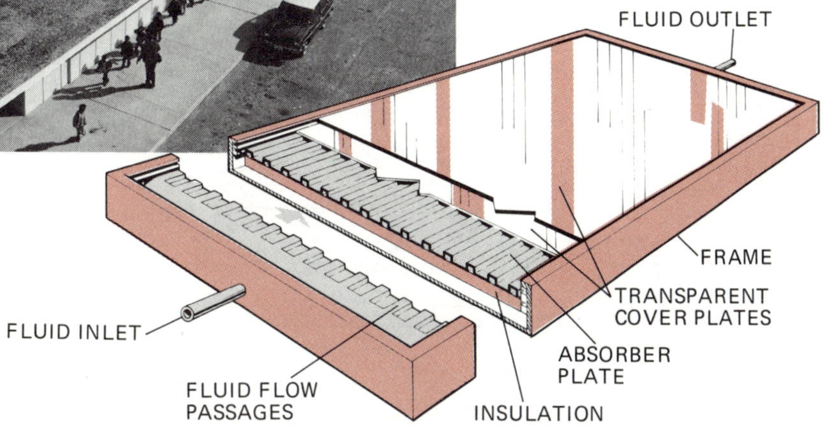

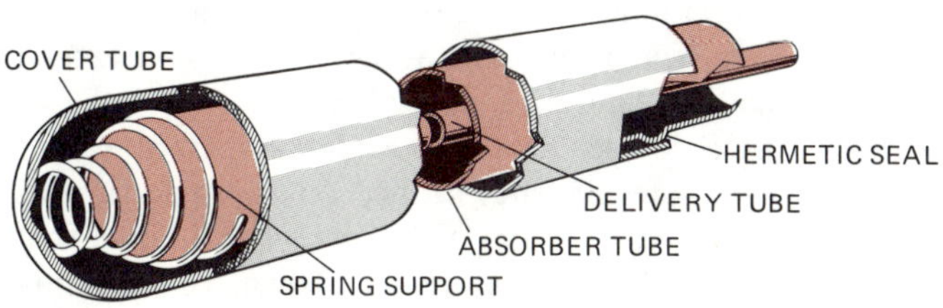

EVACUATED TUBULAR COLLECTOR

EACH UNIT is this townhouse group in the Chicago area uses heat-pump-assisted solar energy for 60 percent of space heating and hot water. Owens-Illinois evacuated tube collectors use liquid to transfer heat.

CONCENTRATORS and vacuum tubes above develop temperatures of 180° F. and up. Northrup unit at right shows prismatic Fresnel lens that focuses sunlight on the copper absorber tube. A tracking device keeps the unit toward the sun.

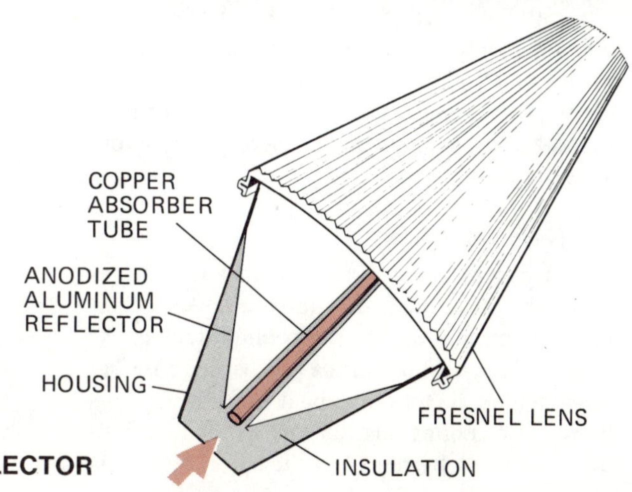

CONCENTRATING COLLECTOR

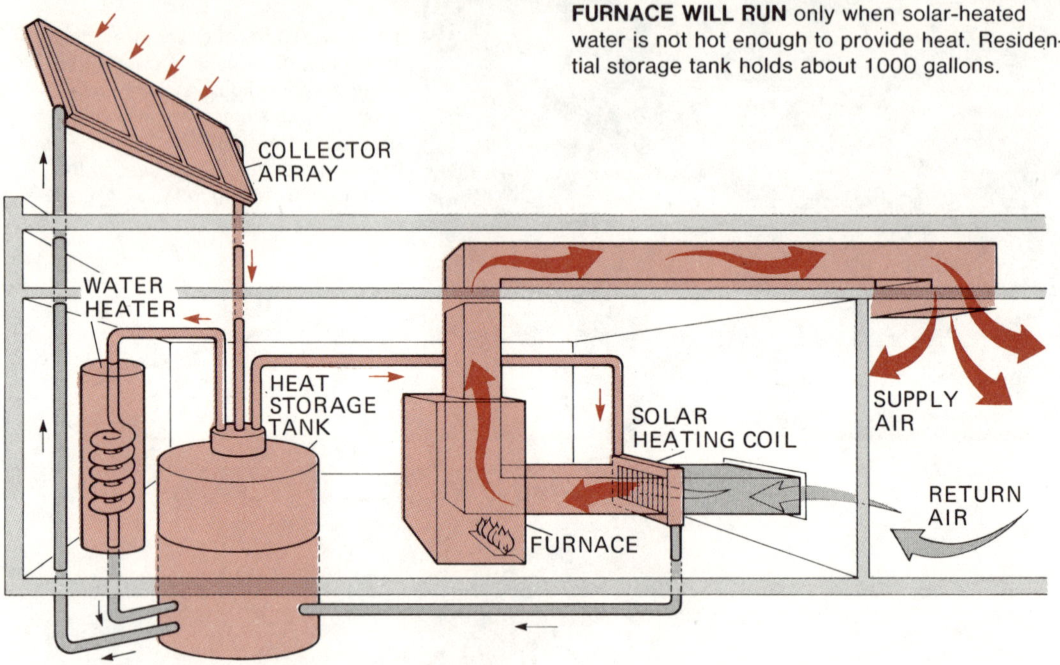

SOLAR LIQUID SYSTEM

FURNACE WILL RUN only when solar-heated water is not hot enough to provide heat. Residential storage tank holds about 1000 gallons.

to provide 50 to 60 percent of space heat and 80 to 85 percent of hot water for a family living in a typical single-family house. Initial cost for such a system can range from $6000 to about $12,000.

The major portion of this cost is tied up in collectors. Flat-plate collectors can run between $6 and $15 per square foot. The amount needed depends on the home's location, construction and size. But as a rule of thumb you can figure that for space heating and hot water the amount of collector needed will equal one-third to one-half the floor space of your home. A 2000-square-foot home could, therefore, require some 700 square feet of collectors. At $10 per square foot, the collectors would run $7000.

Technically, it is feasible to provide 100 percent of all heating needs with solar energy, but in most parts of the country the amount of collector area and storage needed for such a system would not be practical. Therefore, a backup system is almost always used, the most common being a forced-air furnace. Becoming increasingly popular is the heat pump.

heat-pump assistance

Heat pumps are not only making themselves felt in the solar field; they're coming into their own as conventional heating-cooling devices.

Basically, a heat pump is a reversible refrigeration machine. It can pump heat from the indoors outside for cooling just as any other airconditioner does, but by reversing the cycle during the winter, it can draw heat from the outside and deposit it indoors. Surprisingly, cold winter air does have heat in it, and the heat pump can extract that heat and make it usable.

Of course, as the outside temperature goes down, the efficiency of the heat pump declines as well. Compounding the problem is the fact that as outside temperature goes down, your heating load goes up. In conventional operation, when a heat pump can't handle the load by extracting enough heat from the outside air, supplemental electric resistance-heating coils built into the pump come to the rescue.

The efficiency of a heat pump is measured in its coefficient of performance (COP). COP is the amount of energy put out by the pump divided by the amount of energy put into it. If the heat pump is pulling 12,000 B.T.U.s of electrical energy and putting out 36,000 B.T.U.s of heat, the COP is three.

That means money saved. If your heat pump averages a COP of three, your electric bill will be one-third that if you used conventional electric resistance heating only. Unfortunately, as a practical matter, today's heat pumps run an annual COP average of 1.5 to 2.

But this is where solar energy can pay off. If the heat pump can be made to draw B.T.U.'s from a solar system during the cold days of winter instead of from the frigid outside air, then its COP goes up, and conventional energy consumption comes down. One method brings the

SOLAR AIR SYSTEM

A 1500-SQ.-FT. HOUSE needs about 125 cu. ft. of washed rock for heat storage. When sunlight is not available, return air is blown through the rock box for reheating.

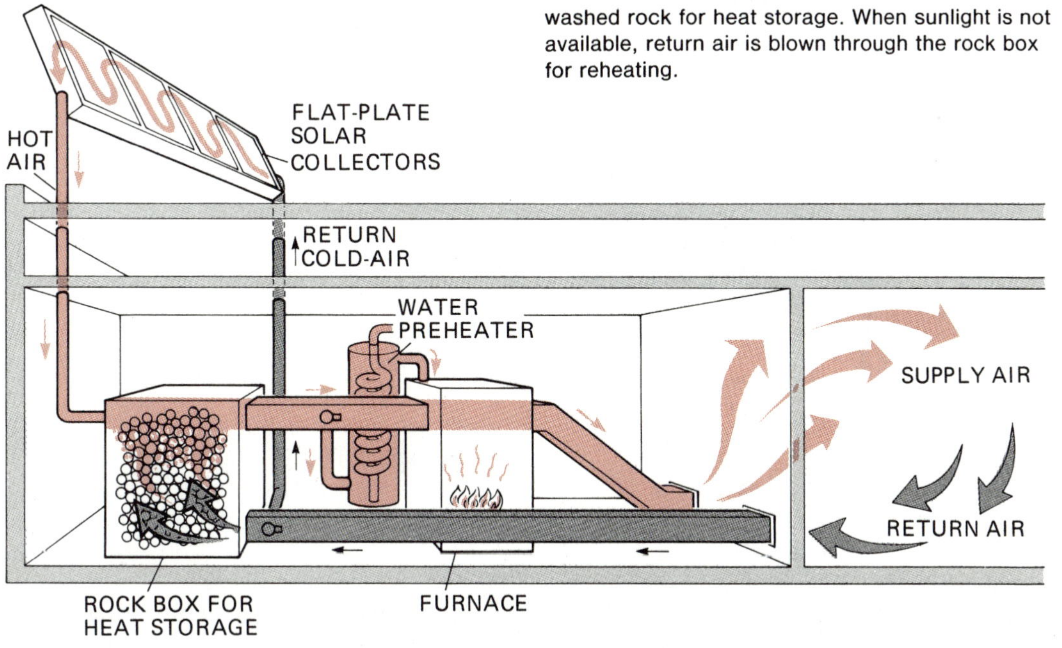

outside condenser coil inside. On cold days, solar-heated water is run through a heat exchanger near the coil unit causing it to operate as though it were removing heat from warm outside air. A duct system allows this coil to draw on outside air when the solar-heated water is not hot enough, as well as during the cooling season.

Other solar-assisted systems use water-to-water heat pumps. Whereas conventional heat pumps are air-to-air, this system allows the pump to draw directly from the solar storage tank.

solar airconditioning

While solar heating is coming of age, the use of solar energy for airconditioning is still in its infancy, but growing fast. Most units are in commercial buildings.

In solar airconditioning, an absorption chiller is used to convert hot to cold by evaporation. The more rapidly it takes place, the cooler you feel—the reason alcohol, for example, feels cool on the skin as it evaporates rapidly.

To operate effectively, absorption chillers need solar-heated water about 200° F. Such installations use high-temperature evacuated tube or concentrating collectors.

Evacuated tube collectors have a vacuum inside and a center pipe through which water flows. The vacuum causes the collector to act like a Thermos bottle and retain heat up to 600° F. Because of its shape, a tubular collector does not expose much of its surface to the sun and is, therefore, not as efficient when used in low-temperature operations.

Another way to go for high levels of heat from sunlight is to use concentrating collectors. These are shaped (generally in a U-type configuration) to concentrate sunlight onto a small area with lenses over the top of the collectors. They need direct sunlight to operate effectively, which means they must have tracking mechanisms to follow the sun across the sky. If you live where there is not much direct sunlight and therefore lower cooling loads, as in the Northeast, the use of concentrating collectors is hard to justify.

On the other hand, in the Southwest, where there is a lot of direct sunlight and a heavy cooling load, concentrating collectors reasonably can be used to drive absorption chillers.

Solar-powered airconditioning is still expensive. A residential-sized absorption chiller runs around $3000 for the equipment alone. Couple this cost with the need for a backup system, and it's not hard to see why solar airconditioning hasn't caught on yet.

electricity from light

Two methods of converting sunlight to electricity are now being developed. One is the central power station concept where mirrors, concentrating sunlight on boilers, produce steam to drive electric generators. To date, this has been prohibitively expensive.

The second method uses on-site conversion

CENTRAL PHOTOVOLTAIC solar power stations are under study by ERDA. Burt, Hill & Associates, Butler, PA, built this model and designed special machines to erect the system.

devices called photovoltaic cells. They use one of two materials: silicon crystals, of which sand (a truly abundant fuel source) is a major component, or cadmium sulfide. While the latter is somewhat less expensive than silicon, it is also less efficient, and even with silicon cells a 10-percent efficiency is considered high.

hot water kits

For the moment though, the largest application of solar energy is for domestic water heating. A number of kits on the market can be installed with existing conventionally fired hot-water systems. The able do-it-yourselfer can purchase such a kit for about $1000 to $1200, and install it himself. If you call in a plumber to do the hard work, your bill will be near $2000.

In the case of space heating, solar architect Rittelmann advises: "If there is enough sunlight and the only alternative is electricity at 5 to 6 cents a kilowatt-hour, or oil at 45 to 50 cents per gallon, some solar space-heating systems are competitive."

From the standpoint of climate, Rittelmann notes: "A space-heating system is more cost-effective in Chicago than in Miami." But even if solar heat is not competitive in your area now, it may be soon—as fuel costs go up and solar-equipment costs come down.

For this reason Rittelmann advises people now building homes to design for solar retrofitting later, if they are not going to install it now. This involves designing for minimum use of energy, providing space for thermal storage equipment (water tank or rock box), and presenting a reasonable southern roof area for collectors.

buyer beware

If you are planning to purchase a solar system in the near future—beware! As Rittelmann warns, "There are systems out today that are making claims that are simply not true. Some even claim they are more than 100-percent efficient."

check legislation

If you are planning to go solar, check local and national legislation. As of this writing, 12 states have enacted legislation providing property, sales or income tax breaks for homeowners installing solar equipment.

CLIMATE AREAS FOR THE HEATING SEASON

MEAN DAILY SOLAR RADIATION (LANGLEY)	HEATING DEGREE DAYS		
	0-2500	2500-5000	5000-9000
350-450	1	2	3
250-350	4	5	6
175-250	7	8	9

Chart shows relationship of heat load (degree days) and available solar energy (mean daily solar radiation). Areas that combine highest number of degree days with most langleys (units of solar radiation) will get most economical use from a solar system.

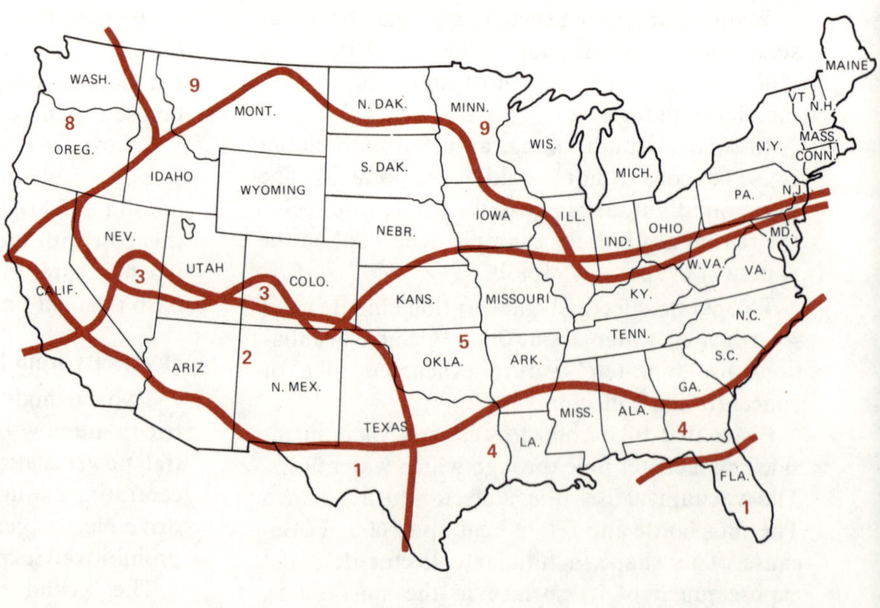

Where to go for solar help

The following sources can answer your questions regarding solar energy and ease your way toward going solar. The list is by no means all-inclusive. Since there is an overwhelming demand for solar information, it's best to check whether a publication is still available before sending money.

Information centers

Environmental Information Center, 935 Orange Ave., Winter Park, Fla. 32789; distributes literature on environmental issues, including solar use; publishes *Enfo Newsletter* (free) and two books: *Build Your Own Solar Water Heater* ($3) and *Solar Heating for Swimming Pools* ($4.50).

National Solar Heating and Cooling Information Center, Box 1607, Rockville, Md. 20850, (800) 523-2929; in Pennsylvania, (800) 462-4983; in Alaska and Hawaii, (800) 523-4700. Center answers questions about solar heating and cooling. It also distributes a range of solar publications; the list is available by requesting *A Reading List for Solar Energy* (Periodicals bibliography, DC 107). The center maintains lists of solar professionals, manufacturers of solar equipment.

Solar Energy Institute of America, 1110 Sixth St. N.W., Washington, D.C. 20001; publishes a newsletter, *Solar Life;* disseminates over 300 brochures, booklets (write for free list); publishes *Solar Energy Sourcebook* of manufacturers and professionals. Yearly membership is $25.

Regional sources

Mid-American Solar Energy Center, 8140 26th Ave. S., Minneapolis, Minn. 55420, (612) 853-0400; services 12 Midwestern states.

Northeast Solar Energy Center, 470 Atlantic Ave., Boston, Mass. 02110, (617) 292-9250; services nine northeastern states.

Southern Solar Energy Center, 61 Perimeter Park, Atlanta, Ga. 30341, (404) 458-8765; services 16 southern states, Washington D.C., Puerto Rico and Virgin Islands.

Western Solar Utilization Network, 715 Southwest Morrison St., Suite 800, Portland, Ore. 97205, (503) 241-1222; services 13 western states.

Service

You can purchase a "Computerized solar domestic hot-water performance estimate" from Solcost, Solar Energy Corp., Box 3065, Princeton, N.J. 08540. It's a computer's estimate of thermal performance and payback time for installing a particular solar hot-water system. The report indicates whether a solar installation, given the particular conditions of your home (i.e., taxes, weather), is a feasible investment. Send Solcost the completed user form and the firm runs the information through a computer and returns the output.

Product catalogs

People's Solar Sourcebook, Solar Usage Now Inc., 420 East Tiffin St., Bascom, Ohio 44809; 200 pages of solar products; $5.

Solar Age Resource Book, Solar Age, Church Hill, Harrisville, N.H. 03450; listing of solar equipment and systems, geographical directory of architectural and design services and product buyer's guide; $9.95.

Solar Components Division Catalog, Kalwall Corp., Box 237, Manchester, N.H. 03103; besides manufacturing Sun-Lite insulated solar glazing panels for home use, Kalwall claims to have the largest solar mail-order house in U.S.; 64-page catalog is free.

Solar Energy Sourcebook, Solar Energy Institute of America, 1110 Sixth St. N.W., Washington, D.C. 20001; 797 pages of solar-energy-related products and services; $15 (free to institute members).

Solar Engineering Magazine Second Annual Solar Product Listing, Solar Energy Industries Assn., 1001 Connecticut Ave. N.W., Suite 800, Washington, D.C. 20036; 232-page listing of products from 655 manufacturers in 20 countries; geographical listing of manufacturers and services; $10.

Periodicals

Solar Age, Solar Vision Inc., Church Hill, Harrisville, N.H. 03450; monthly magazine that focuses on solar applications, innovations, energy conservation; yearly subscription is $18; single copy, $1.95.

Solar Engineering Magazine, Solar Engineering Publishers Inc., 8435 North Stemmons Freeway, Suite 880, Dallas, Tex. 75247; monthly magazine covering industry news, products and applications; subscription is $29 for 13 issues; single copy, $3.50.

Solar Times, 3 Old Post Rd., Madison, Conn. 06443; monthly publication reports industry news; yearly subscription is $12.50; single copy, $1.50.

Literature catalogs

Environmental Action Reprint Service, 2239 E. Colfax, Denver, Colo. 80206; $1.

Solpub, Box 9209, College Station, Tex. 77840; free.

Total Environmental Action, Church Hill, Harrisville, N.H. 03450; free.

U.S. Government Printing Office Publications, Superintendent of Documents, U.S. Government Printing Office, Attn.: inquiries, Washington, D.C. 20402; request list of solar-energy publications, subject bibliography No. 9; free.

Books

At Home in the Sun, by Norah Deakin Davis and Linda Lindsey, Garden Way Publishing Co., 520 Ferry Rd., Charlotte, Vt. 05445; $10.95 postpaid; a tour of solar homes.

The Complete Energy-Saving Home Improvement Guide, Revised Edition, James W. Morrison, Editor, Arco Publishing, 219 Park Ave. S., New York, N.Y. 10003; $1.95.

Consumer Handbook of Solar Energy, by John H. Keyes, Morgan & Morgan Inc., 145 Paradise St., Dobbs Ferry, N.Y. 10522; $11.70 postpaid, softcover.

A Design and Construction Handbook for Energy-Saving Houses, Alex Wade, Rodale Press, Emmaus, Pa. 18049; $12.95 postpaid, paperback.

Designing and Building a Solar House, Donald Watson, Garden Way Publishing, 520 Ferry Rd., Charlotte, Vt. 05445; $10.95 postpaid.

Energy Future, Report of the Energy Project at the Harvard Business School, Robert Stobaugh and Daniel Yergin, editors; Random House, 201 East 50th St., New York, N.Y. 10022; $12.95.

Home Energy for the Eighties, by Ralph Wolfe and Peter Clegg, Garden Way Publishing Co., 520 Ferry Rd., Charlotte, Vt. 05445; $11.95 postpaid.

How to Build a Solar Heater, revised edition, by Ted Lucas, Crown Publishers Inc., 1 Park Ave., New York, N.Y. 10016; $6.95.

Present Value, by Gigi Coe, Friends of the Earth, 124 Spear, San Francisco, Calif. 94105; $6.55 postpaid; 20 buildings that use solar energy.

Solar Energy in America, by William D. Metz and Allen L. Hammond, American Assn. for the Advancement of Science, 1776 Massachusetts Ave. N.W., Washington, D.C. 20036; $8.50, paperback.

Your Solar Energy Home, by D. Howell, Pergamon Press, Fairview Park, Elmsford, N.Y. 10523; $10.25, paperback.

WHEN YOU FIND it necessary to drive a stud, but don't have the proper tools at hand, try improvising a driver from a matching nut. Drill a hole completely through the nut and drive a tapered pin into it. Be sure to leave enough room below the hole to allow for a good grip with the wrench. The pin stop will prevent the nut from jamming on the stud. To remove, just back the nut off the stud.

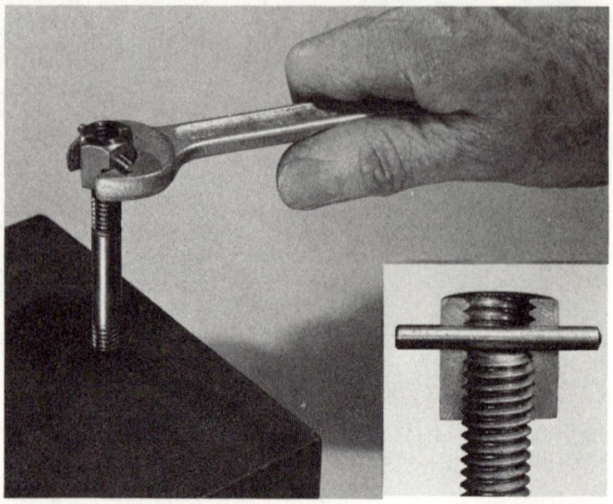

SOME GLUE is always squeezed out of a joint once clamping pressure is applied. To eliminate the job of scraping away this excess, mask both sides of the joint with cellulose tape. Lay the tape close to the edge of the joint and press it firmly to insure good contact. Once the glue hardens, pull off the tape and the glue will come with it. This is especially good when regluing finished joints which might be scratched during cleanup.

WHEN WORKING with your metal lathe, you can forget about the need to oil the tailstock center repeatedly if you slip an oil-saturated felt washer on the spindle before you clamp the work in the lathe. If the job is very large, it may be necessary to give the washer an occasional extra dose of oil. However, for the average job, the original oiling is sufficient. When not in use, store washers in a small bottle with enough oil to cover them.

USE OF THE STEP BLOCK shown at right is a big improvement over the usual practice of placing a scrap of wood under the hammerhead when pulling nails. As a nail is pulled, you can move the hammerhead up the steps for the best possible leverage. The block shown was cut with steps slightly less than 1 in. high. For stubborn jobs, make shallower steps. Another advantage of this block is that nails come out straight so they can easily be redriven if the job requires it.

AUTHOR CHECKS lines on the completed installation. The compass (inset) shows panel relation to true south.

How to install a solar water heater

By HARRY WICKS

■ THERE WERE two reasons why I installed a solar-assisted domestic water system this summer: My oil-fired water heater had sprung a leak and was wearing out, and knowledgeable trade sources were predicting even higher fuel prices. So I moved when my pocketbook was pinched.

As my first step, I selected a closed-loop solar fluid system. In it a transfer fluid transports heat from sun rays to the water heater where a heat exchanger transfers it from solar fluid to the potable water. An alternative is to run the potable water through the lines and collector plates, and back to the water heater.

Since Department of Energy figures rate solar efficiency less than 50 percent efficient in my area (near New York City), I also needed a backup system for sunless days and periods of heavy water use. I tossed out the oil guzzler and installed a gas-fired unit and glass-lined, insulated tank. The preheater tank, with exchangers is also insulated.

After some price comparing (I didn't want a system that would take 30 years before it paid off), I picked the Conservationist System made by A.O. Smith Corp. Like those of its major competitors, this system is well designed. Quality parts include components made by others, such as collector plates by Revere and circulating pump by Grundfos. Here are job costs: three collector plates, $930; preheater and heat exchanger, $800; backup gas-fired water tank and heater, $300 (not needed if your existing system is in good shape). A plumber charged $800 for labor and piping; carpentry was do-it-yourself free, but would have added $300 if contracted. (All prices were current at the time this was written.)

choosing collectors

Solar collector panels may be almost out of sight on the roof, but you should give them special thought. These plates can be exposed to severe temperature extremes. A flat-plate collector can be hit with temperatures below 0° F. on winter nights and over 400° F. (if not operating) on summer days. And they contend with wind, snow, sleet, rain and hail. Although there is similarity in operating principles of many solar domestic hot-water systems, each maker has certain unique or unusual features.

SEE ALSO

**Dishwashers . . . Energy, saving . . .
Heaters, solar . . . Heaters, water . . .
Solar energy . . . Washing machines . . .
Winterizing, homes**

laying out your panels

Collectors should be placed to receive unshaded sun during the "solar day"—9:00 a.m. to 3:00 p.m. Check your roof to see that trees or neighbors' homes won't shade your collectors. Remember, the sun changes position significantly. In winter, for example, it is much closer to the horizon and casts longer shadows.

Don't position collectors near the roof ridge because of a greater risk of damage by high winds. Locate the plates with horizontal midlines slightly below mid-height of the sloped roof. Keep plates close as possible to storage tanks to

INSTALLING THE COLLECTOR-PLATE HARDWARE

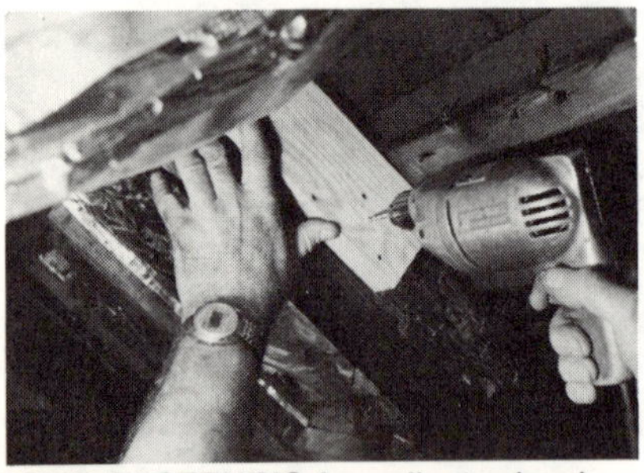

SOLID FASTENING for collector hardware is a must. Here, cat is located.

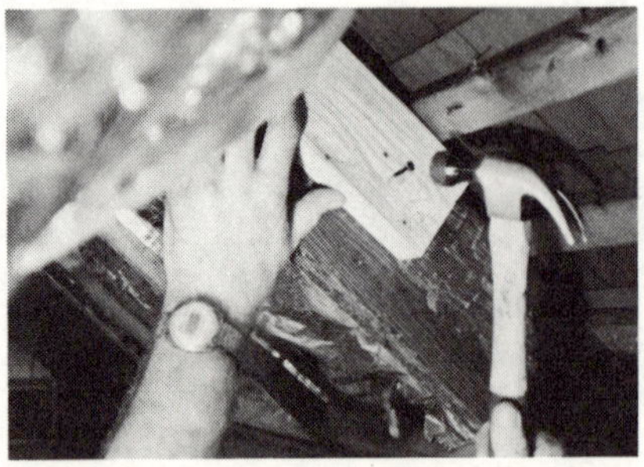

USE 16D NAILS to secure the cat. See drawings for blocking technique.

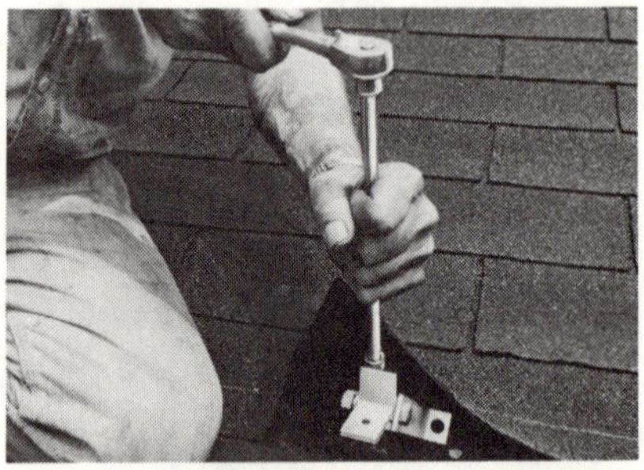

ALL BRACKETS on the job were lag-screwed into rafters, cats or blocking.

HOW THE CONSERVATIONIST SYSTEM WORKS

Hot rays from the sun are absorbed by the roof-mounted collector panels to heat a special antifreeze fluid that circulates through integral copper channels. The propylene glycol eliminates any chance of freezing in cold climates during the unit's downtime (i.e., at night). The Conservationist System utilizes a closed-loop design for transfer of heated solution of the preheater and its return. The heater-mounted differential controller has a modulating output (speeds up or slows down glycol solar fluid flow depending on available energy) to collect the maximum amount of heat from the solar panels, even on cloudy days.

The house water service flows to the preheater tank in which the Corona heat exchanger is submerged. The heat exchanger is double-walled and electrically isolated from the tank for safety. As the solar fluid flows through the exchanger, the heat is transferred through double-walled pipes of the exchanger to the domestic water supply.

Installation can include an electric backup heat system as shown. This unit fires up to bring water temperature to preset use temperature, usually from 120° to 140° F. I opted to eliminate the electric backup system because of high prevailing rates in my area, and installed a backup gas heater and water tank instead.

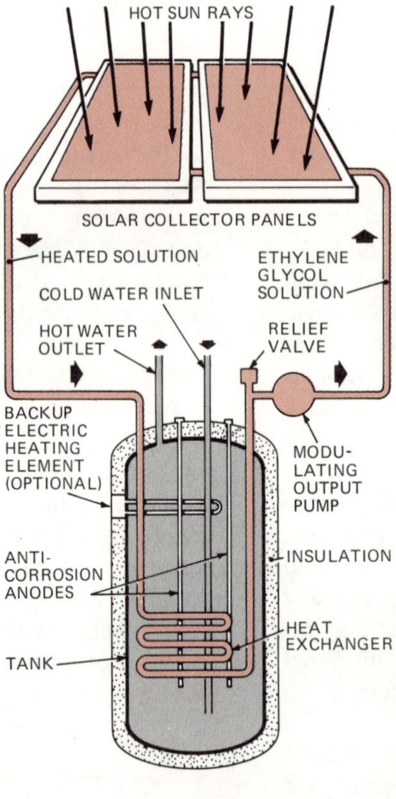

SECOND bottom bracket is located so that blocking can be installed inside.

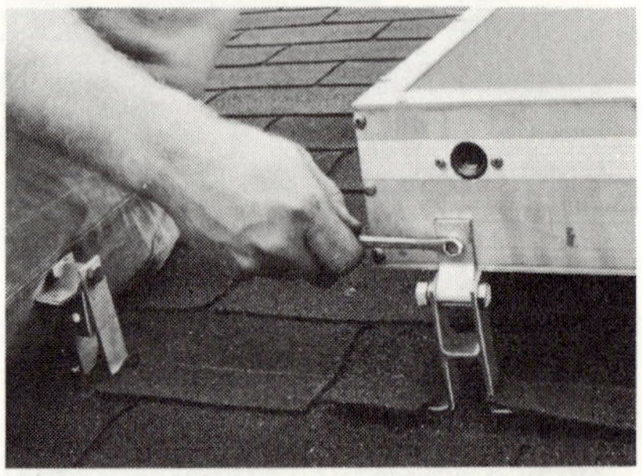

NEXT, the collector is hoisted to the roof and secured to brackets.

SINCE ROOF is pitched 42°, short legs at top bring panels to desirable 45°.

reduce heat loss during circulation of solar fluid.

Make certain you or your contractor check that hazards aren't created for house occupants. Points to think about:

■ Antifreeze fluid, waterproofing and insulation should comply with local codes for fire safety and health under operating and nonoperating conditions.

■ Storage tanks and piping that may reach temperatures above 140° F. should be insulated so passersby will not be burned should they contact those elements. Identify pressure and temperature relief valves with appropriate warnings.

■ The system should withstand pressures of 150 pounds per square inch. The hot-water side should be protected against excessive temperatures.

■ Equipment design should fully protect the potable water supply.

installing the system

I handled all carpentry and brought in a local plumber for piping. Ripping out the old heater and installing plates, preheater and tank with gas heater took three men 3½ days. My guess is that contractors experienced with a system's installa-

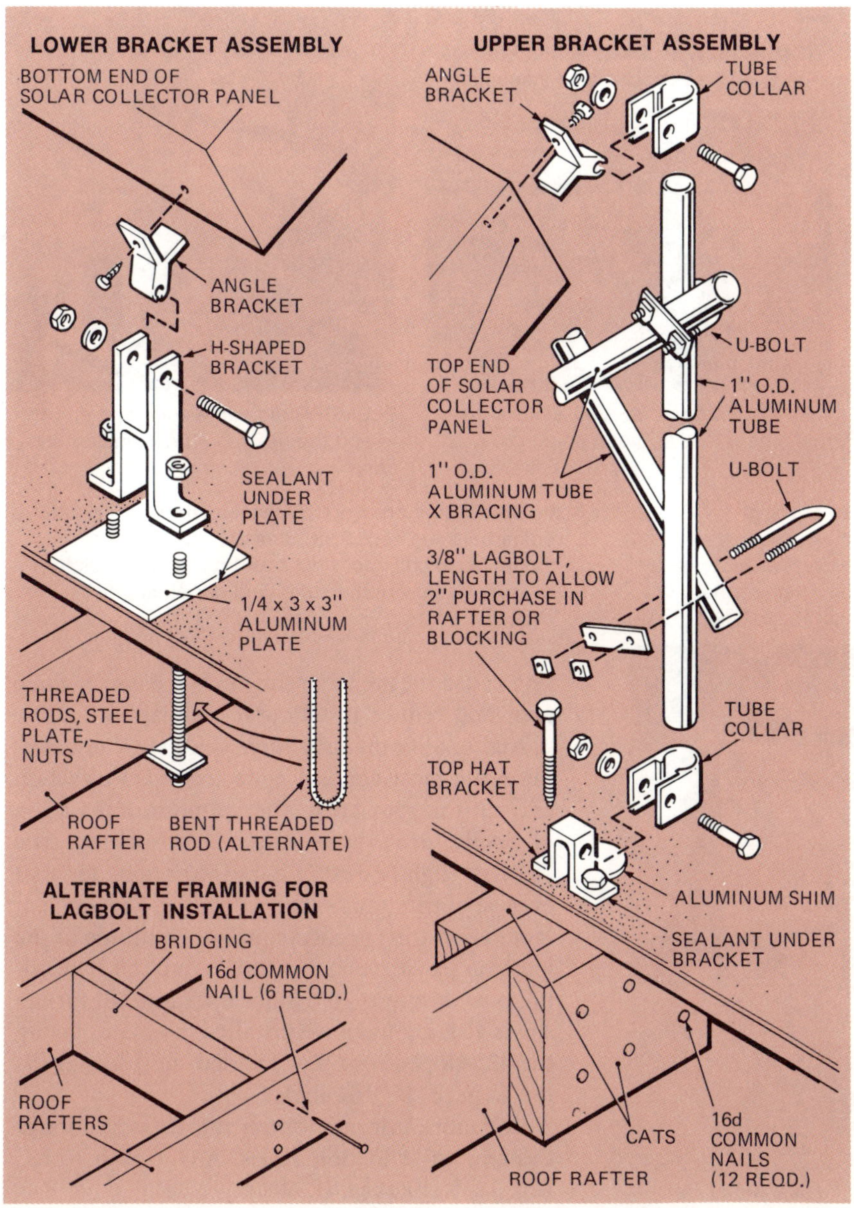

DRAWINGS (left) show the standard panel installation method that was used. When bracket misses a rafter, you must install either cats or blocking.

AUTHOR FOUND collector weight tilted brackets, which then cut into shingles.

A ¼ x 3 x 5-IN. aluminum plate under the bracket distributed the weight.

INSTALLING THE SOLAR FLUID LINE

COPPER PIPING for solar fluid was run on the outside of house.

PIPE ELBOWS around gutters. Straight run requires holes through cornice.

TO MINIMIZE heat loss as fluid travels, pipe must be wrapped with insulation.

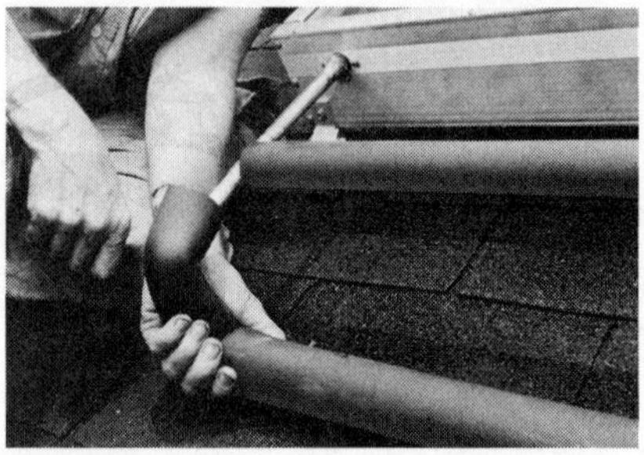

ARMAFLEX taped around elbows prevents heat loss at these points, too.

ALL JOINTS are soldered to eliminate joint hardware and the chance of leaks.

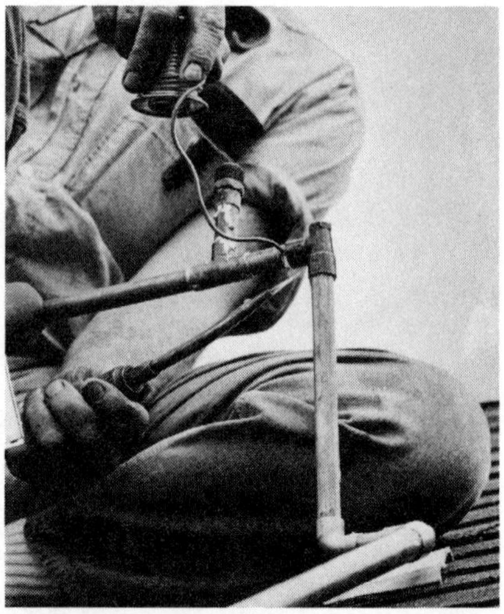

PLUMBER did some soldering on roof to end the need to lift assembled sections.

IMPRESSIVE ARRAY of gauges (more than maker calls for, in fact) provide these readings: **A,** Pressure/temperature of preheated water to water heater; in closed loop—**B,** pressure/temperature of fluid collectors; **C,** pressure/temperature, fluid to preheater; **D,** line pressure. **E** senses temperature differential between sensor in preheater and sensor mounted on collector plates and turns on circulator **F** to vary the flow of the solar fluid depending upon the available energy.

tion could cut the labor time to two days for three men and reduce installation costs at least $200.

Any quality manufacturer will help you determine the most efficient collector panel direction and tilt for your area. The optimum orientation of a collector in the Northern Hemisphere is true south or slightly west of it, but variations 15° east or west of true south are acceptable. The angle of inclination (tilt) needed equals the latitude of the location (in degrees) measured from the horizontal, plus or minus 10°. Since optimum tilt for my site is 45°, I could have installed my plates flat on the 42°-sloped roof. But I added short legs at the top to get a 45° tilt angle.

For more information on the Conservationist System, write to Bob Jones, A.O. Smith Corp., Box 28, Kankakee, IL 60901.

How to solder wiring

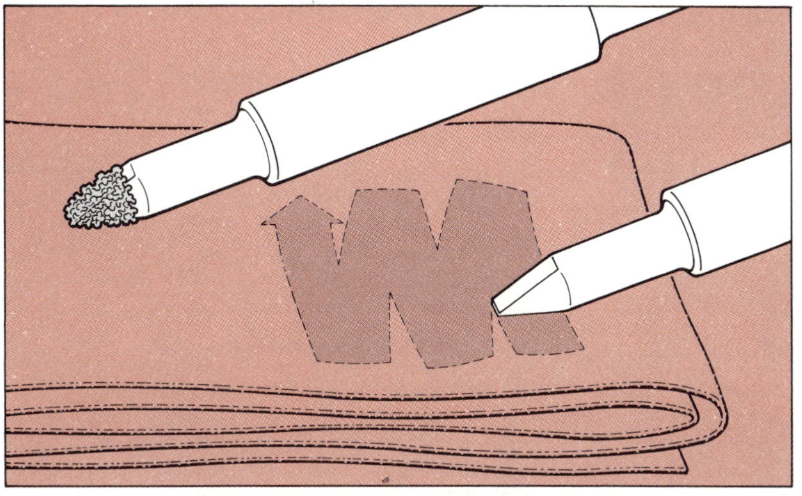

Keep your iron clean

A dirty iron won't transfer its heat to the joint efficiently. For best results, "tin" your iron's tip with a thin, shiny coating of solder before using it. After every few joints, clean the tip with a damp cloth or sponge—more often, if it acquires a dirty, dark or charred look, like the one shown at the far left. After cleaning, if the tip has lost its shiny appearance, re-tin it with another thin coat of solder. When the job is finished, clean and re-tin your iron again before you put it away

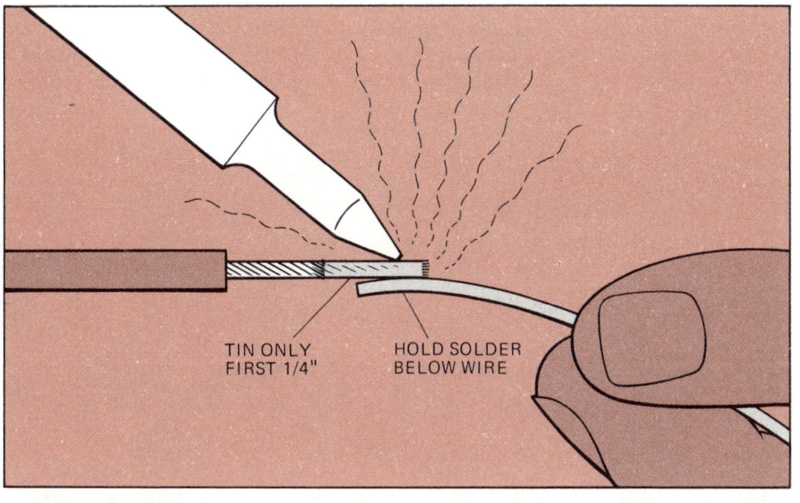

Tin wires carefully

Tinning any wire with a thin coat of solder makes it easier to solder to a joint. Tinning stranded wires also helps hold the strands together at the tip. Hold the solder below the wire so it will soak in, not drip on, and remove it and the iron once the solder has soaked into the first ¼ inch of the wire. Don't tin the remaining wire—it could become brittle and the joint break if wires are flexed or pulled. When soldering shielded cable, be careful not to melt the insulation by applying too much heat

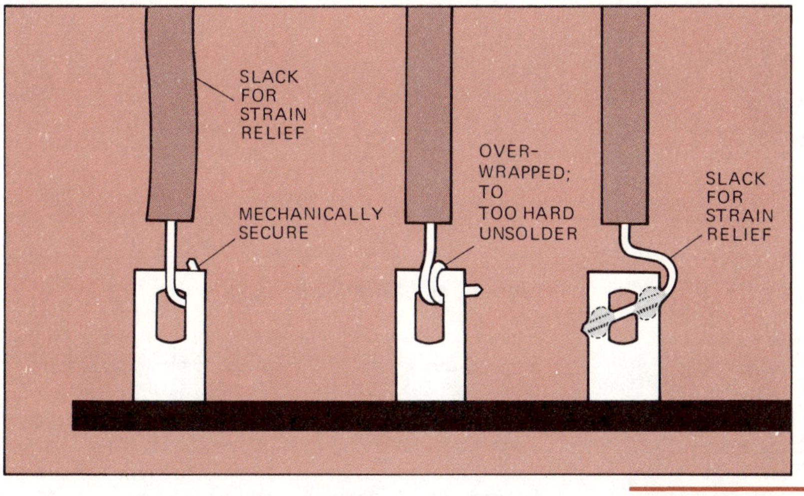

Make solid connections

Before soldering, wires should be bent to form mechanically secure connections (far left) that can stay in place even without solder; the solder's job is to maintain good electrical contact, not to glue wires in place. Leave some slack in the wire too, to prevent strain on the connection. Too complex a wrap (center) makes it harder to unsolder the wire for servicing. But a solder-only connection, with no wrapping, will usually yield a "cold-solder" joint

SEE ALSO

Doorbells . . . Electrical wiring . . . Lighting . . . Testers, continuity . . . Wiring, electrical . . . Yard lighting

Keep wires stationary while cooling

Wires that move while the solder cools cause unreliable "cold-solder" joints. If you can't hold the wires in place with a good mechanical connection (as shown above, where a component lead is too short), hold them in place with soldering aids or other tools until the joint is cool. Brace your hands if necessary, to prevent shaking. Don't try to hold wires in place with the soldering iron—they'll spring up again as soon as you take the iron away. Soldering aids, of metal that solder doesn't stick to, also have many other uses

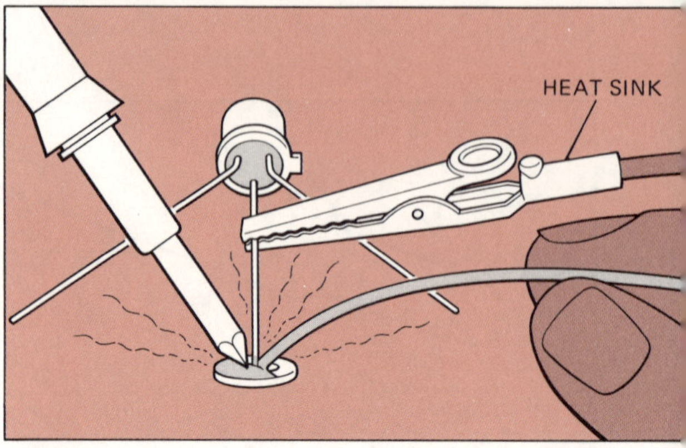

Heat sinks protect transistors

The heat of soldering can cook transistors and integrated circuits. If you're not using sockets, clip a heat sink between the joint and the transistor body to prevent this. Commercially made heat sinks are good, but you can also make your own from an alligator clip with a stub of heavy copper wire attached; or cement some felt into the clip's jaws and moisten it before each use. With no heat sink, use the least-powerful iron that will bring the joint quickly to soldering temperature. Too-small irons will cook more transistors than you'd think

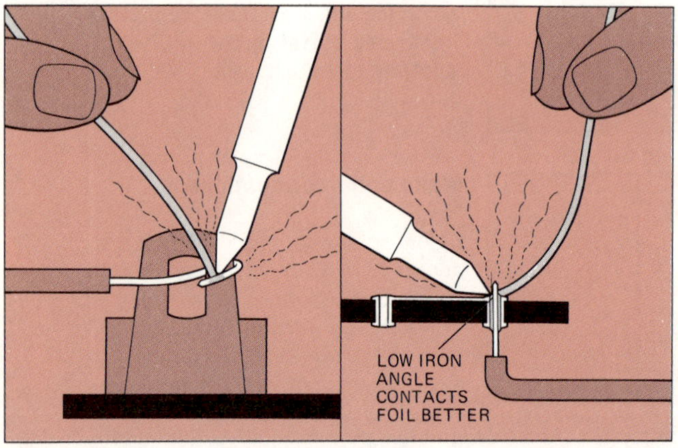

Heat the joint first, then solder

Don't just melt the solder and drip it onto the joint. First, heat the joint with the iron for a few seconds, then move the solder into contact with both the iron tip and all the parts or wires to be soldered. When the joint is hot enough, the solder will flow over and into it, wetting it evenly, filling in spaces, and cooling to a smooth, silvery sheen. If the joint takes more than three or four seconds to heat, though, you're using too small an iron for that job

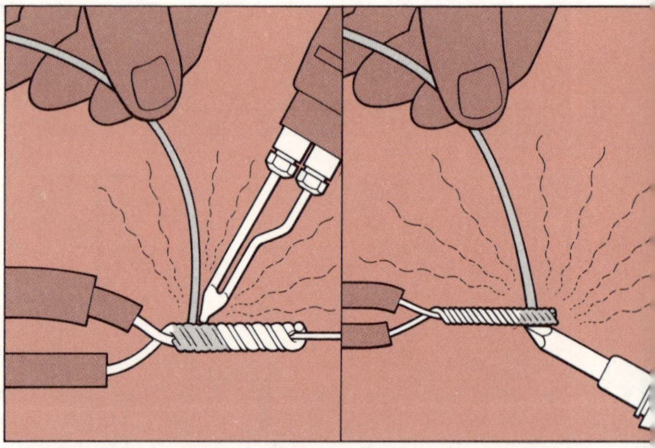

Use the right iron for the job

Electronic soldering is usually done best with medium-wattage pencil irons—hot enough to heat fine electronic wires quickly without cooking components. Heavy household wiring jobs are best done with high-wattage guns, powerful enough to heat the joint rapidly without having to bake wires and insulation for minutes; guns, which cool off between joints, are also handier than continuous-heating irons in the awkward places typical of house-wiring and other electrical situations

How to tell good solder joints from bad ones

Good solder joints (A) are smooth and shiny, with the outlines of all wires and contacts clearly visible, but with rounded fillets of solder filling in the gaps and corners where wires meet. Insufficient solder (B) leaves no fillets and may not maintain a reliable connection. Too much solder (C) covers a connection with big blobs (which sometimes cause short-circuit bridges between conductors on circuit boards); there may be a good joint underneath, but you can't see it to tell. Overheating (D) chars wire insulation and may lift solder pads from circuit boards or harm delicate components. Cold solder joints may have a jagged, crystalline look (E), a dripped-on, blobby appearance not conformant to outlines of the joint (F), or merely a hazy, milky sheen (not shown)

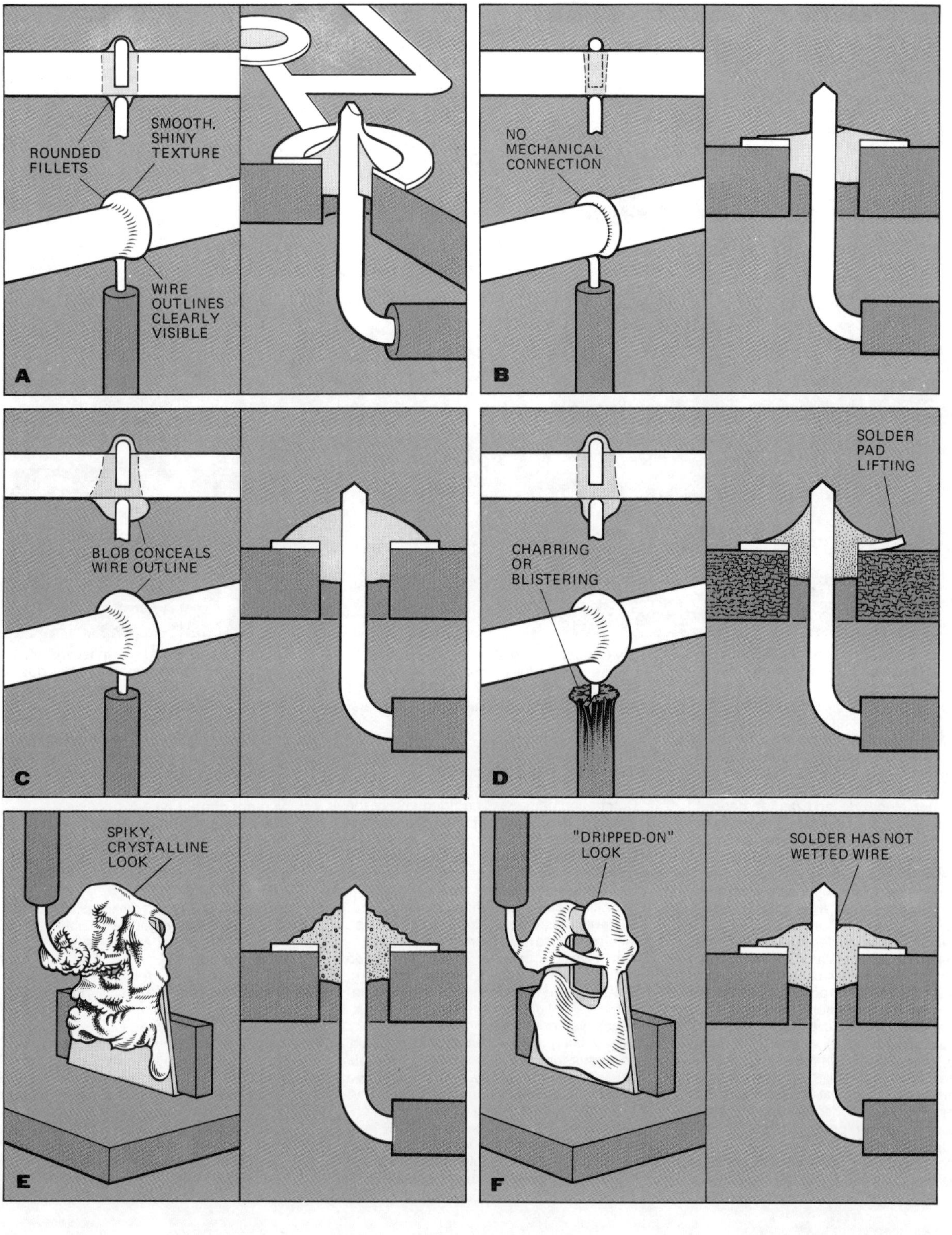

SPARKPLUGS THAT INDICATE NORMAL ENGINE OPERATION

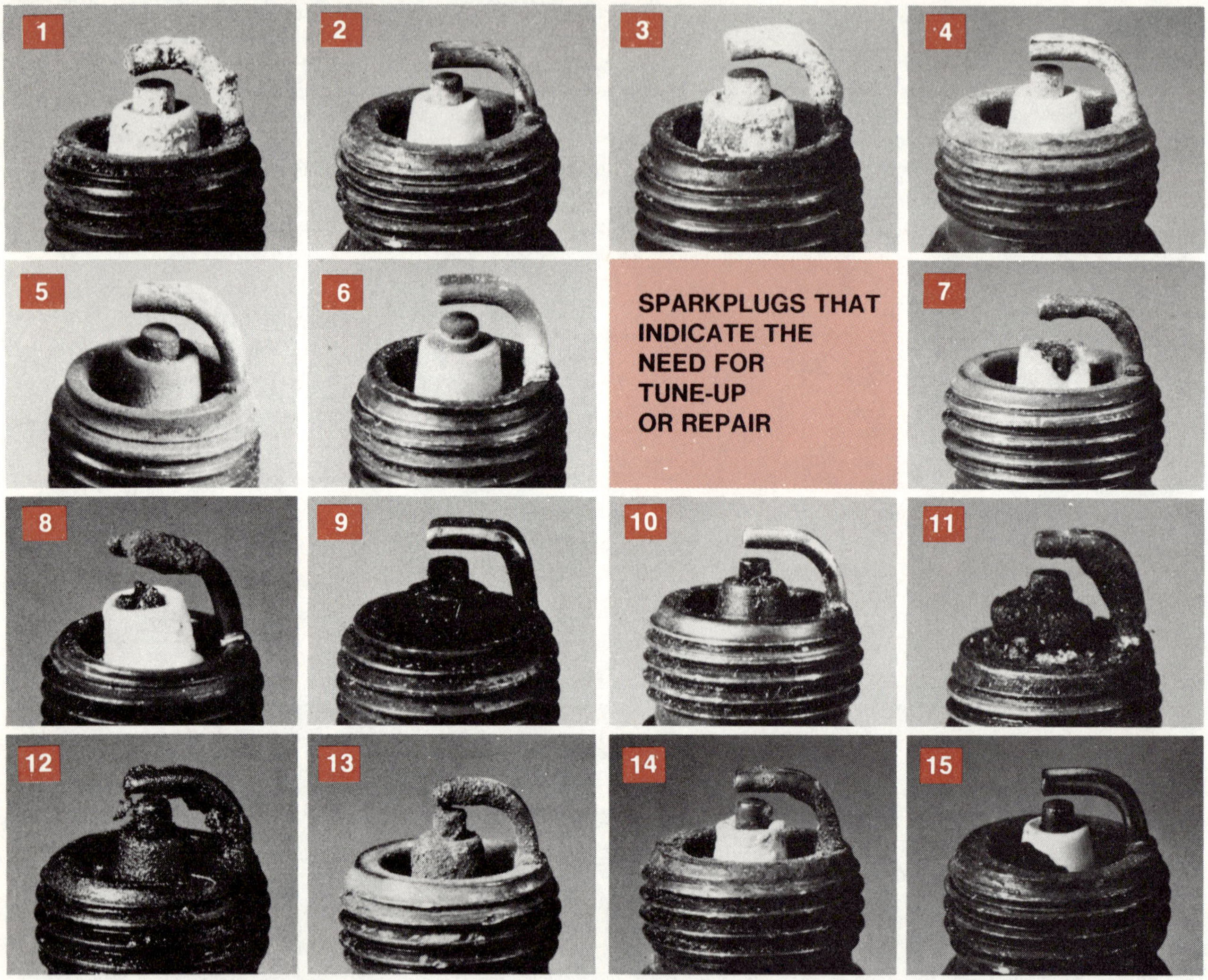

In the photos above are sparkplugs taken from 15 different engines. Here's how to "read" them.

1. Almost white, fluffy gray deposit on insulator tip and side electrode is normal for emission-controlled engines using lean mixtures and no-lead fuels. This plug has high mileage and should be replaced.
2. White with light tan tint: The soft deposits on center electrode and darker deposit on side electrode indicate proper heat range for the way this engine is being used—at moderate speeds and loads.
3. Light tan deposits on a well-used plug. The yellow deposit on the side electrode is normal and comes from metallic additives.
4. Yellowish, soft white deposits on the center electrode and insulator are normal for an engine using fuel containing certain metallic additives. Deposits on the shell are normal and show no signs of over-rich or over-lean fuel mixtures.
5. Classic example of a normal plug with fluffy, chocolate brown deposit on the insulator. Note slightly lighter color on side electrode showing that it's running a bit hotter. Sooty black deposit on shell suggests rich mixture, perhaps need for new air filter.
6. Fluffy red deposits are normal in engines using fuels with MMT additives. Slightly oily deposit on the shell may be due to an engine not yet fully broken in. In an older engine it might indicate the beginning of wear on piston rings, valve guides/seals.

Problem sparkplugs 7 through 15:

7. Detonation damage: The firing end of the insulator is broken and metal transferred from center electrode to the side electrode. Possible causes: a. Overadvanced ignition timing. b. Fuel too low in octane. c. EGR system malfunctioning.
8. Preignition damage. White deposits on a blistered insulator, along with burned electrodes, reveal extreme heat condition. Possible causes: a. Sparkplug too hot. b. Overadvanced ignition timing. c. Glowing deposits in combustion chamber. d. Cooling system clogged. e. Exhaust system blocked.
9. Soot fouling. Fluffy, black soot deposits on insulator and electrodes. Possible causes: a. Excessively rich mixture due to sticking choke or defective carburetor. b. Faulty ignition primary circuit or defective sparkplug wires. c. Excessively cold starting without engine warm-up.
10. Oil fouled. Oily, usually black deposit covering insulator and electrodes. Possible causes: a. Excessive passage of engine oil into combustion chamber due to piston ring or valve guide seal leakage. b. Defective PCV system.
11. Carbon fouled. Hard, black carbon deposits on insulator and electrodes. Possible causes: a. Moderate amount of oil passing rings or valves. b. Defective PCV system. c. Sparkplug too cold. d. Sparkplug not correct type for engine.
12. Dirt fouling. Carbonized and sometimes granular deposits on and around the insulator and electrodes. Possible causes: a. Air cleaner missing. b. Defective air-cleaner mountings.
13. Bridged gap. Carbon particles are lodged in the sparkplug gap. Possible cause: Combustion chamber deposits accumulated during low-speed, light-load use break loose during demand for full power.
14. Glazed insulator. Glassy surface on the insulator as a result of deposits melting on plug. Possible causes: a. Sparkplug too hot. b. Local overheating due to cooling system-blockage or similar defect.
15. Splashed insulator. Splotches of black, almost paint-like deposits on the insulator. Possible causes: Delayed correction of an engine miss allows soft, oily deposits to accumulate in cylinder. After tune-up these deposits break loose and foul plug.

PARTS OF sparkplug are shown in this cutaway.

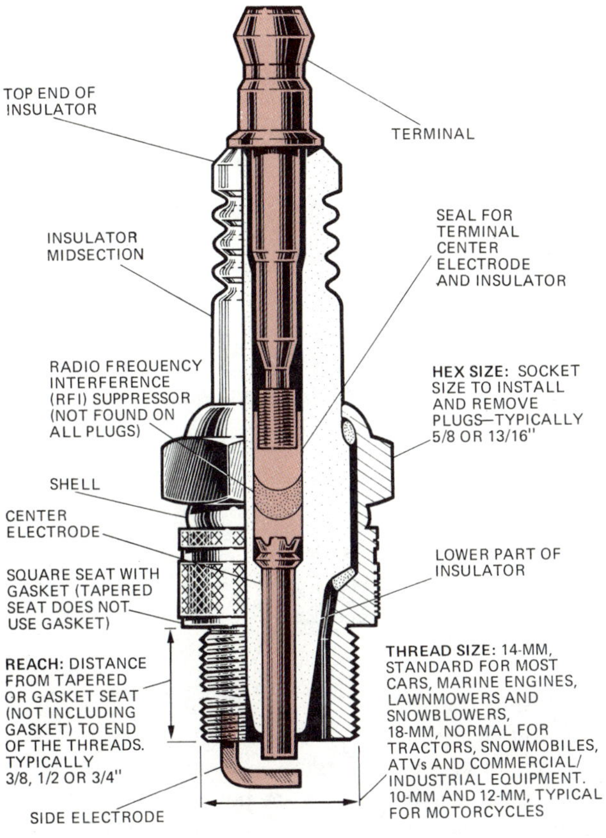

How to 'read' your sparkplug

They're sensitive indicators to all kinds of conditions inside your engine, so begin by learning to recognize exactly what they're trying to tell you

By MORT SCHULTZ

■ ARE YOU SPARKPLUG smart? Anyone who thinks he knows everything about sparkplugs ought to see if he can answer these questions:

■ What has gone wrong when the top part of a sparkplug insulator shows vertical black streaks?

■ What's the problem when a sparkplug's center electrode shows burning and extreme wear?

■ What is corona, when is it most likely to occur and what should be done about it?

■ How would you go about removing sparkplugs from a late model Chevrolet Monza with a V8 engine?

■ Back in 1908, a fellow who was to give his name to two present-day sparkplug companies started his own outfit. Who was he and what are the two companies that took his name?

Here are the answers:

1. The plug was improperly installed. In all likelihood, it was overtightened or an open-end wrench was used that distorted the shell, which led to the blowby that caused the streaks.

2. This condition is usually caused by improperly compressed or corroded gaskets which had been tightened down onto dirty seats. The normal flow of heat away from the sparkplug was prevented, resulting in overheating.

3. Corona is a high-voltage electric phenomenon that makes sparkplugs and sparkplug cables glow. It most often occurs in damp weather and is especially visible in the dark. Nothing has to be done about it.

4. Certainly not in the conventional manner. You will never get the No. 3 plug out of the engine. The entire procedure is outlined later under the heading, *Removing Monza plugs.*

5. The fellow was Albert Champion. The companies are Champion and AC.

Sparkplug—that's an electrical component used in a gasoline engine's ignition system to provide a high-tension-voltage spark for igniting the fuel mixture.

when new plugs are needed

No one can argue with the fact that worn sparkplugs are a chief cause of hard starting, poor engine performance and increased fuel use.

"Sparkplug performance is the most important

SEE ALSO
**Auto batteries . . . Cables, auto . . .
Electronic ignition, auto . . . Engines, auto . . .
Ignition systems, auto . . . Tune-up, auto**

WHY SPARKPLUGS MISFIRE

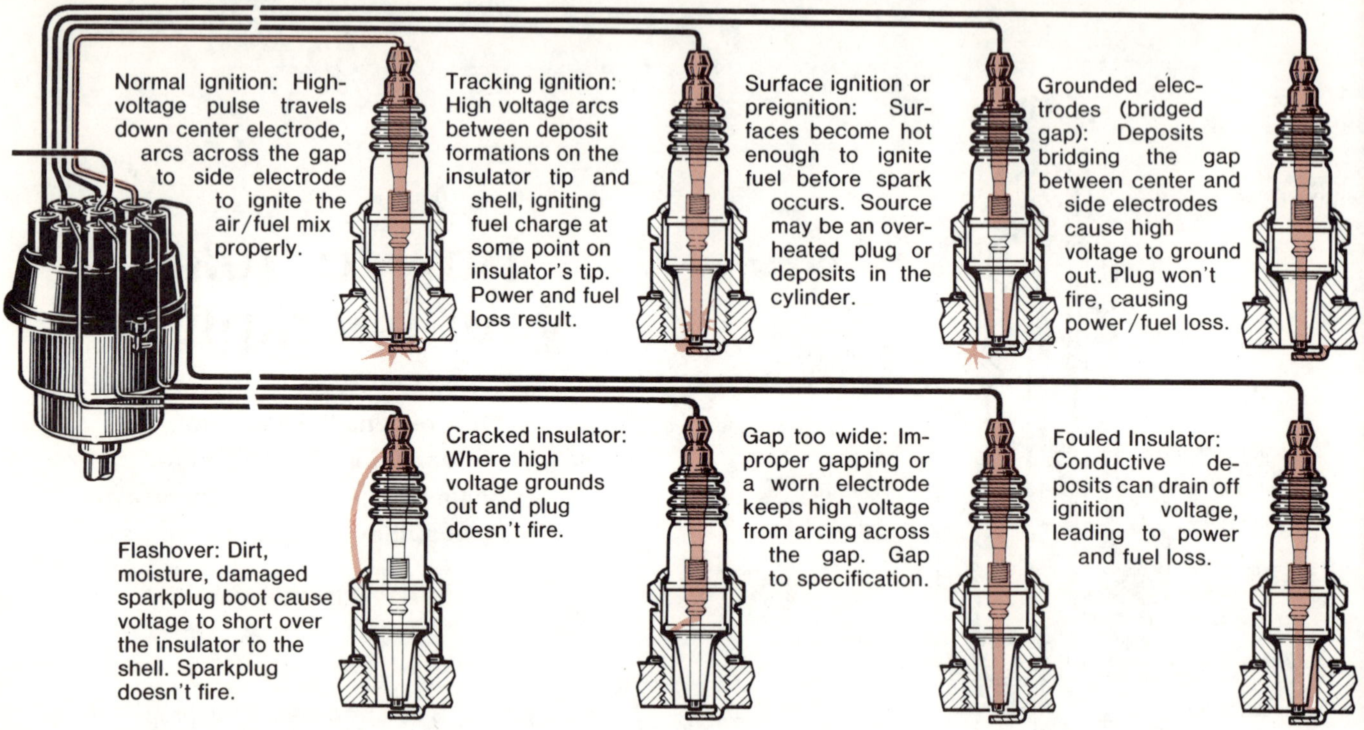

single factor in maintaining your gasoline mileage and engine efficiency," the AC Spark Plug Div. of General Motors contends. "AC tests show that if only one sparkplug out of eight is misfiring, gasoline mileage may fall off as much as 15.2 percent."

However, sparkplugs are frequently blamed for poor engine performance which they don't cause. The story of a car owner who installs a set of new sparkplugs to cure engine misfiring and power loss is typical.

The remedy works, but only for a few hundred miles. What's happened is that the new plugs temporarily improve engine performance, because new plugs make less of a demand on the ignition system.

But new sparkplugs cannot permanently rectify poor engine performance that is being caused by worn distributor contact points, cracked distributor cap, unspecified ignition timing or a weak coil. Or for that matter, by worn rings or cylinders, or faulty carburetion.

The best way to tell if sparkplugs are to blame for your problem is to examine them carefully when you take them from the engine. Look for conditions shown on page 2746. If one exists, then a sparkplug or sparkplugs are causing trouble.

You should also analyze the tips of used sparkplugs carefully. They can provide clues to

SPARKPLUGS are cleaned by inserting tip into a sandblasting machine.

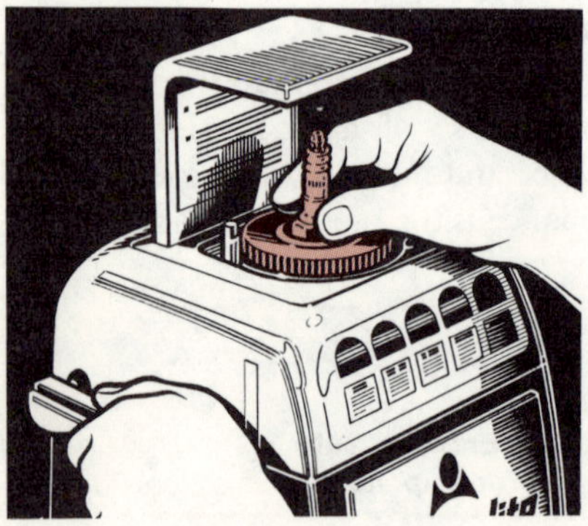

FILING ELECTRODES may be necessary to remove stubborn deposits.

CLEANING THREADS is important to insure proper seating of plug in block.

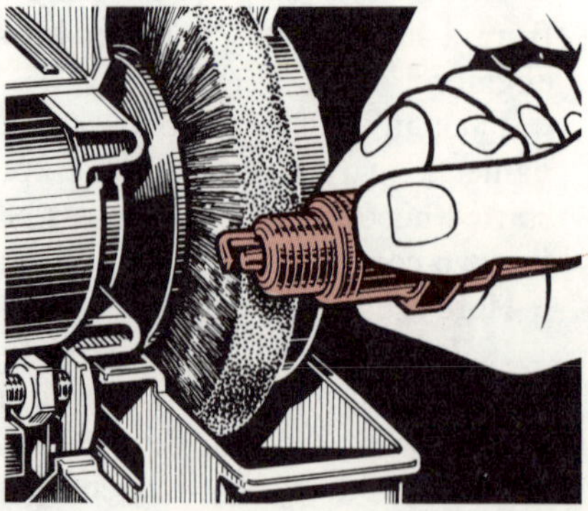

HOW TO TIGHTEN SPARKPLUGS

PLUG SIZE	WITH TORQUE WRENCH (ft.-lbs.) Cast Iron Head	Aluminum Head	WITHOUT TORQUE WRENCH Cast Iron or Aluminum Head
10 mm	8-12	8-12	⅜ to ½ turn
12 mm	10-18	10-18	¼ turn
14 mm, gasket seat	25-30	18-22	½ to ¾ turn
14 mm, tapered seat	7-15	7-15	*
18 mm, gasket seat	32-38	28-34	½ to ¾ turn
18 mm, tapered seat	15-20	15-20	*

*Champion suggests that tapered-seat sparkplugs be turned 1/32 to 1/16 turn beyond finger tight.

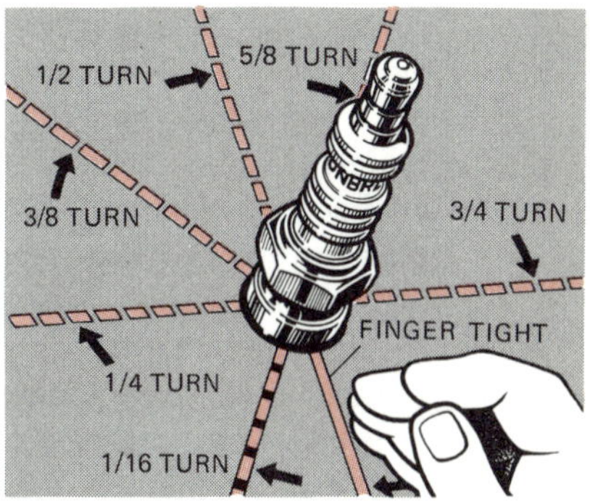

THE ART of tightening plugs without a torque wrench is aided by diagram.

TWO TYPES of plugs for rotary engines use two outer electrodes.

FLAT FEELER gauge won't give an accurate reading; use the round wire type.

what's happening in the engine and to the plugs themselves.

removing plugs correctly

In most cases, the tools you need are a 13/16-in. hex or ⅝-in. hex sparkplug socket, a ratchet wrench and an extension.

You can find out the hex size you need by checking service data in a manual or asking a dealer selling your make of car.

Don't confuse hex size with two other sparkplug dimensions—thread size and reach. The lead illustration has an explanation of all three.

In some cases, "conventional" tools won't do. Where quarters are too close to get a wrench and extension onto a plug, use a flexible sparkplug wrench. It consists of a socket on the end of a flexible hose-type extension with a T-bar handle, sold where auto tools are sold.

The following procedure is the conventional,

GASKET ON plug at left should be seated tightly.

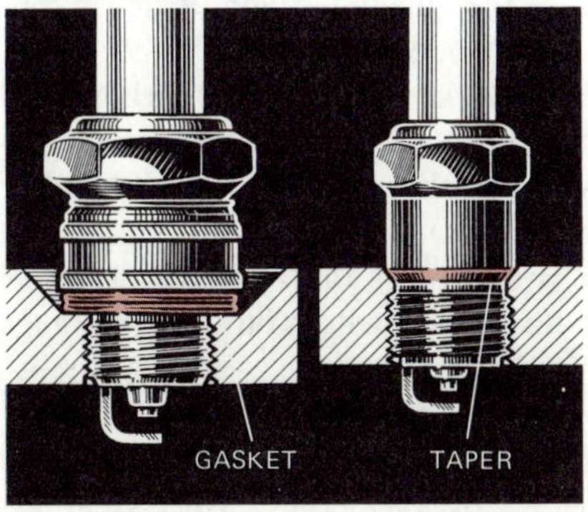

HOT AND COLD plugs are illustrated here. Plug at left is a hotter type since it dissipates heat slowly (a longer path). Plug at right, a cold type, dissipates heat quickly because of its short path.

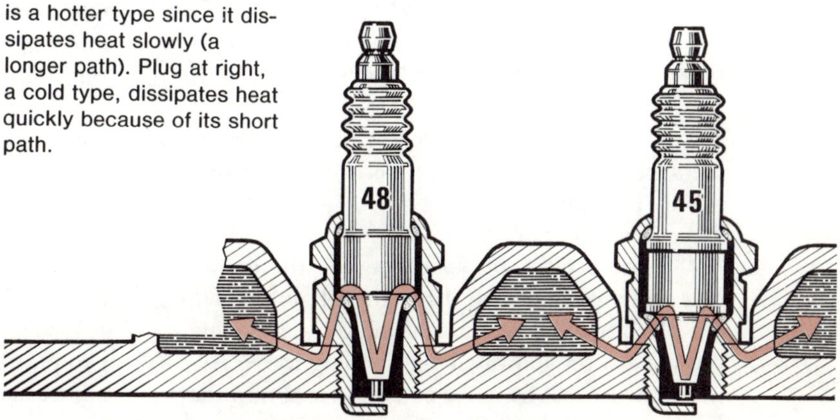

correct way to remove sparkplugs from an engine:

1. *Mark each sparkplug wire* with some identifying symbol so it can be reinstalled in its correct cylinder. Accidentally switching wires leads to plugs firing out of sequence which can cause serious engine damage.

One method you can use to mark wires is to attach a clip-type clothespin or masking tape marked with a number to each wire as you remove it. The numbering system you use in the case of a V8 engine may be R-1, R-2, R-3 and R-4 for plug wires on the right (passenger) side of the car, and L-1, L-2, L-3 and L-4 for plug wires on the left (driver) side.

2. *Rotate the sparkplug boot* about one-quarter turn while pulling it off.

Caution: Never pull on the sparkplug wire itself. Rough handling will cause separation of the conductive strands, which will lead to an open circuit, poor conductivity, excessive resistance and sparkplug misfire. Pull only on the boot.

3. *Loosen each sparkplug* one turn only after cables have been removed.

Caution: Aluminum-head engines must be cool before removing plugs since plugs in a warm engine will seize and be difficult to unscrew.

4. *Blow away carbon and dirt* from around each sparkplug. Compressed air is best to use, but if an air hose isn't available use a length of vacuum hose. Aim one end at the area and blow through the other.

5. *Remove each plug* and place it in its appropriate hole in a sparkplug tray that is numbered to coincide with the number of cylinders in your car. Proper identification is important so you can relate the particular plug with the cylinder to make a proper diagnosis of sparkplug condition.

Service tip: If a sparkplug is difficult to remove, unscrew it slightly to expose a few threads. Drip some light oil on the threads and screw the plug back into place. Let oil soak the threads before you try removing the plug again.

removing Monza plugs (V8 engine)

1. Raise the car.
2. Loosen the two engine mount-to-cross-member attaching bolts on left side approximately four turns.
3. Lower the car.
4. Place a block of wood between the crankcase and a jack, and lift the engine about ½ inch.
5. Remove the No. 3 sparkplug by attaching the wrench set and breaking the plug loose. Remove the ratchet from the extension and turn the extension by hand until the plug is removed. Reverse this procedure to install the plug.
6. Lower the engine.
7. Raise the car and tighten the engine mount-to-cross-member attaching bolts.
8. Lower the car.

Plugs other than the No. 3 plug can be removed conventionally.

servicing plugs

It is extravagant to throw away a set of plugs that can be cleaned, adjusted and put back in service. However, to do a thorough job of cleaning use a sparkplug cleaner.

Where do you get a sparkplug cleaner? You can buy one made for home garage use for about $20. If you don't care to do this, take the plugs to a local service station and pay the man to do the job for you.

To service plugs correctly, proceed as follows:

1. *Wipe the plug clean* to remove moisture, oil and dirt.

2. *If the firing end* of a plug is oily or coated with wet deposits, wash the plug in a cleaning solvent, such as kerosene. Use a brush to work solvent into the lower insulator cavity. Dry the plug with compressed air—even if you have to beg an air hose. If the tip of a freshly washed plug isn't dried thoroughly, the cleaning solvent can cake deep within the plug and hinder plug performance.

3. *Clean plugs* in the cleaning machine.

Caution: Don't blast a plug for more than five seconds. Longer application could wear down the insulator and electrodes.

4. *Open the outside electrode* enough to slip a sparkplug file between electrodes. Use the gap adjusting tool of a sparkplug feeler gauge tool. Do not use pliers or any tool except a sparkplug tool to spread the electrode. If you do, irreparable damage may be done to the plug.

5. *File the center* and outside electrodes clean. Only one or two passes are necessary. Filing is important since the cleaning machine doesn't always remove electrode scale.

6. *Examine threads closely* for carbon and scale that could keep a sparkplug from seating itself properly. Clean threads with a small hand or machine-powered wire brush.

Important: Be careful that you don't touch electrodes with the brush. You may damage them.

7. *Use a sparkplug wire-type feeler gauge* to gap plugs. A flat feeler gauge of the type used to adjust distributor breaker points will give an er-

roneous adjustment. Use the gap adjusting tool to set gap by bending the side electrode.

Caution: Do *not* bend the center electrode. If you do, you will have to discard the sparkplug.

Set gap to the exact specification in your manual or to that shown on the servicing decal in the engine compartment of your car. Gap is set properly when you feel a slight amount of friction as you move the feeler gauge back and forth between electrodes.

Important: Whether you are installing reconditioned or new sparkplugs, the gap of each one you put into your car's engine must be set before installation.

installing plugs

If your engine has an aluminum head, apply a *thin* coat of graphite grease to the first two or three threads of each sparkplug. This helps prevent seizing.

Clean the cylinder head threads with a thread chaser, which you can buy in an auto-parts store, or with a small brush. If plugs use gaskets and are being put back in service, replace the old gaskets with new ones. Seat the gasket fully by threading it on so it fits flush against the base of the shell.

Tapered seat sparkplugs do not use gaskets.

If your engine uses tapered seat sparkplugs, it cannot use sparkplugs with gaskets. If your engine uses sparkplugs with gaskets, it cannot use tapered seat sparkplugs.

Screw the sparkplugs finger tight into the cylinder head and stop. Here is where we come to an impasse.

AC Spark Plug Co. and Prestolite are two leading companies that recommend the use of a torque wrench to tighten sparkplugs. Champion, on the other hand, contends that "practically no one uses a torque wrench on sparkplugs, and it is not really required."

What do *you* do? I suggest that if you have a torque wrench, use it. If you don't, use the "feel" method.

In either event, sparkplugs must be tightened *exactly* to the specifications given here which have been devised by the International Standards Organization and Society of Automotive Engineers. Although plugs won't seem to be tight, they will be tight enough. If you take liberties with these specifications, you will overtighten the plugs.

Caution: Be very careful that you don't cross-thread plugs when putting them into the cylinder head. You could ruin the threads of sparkplug ports.

selecting sparkplugs

This should cause you no problem. You start by choosing the sparkplug recommended for your engine by the car's manufacturer. This recommendation is in the owner's manual and on the service decal in the engine compartment.

We aren't going to discuss the numbering systems of sparkplugs here. It's interesting, but irrelevant since each sparkplug manufacturer has devised his own. All we want to do is emphasize that you start with the number that your car's manufacturer says to use.

Now, if this plug doesn't operate satisfactorily for the driving conditions you encounter, a plug that is colder or hotter in the heat range may be substituted. The heat range of a sparkplug is determined primarily by the length of the lower insulator. The longer the insulator is, the hotter the plug will operate. The shorter the insulator is, the colder the plug will operate.

There are three rules to follow in selecting the exact heat range plug that will operate best in your engine:

1. Select sparkplugs having the heat range specified by the car's manufacturer.
2. If plugs overheat (lower insulator blisters or turns ghostly white, and/or electrodes wear prematurely), switch to sparkplugs of the *same* make of the next lower (colder) heat range.
3. If plugs foul (firing tips get oily or sooty), switch to sparkplugs of the *same* make of the next higher (hotter) heat range.

suppression vs. non-suppression

Automotive electrical systems have long been recognized as a major source of radio frequency interference (RFI). With almost 150 million cars, trucks and buses on the road, there's a lot of radio and TV interference. To keep it in harness, all vehicles are equipped with suppression devices at the factory.

As far as cars are concerned, these suppression devices take the form of so-called resistor sparkplugs, suppressor-type secondary cables or external suppressors. Frequently, resistor sparkplugs are combined with suppressor cables or external suppressors. Suppressor cables and external suppressors are not recommended for combined use.

Regarding the selection of sparkplugs, if the manufacturer's original equipment calls for resistor-type sparkplugs, then it is suggested that you use them.

Paint preservative

Is there a way to preserve the enamel finish on a yard shed made of steel? Mine has become unsightly with mildew and rust.—James Robbins, Montgomery, Ala.

There's a great range in price and quality among yard sheds. On even expensive models, often the inside of bolt or screw holes aren't coated with enough paint. Scratching assembly bares metal and invites rust.

A new steel structure should have all scratches and bolts touched up with a rust-deterrent paint, like Rust-Oleum. A coating of auto wax helps, too, but it's almost impossible to wax all the vulnerable areas that water reaches.

Leaky tar roof

My building has a flat roof made with tar paper and tar but no gravel. The roof expands and contracts, causing breaks and leaks. I need something soft and pliable to "give" with the structure. I've tried most types of roof coatings, but they always end up as temporary patches. The building has a history of leaking.—Glen L. Zabel, Cleveland, Minn.

It sounds as if you need a new roof. If your substrate (wooden decking) is in good condition, you may want to try a product by Water Guidance Systems Inc., Branford, Conn. 06405. Send for their brochure. The product is a polyvinychloride membrane laminated to each side of a nylon reinforcing cloth or scrim for added strength. Applied with adhesive, it "gives" with the roof's movement. (It's available in 54-in.-wide strips, 32 mils thick.)

To prepare your roof for application, scrape it clean of all curled edges, pierce and nail flat all bubbles. Brush the roof clean. No ballast (stone) is used in the application. Use the special tape to seal the joints, followed by a top coating (with color choice) to protect the roof from ultraviolet rays. You don't have to rip off your old roofing, but for energy conservation, consider adding 1-in. rigid insulation to the roof.

Sticky predicament

I'm attempting to remove a pressure-sensitive foam-rubber-backed carpet from a hardwood floor. Most of the backing remains stuck to the floor. How do I remove the mess?—Raphael Bostic, Delran N.J.

I assume you want the wood floor exposed. Otherwise, I would suggest you carpet right over it. Armstrong, a leading carpeting manufacturer, suggests you apply warm water with a small amount of detergent (about 1 tablespoon per gallon). Use a sponge to moisten the backing for 30 to 60 minutes, but don't drench the rubber or you'll saturate the hardwood floor below. As the bonding agent appears to be "cut" by the water and heat, carefully remove the rubber backing. Although I haven't tried it, I think a steam iron would also be effective—much like it is in removing wallpaper. Since you already have a "mess," if the warm water and steam don't work, I'm afraid you'll have to call a professional floor refinisher for a scraping and sanding job.

Plastic sheet

I plan to replace my entire ceramic tile shower stall as dry rot has attacked the subfloor. Books from the library refer to a plastic sheet to be installed under the mortar mix for the shower pan. No one seems to carry this item. Also, what's a simple way to get the desired pitch for water to drain?—H. Lucas, San Carlos, Calif.

The plastic is polyethylene, such as you might buy for temporary storm windows or cold frames for your garden. Use a 6-mil thickness, but take care to fold it carefully at the corners; the material is somewhat stiff and could keep the mortar from filling the form.

Polyethylene is installed to prevent any water from penetrating and rotting the subfloor. The shower floor should pitch ¼ in. per foot toward the drain outlet. With the bubble centered and one end of the level resting on the high point of the line, the clearance at the opposite end should be ½ in. for a 2-ft. level; ¾ in. for a 3-ft. level and so on.

Loosening wood joints

I have to take some dining room chairs apart to make repairs. How do I loosen the glued joints?—Stephen Pinchot, Youngstown, Ohio.

Since most queries regarding wood joints are just the opposite of yours, you've hit upon a good one! Methods I've used involve moisture and therefore must be done carefully. I loosened one joint by applying warm water with an eyedropper—four applications, about five minutes apart. But to avoid damaging adjacent finishes, take care to wipe up the excess water that spills out of the joint.

You can also boil water to create steam. Then hold the joint in the steam for several minutes. (Longer exposure could damage the wood.) Tap gently with a rubber mallet to hasten breaking the glue line.

How to install car stereo speakers

By EUGENE WALTERS

There's no special trick to making your car into a total sound stereo system. The speakers can be located on the rear window deck or the front door panels and hooked into your radio or tape deck

■ YOU DON'T HAVE to have a pro install your car speakers to get a professional-looking job like the one above. But it pays to do it like the pros do.

First, decide where you want your speakers. Rear-deck speakers are often easiest to install, since many U.S. cars already have the necessary holes. But front mounts—in the doors or front kick panels—give you the best stereo effect in the front seat. And that's the seat most likely to be occupied.

Probably the hardest part of mounting speakers in a door is finding a spot where they won't interfere with structural members or the window mechanism and at the same time won't be placed where the seats will swallow up their sound. Pros (like the ones at Wally's Tape City in New York, where the pictures on following pages were taken) know these spots, but you'll have to find them. Loosen the door trim panel, and check out possible speaker sites as you raise and lower the window. Then measure carefully and cut your hole. Use a sabre saw or hacksaw, or drill a circular pattern of holes and saw from one hole to the next. But don't use a power drill or saw on carpet-covered doors—the carpet may tear or run.

To run the speaker wires, remove the inner kick-plate trim (just in front of the door) and drill holes opposite each other in the door edge and door pillar. Line the holes with grommets, so their edges won't cut the insulation. Run wire through the holes to the speakers, and solder them so they can't vibrate loose. Make sure the "hot" leads from each channel of your tape deck go to the same terminal on each speaker, or you'll lose bass response.

For rear-seat speakers, snake the wires unobtrusively through the car by tucking them under the edge of the carpet or floor mats. Where the wires pass the doors, run them under the door saddle (first removing the saddle to clear away gravel or debris that might cut the wires).

To get the wires into the trunk, you must usually remove the rear seat cushion, which is easy. But getting it locked back in again is usually a two-man job. The holes that pass the wire into the trunk should also be grommeted to prevent chafing; it's not a bad idea to caulk the space around the wires, too, against the possibility of exhaust-fume leaks.

Wedge-type, surface-mounting speakers are easiest to mount on the rear shelf, requiring only screw holes for attachment and a grommeted hole for the wire. If the wedge has an open bottom. cutting a larger hole under the speaker will give you better bass response, by letting the trunk act as a resonator.

But wedge speakers can obscure rear vision. and their plastic cases can warp in sunlight. So flush-mount speakers are usually preferred (and many wedges' grilles and speakers can be disassembled and flush-mounted, if you prefer).

Most American cars now have 6x9-inch speaker ovals cut in the metal frame under the rear shelf, often with the deck's fiber covering perforated to form a grille. If your car lacks these perforations, you'll have to cut the fiber. A sharp knife does the cleanest job, but the speaker grille should cover ragged saw-cut edges. If the metal

SEE ALSO
Amplifiers . . . Cassette recorders . . . Cassette tapes . . . Citizens band radio . . . Hi-fi centers . . . Mixers, audio

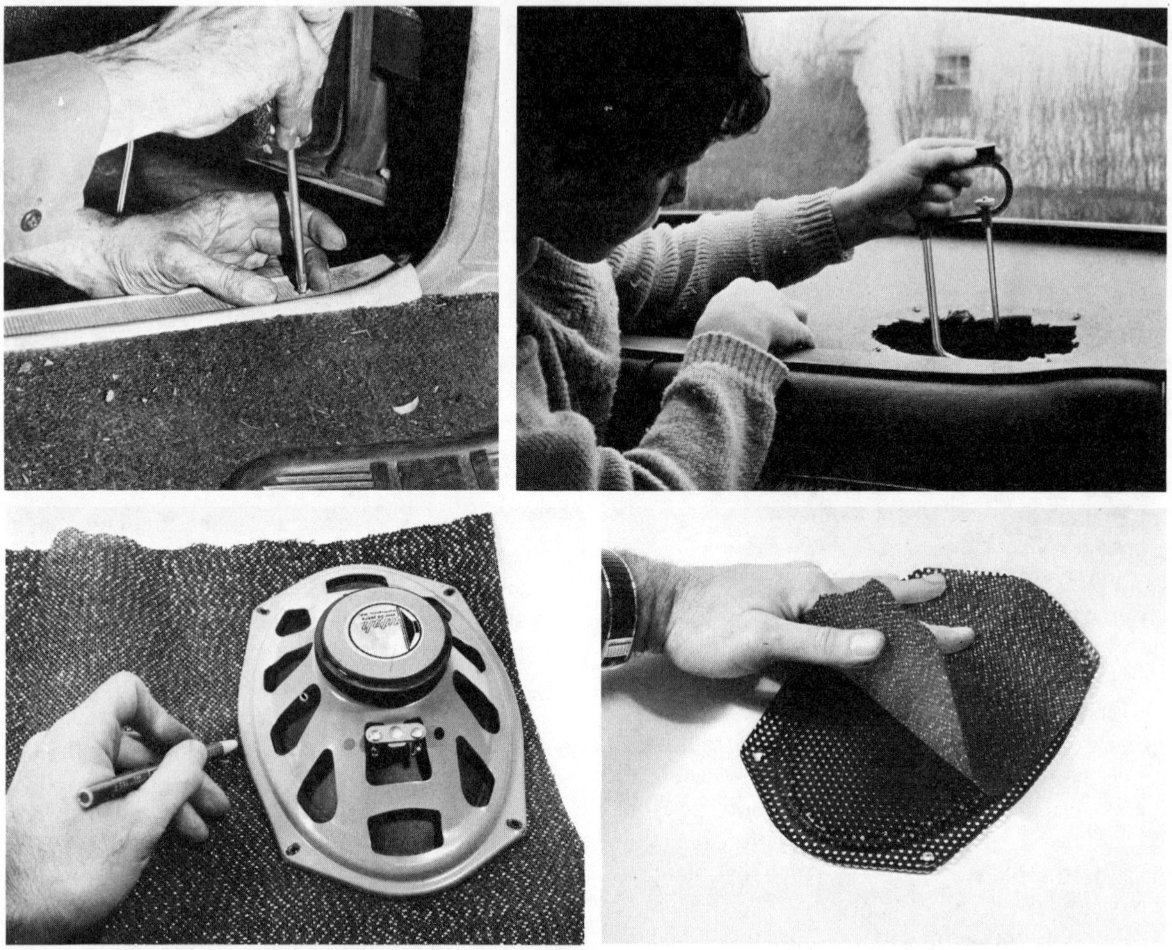

REAR-DECK SPEAKERS ARE EASY TO INSTALL

REAR DECK SPEAKERS' leads go past the doors most neatly if you unscrew the door saddle (upper left), clear out rough debris that could damage the wires, and run wire under the saddle. Rear-deck mounting is often eased by holes precut for 6x9-in. speakers. If you must cut your own hole, hacksaw work (upper right) can be reduced by drilling a series of holes and sawing between them. Slanting rear windows often prevent the use of a sabre saw from the top of the deck, but you can approach the deck from in the trunk below. Grille cloth can keep small holes from focusing sun on the speaker. Cut it to fit the speaker (lower left) and apply it under the grille (lower right). Avoid plastic grilles on the rear deck. The location is too hot and some housings can melt or warp if located there.

is not precut, you'll need a hacksaw or sabre saw. Window overhangs make sabre saws impossible to use from above the shelf on many cars, but if so, you can get in the trunk and cut upward from there. Speaker attachment holes can be poked through the fiber with an icepick; if you have to drill the metal yourself, drill from inside the trunk until the metal is holed, then finish with the icepick. Bolting the speakers in place is easiest if you have a helper in the trunk to hold the speaker nuts and lockwashers as you tighten the screws from above.

Rear-deck speaker grilles should be dark to avoid annoying reflections and preferably not be plastic, which can warp. But metal grilles' small holes (or those in some deck perforations) can focus the sun's rays like pinhole lenses, sometimes damaging speakers. Here's where an ounce of prevention (or an ounce of grille cloth) is worth lots of cure. Before attaching a metal grille. cover its underside with speaker grille cloth. Cut the cloth to fit the grille and tack it in place with beads of cement around the grille edge.

If you're wiring stereo speakers in both the front and rear of the car, use identical speakers mounted at identical heights for best sound balance. Add-on front-rear stereo balance controls may cause distortion in some installations, but they're cheap, so try them if you like. Four-channel tape decks (and some stereo ones) have built-in connections and balance controls for four speakers.

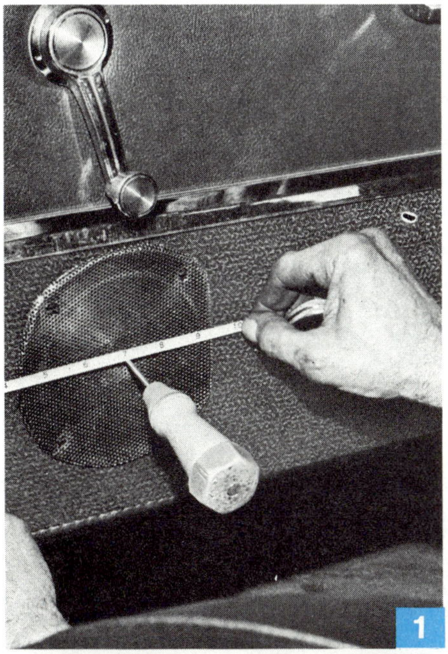
1

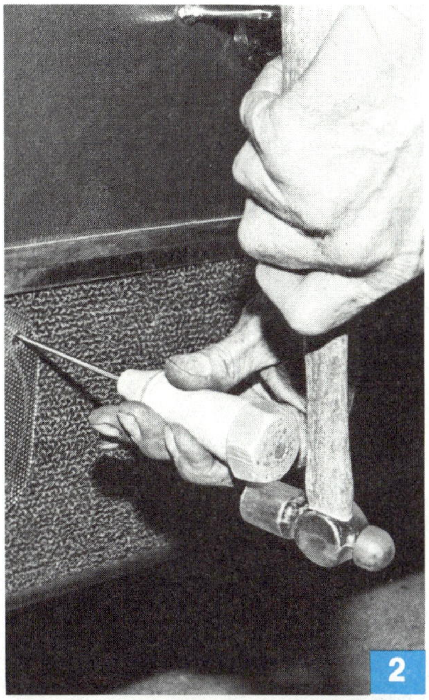
2

3

4

5

OPEN UP THE DOOR PANEL. IF YOU'VE NEVER DONE IT BEFORE, YOU'LL FIND IT'S EASY TO DO, AND HELPS YOU PINPOINT THE BEST SPEAKER LOCATION

AFTER OPENING THE inside door panel to find the best speaker location, measure the distance on the panel (1); mark, punch and drill mounting holes operating from the most reasonable working position you can find (2); then cut the speaker hole (3). Use care; carpeted door panels are often vulnerable to power tools. Now remove the car's inner kick-plate panel (4); drill the panel and door edge; and thread the wire (4 and 5). Grommets are a smart idea. Run leads to the speaker (6) and solder them, positive to the same post on each speaker. Position the speaker, align the holes (7), and mount the speaker and grille (8). Use self-tapping screws if the door is metal, speed nuts or washers and lockwashers if it's fiber. The grille shown here matches the car's interior, but a chrome grille such as the one shown on page 2753 is significantly more scuff resistant.

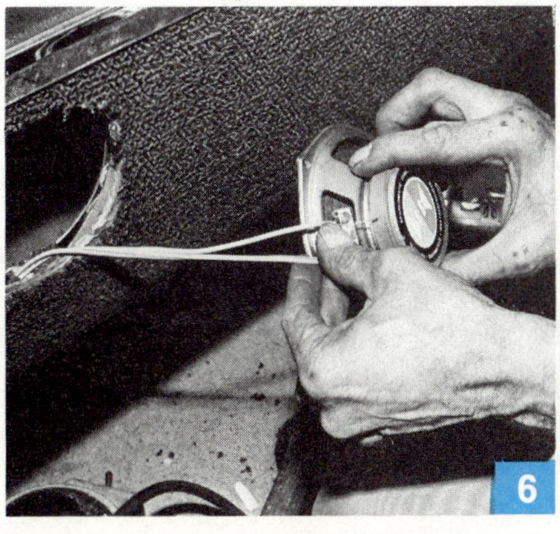
6

7

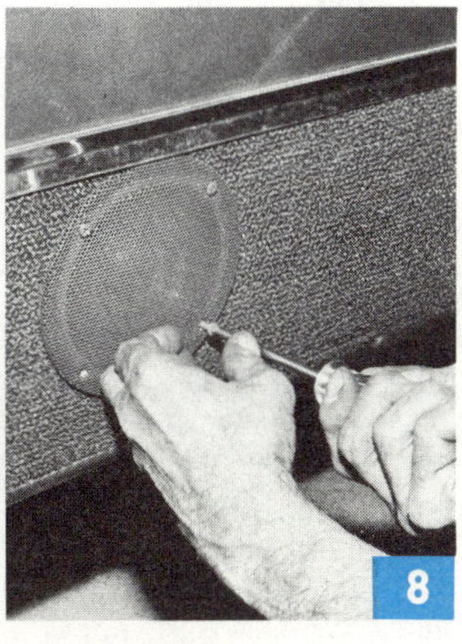
8

■ NOW YOU CAN TRY those mid-air tricks that daredevils do when schussing down a mountainside of snow. Freestyle hot-dogging has hit water-ski level and, with practice, you can take off from a towboat wake for the new sport of aqua-acrobatics.

A mistake on water skis is more likely to end up in a splash than in traction at a local hospital, but Ricky McCormick, considered the country's top trick skier, recommends perfecting your water-ski fun-

UP AND OVER as towboat cuts away from jump ramp, Carl Lyman performs his specialty, a feature of his routine at Cypress Gardens.

PROPERLY OUTFITTED in life vests and helmets, freestyle skiers practice trick Spread Eagle maneuvers that are part of aerials.

Try acrobatic skiing on the water

By BILL McKEOWN

WORLD CHAMPION jumping, slalom and trick skier Ricky McCormick tunes up for performance in the freestyle with some slalom practice.

BEFORE TRYING Forward Flips and Back Flips, riding up outside of one tow wake and landing on the other, Lyman performs ramp jump flip.

BACK-TO-FRONT one-ski stepover is practice for forward or backward spins.

PRACTICING ASHORE, freestylist Carl Lyman shows Aquamaid Callie Beatty the towline and balance position for front-to-back stepover.

GETTING MORE difficult, trick requires proper toehold for 360° turn.

PRACTICING CORRECT form for skiing backwards, Beatty leans her weight away from boat's direction of pull. Such dry runs on beach simplify things on the water.

damentals before taking to the air. For this ultimate test of your technique, there's the challenge of the Spread Eagle—where skis are spread wide apart and then brought back together just in time for a graceful touchdown. Then try the Daffy—scissoring the legs by lifting one ski up in front of you while the other points down and back. The Back Scratcher swings the aft end of the skis up to touch your back while the front tips point straight down—with legs tight together, please.

Front Flips and Back Flips are forward and back somersaults that end in skiing position. Then go around in the air twice before you land.

Recently, rules for championship water-ski aerobatics have become more formalized:

- Tow rope length must exceed 46 feet, and a safety jacket may be required.
- A skier will get three jumps per pass, and be allowed three passes. Between jumps, the skier may perform one double-wake or surface trick.
- Skiers may execute aerial tricks from a ramp at 20, 25 or 30 MPH.

Early hot-doggers used 42-inch trick skis without rudders and little bend in the ends. Newer freestyle models have turned-up tips, and may be wood, fiberglass or graphite laminates. Back ends are squared off and lengths run from 45 to 49 inches with widths ranging from 8½ to 9½ inches. Small 4-inch rudders help the hot-dogger to cut sharply.

First step is to decide which foot comes first. As you graduate from two skis to one, try lifting one foot to determine which gives better balance. Try standing on land with eyes closed and leaning forward. The foot that keeps you from falling will be your front steering foot.

One-ski deep water starts, slalom runs and wake jumps all deserve extensive practice. A boat speed of 20 to 25 mph should give the sharpest wake.

Tricks over wakes and off the jump ramp are the final hot-dogging tests. And now you think you're ready for the Worm Turn? Simply fall on your back at 35 mph in a shower of spray. Ride there a moment, spin upright and leap to your feet again as if nothing had happened.

The easy way to make 'stained glass' projects

By PENELOPE ANGELL and CONSTANCE SPATES

■ YOU CAN GIVE the distinctive look of stained glass to your workshop projects with very little effort and no special tools. The modern version, using liquid lead squeezed from a bottle, combined with glass stains applied with eyedroppers, eliminates the time-consuming, exacting

SEE ALSO

Bottle craft . . . Carving, wood . . . Clay pottery . . . Hobby centers . . . Jewelry . . . Lapidary . . . Marquetry . . . Metal casting . . . Potter's wheels . . . Tin-can crafts

EACH SQ. = 2"

MATERIALS LIST—CASA LIGHT BOX

Key	No.	Size and description (use)
A	2	¾ × 3⅜ × 25 9/16" pine (sides)
B	1	¾ ×3⅜ × 37 9/16" pine (bottom)
C	1	¾ × 3 × 37 9/16" pine (top)
D	1	1⅛"-dia. × 11′ round; cut 4 pieces to size (molding)
E	2	¼ × ¼ × 36" pine (top, bottom cleats)
F	2	¼ × ¼ × 23½" pine (side cleat)
G	1	⅛ × 24½ × 36½" hardboard (back)
H	1	¼ × 24 × 36" opal/frosted acrylic (glass stain panel)
I	4	⅛ × ½ × 4" hardwood (spline)
J	2	24" General Electric Bright Stik (light)
K	2	L-hook (back fastener)
L	1	canopy switch
M	3	solderless connector
N	1	power cord and plug (with Bright Stik)
O	4	medium-size screw eye (for hanging)
P	1	55" picture-hanging wire.

Misc.: 1" brads; ¾" brads; lamp wire; 6d finishing nails; wood filler; white glue; pigmented shellac and glossy white paint. To stain the panel, you'll need eye droppers; full-size pattern; toothpick; four 4-oz. bottles of Titan's Liquid Lead. Also, 2-oz. bottles of Glas Stain in the following colors: Royal Blue, 2 bottles (1)*; Hot Orange, 1 bottle (2); Red, 1 bottle (3); Lemon, 2 bottles (4); White, 2 bottles (5); and Black, 1 bottle (6).
*Numbers in parenthesis match color code in pattern, left.

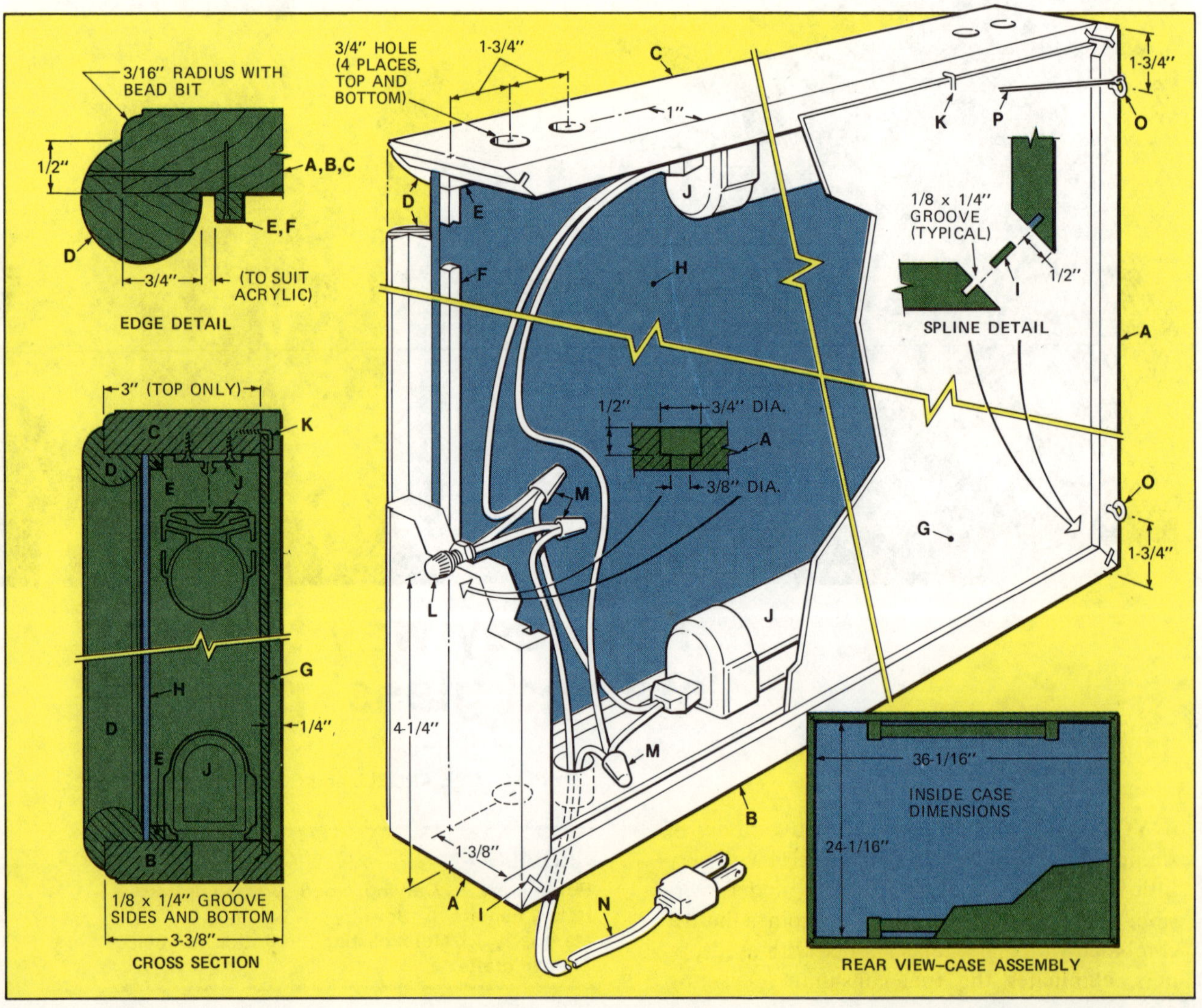

techniques of cutting glass and fusing pieces. Yet the effects are comparable in beauty to real stained glass.

To introduce you to this colorful craft, we've designed three shop projects around stained-glass panels. Following are glass-staining tips.

wash glass with vinegar

To stain a pane of glass or a mirror, wash it thoroughly with a vinegar-and-water solution or alcohol. For an acrylic panel, first remove the protective paper and wash the plastic with warm water. Dry with a soft, lint-free cloth. Enlarge the pattern to full size.

To stain a mirror or frosted acrylic, transfer the pattern to it with carbon paper. On clear acrylic or glass, place the pattern underneath on a flat surface. Apply liquid lead (black) or liquid pewter (gray) following the pattern lines.

Cut the tip of the liquid lead applicator, taking care not to cut too large a hole. You can enlarge it later if necessary.

test size of bead

Squeeze the lead onto scrap paper to check the size (diameter) of the bead that is formed. Once the hole size is correct, you can use the top on subsequent bottles. Store it after each project for use on the next one.

Outline the design on the panel with liquid lead, being careful that every bit of the line adheres. Each section must be a tight well so the stains cannot run together. Use a toothpick to dab the bead down where it's not secure. Let the leading dry overnight. Note: Don't expose this water-based material to the outdoors.

applying the glass stain

Place the outlined piece on a *level* surface so the stain won't flow beyond its enclosure. Apply the stain with eye droppers, using a different dropper for each color.

To avoid accidents, hold a tissue under the dropper until it is directly over the area to be filled. To achieve the best color, fill each area with stain as far as possible, without letting the stain overflow.

If any bubbles should appear during the application, use the dropper to remove them. If you expel as much air as possible from the dropper before inserting it into the stain bottle, the bubbles will be negligible.

casa light box

Begin work by cutting frame parts (A,B,C) to size. Cut grooves in these parts to hold backing (G). Also miter the ends and cut grooves for splines (I). Sand these parts smooth.

Cut hardwood splines and assemble the frame with glue and clamps. Check that it is square; let the glue dry overnight. Next day, secure with well-set 6d finishing nails at joints. Fill holes with wood filler.

install cleats

Cut and temporarily install cleats (E,F). These are removed later for painting. Bore vent holes at top and bottom. Cut and test-fit back (G).

Rip a length of 1⅛-in. round to suit for molding (D). Sand smooth.

Temporarily install panel (H) and tack-nail molding (D) to check fit. Note: If your decorative panel is sheet acrylic, allow expansion space when installing molding and cleats to prevent stress. Install hardware at back. Check parts for fit and disassemble.

install lamps

Install the fluorescent lamps, making the connections as shown in the drawing. Carefully locate lamps (J) to allow clearance between them and the front and back panels. Cut the lamp wires to length *after* fixtures are in place. Make the splices as shown and secure them with solderless connectors (M). The connectors, canopy switch (L) and extra lamp wire are hardware and lamp-store items. After testing, remove the fixtures from the box. Permanently secure molding (D) to the frame with 1-in. brads (two per strip), and use wood filler in holes.

apply sealer

Sand again if needed. Dust and wipe with a tack rag. Apply a coat of sealer (pigmented shellac such as Bin or Enamelac) and let dry overnight. Sand lightly, dust and wipe with a tack rag. Apply paint, covering the inside, too, to aid reflectivity. Paint cleats (E,F) out of the box. They are easier to paint that way.

When parts are dry, lay the box face down and reassemble in this order: Install Casa panel. Install cleats (E,F) using ¾-in. brads. Install the lamps and arrange the wires around the frame. Keep them in place with insulated staples, being careful that the staples don't penetrate the insulation.

Install the back, remount the hardware and hang the unit from a pair of hefty picture hangers. Note that lower screw eyes (O) act as spacers to keep the box parallel with the wall; otherwise it would hang at an angle.

A DRAGONFLY in brilliant blues presides over this glass-stained mirror. The handsome frame, made from conventional wooden moldings, is an original design from our workshop.

dragonfly mirror

Start work on the mirror frame by cutting base frame (A). Sand, and then cut the frame molding (B), beginning with the inside pieces. These four pieces overhang the inside of the base frame by ¼ in. and form the rabbet that holds the mirror (E). Measure carefully and cut the miters on the inside molding pieces so that they are ½ in. less than the length and width of the base cutout. This creates the glass-holding rabbet. Attach with glue.

attach molding

Measure, cut and attach the remaining molding pieces (B,C) using glue and 1¼-in. brads. Set brads slightly and fill holes with wood filler. Temporarily position the completed dragonfly mirror. Cut and test-fit molding (D); then remove mirror.

Sand the frame, if needed, before finishing it. Dust and wipe with a tack cloth. Apply two coats of McCloskey Heirloom Satin Varnish as directed, sanding, dusting and wiping with a tack cloth between coats. Reinstall mirror and back molding. Attach screw eyes (F) and picture wire (G).

PRACTICE on scrap until you can apply liquid lead in a uniform line.

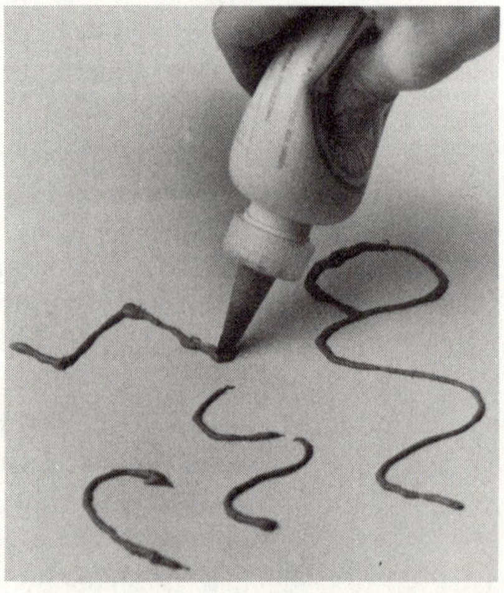

PLACE full-size pattern under the panel; trace the lines with liquid lead.

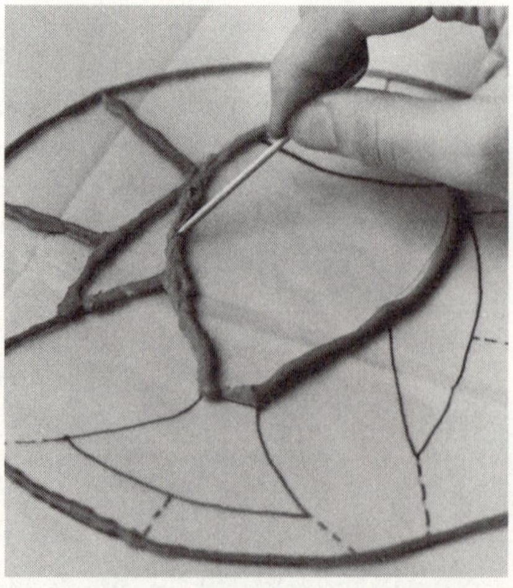

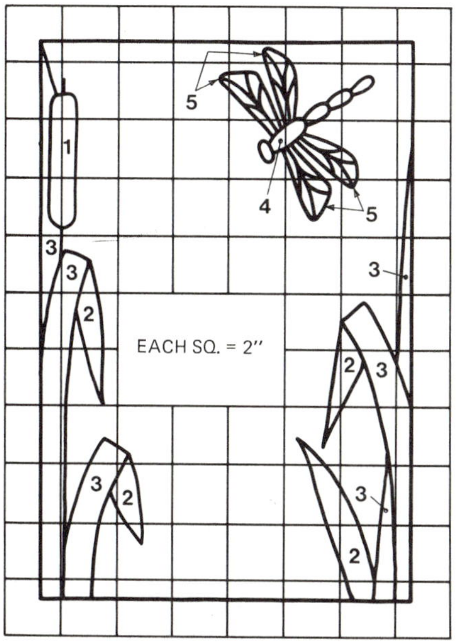

MATERIALS LIST—MIRROR

Key	No.	Size and description (use)
A	1	¾ × 20 × 26″ plywood (frame base)
B	1	9/16 × 1⅛″ × 24′ half round, cut to size (molding)
C	1	⅜ × ¾″ by 8′ half round; cut to size (edging)
D	1	½ × ½″ × 8′ quarter round, cut to size (back molding)
E	1	¼ × 14¼ × 20⅛″ mirror (decorative panel)
F	2	small-size screw eye (for hanging)
G	1	30″ picture-hanging wire

Misc.: ¾″ brads; 1¼″ brads; white glue; wood filler and McCloskey Heirloom Varnish. To glass-stain the mirror, you'll need: eye droppers; carbon paper; full-size pattern; pencil; toothpick; one 4-oz. bottle of Titan's Liquid Lead. Also, one 2-oz. bottle of Glas Stain in each of the following colors: Amber (1)*, Lime (2), Emerald (3), Turquoise (4), Light Blue (5).
*Numbers in parenthesis match color code in pattern above.

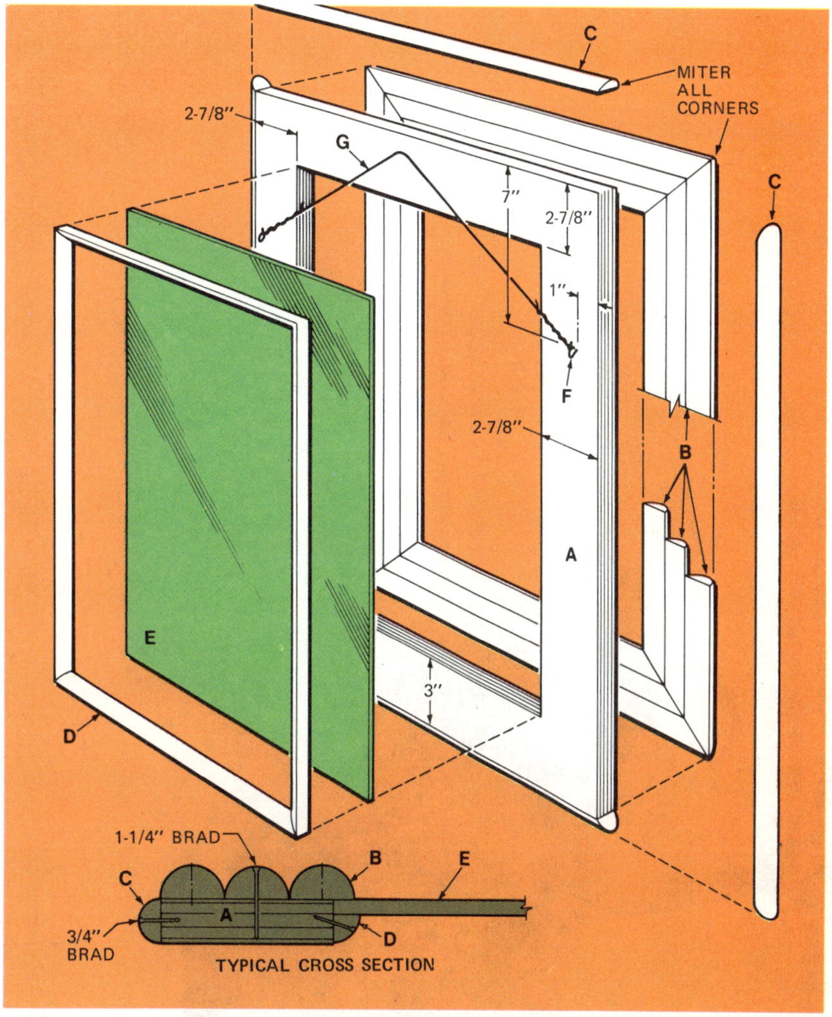

PRESS DOWN on the lead with a toothpick so all areas adhere to panel.

APPLY GLASS STAIN with eyedroppers. Hold tissue under dropper.

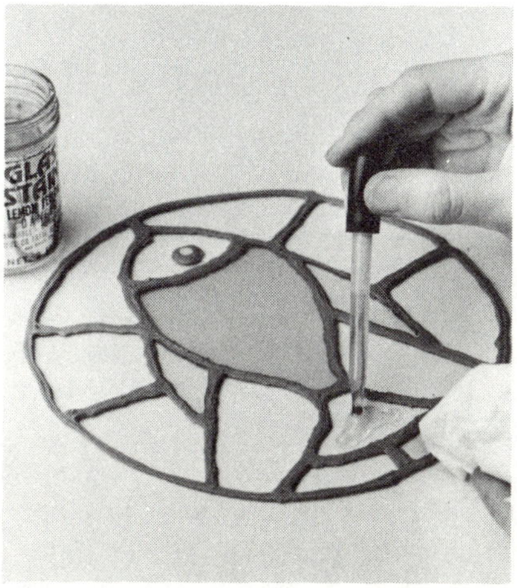

HOW TO ORDER GLASS STAIN PATTERNS

You can order full-size patterns of the decorative glass-stain panels used in these projects. Send check or money order payable to Popular Mechanics to Dept. GSP, Box 1014, Radio City Station, New York, N.Y. 10019. Specify pattern: Dragonfly ($1.25 each), Casa ($1.75 each) or Zodiac ($1.95 each). Allow three to four weeks for third-class mail delivery. For faster, first-class mail, add 35 cents.

YOU CAN SECTION off living space and still maintain an open feeling with this colorful zodiac panel. To separate areas, suspend the panel over a bookcase.

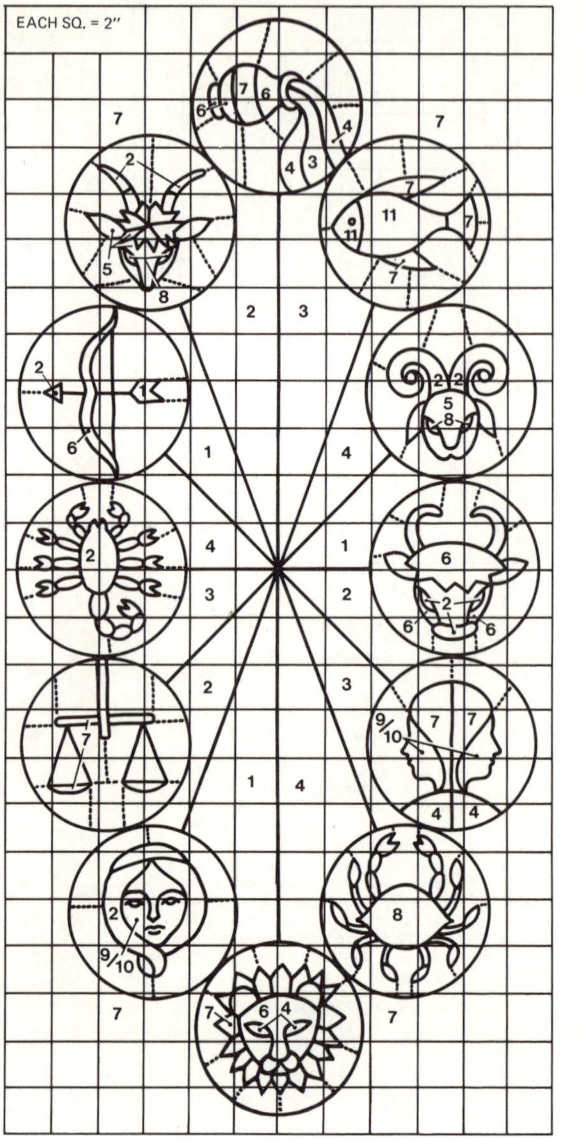

zodiac hanging divider

When you stain the zodiac panel, be certain that the edges of the circles are touching so that the background yellow doesn't flow into the center. Spindles (A,B,C) are ready-made and available at many lumberyards.

Rip four strips of hardwood (E,F) for the frame. Cut a $^3/_{16}$x$^1/_4$-in.-deep groove down the centers to hold the zodiac panel. Note: Acrylic expands and contracts, so make sure the panel is loose in the grooves to prevent stress.

cut the cross members

Cut the shaped upper and lower cross members (D) with a band or sabre saw. Sand the ripples smooth. Mortise recesses in D to receive sides (E). Bevel edges of D using a router with 45° bevel cutter.

Test-fit the frame parts with the zodiac panel in place. Nail and glue parts (F) in place. Trim spindles (C) to fit the assembly. Mark them before cutting so you can produce an accurate fit.

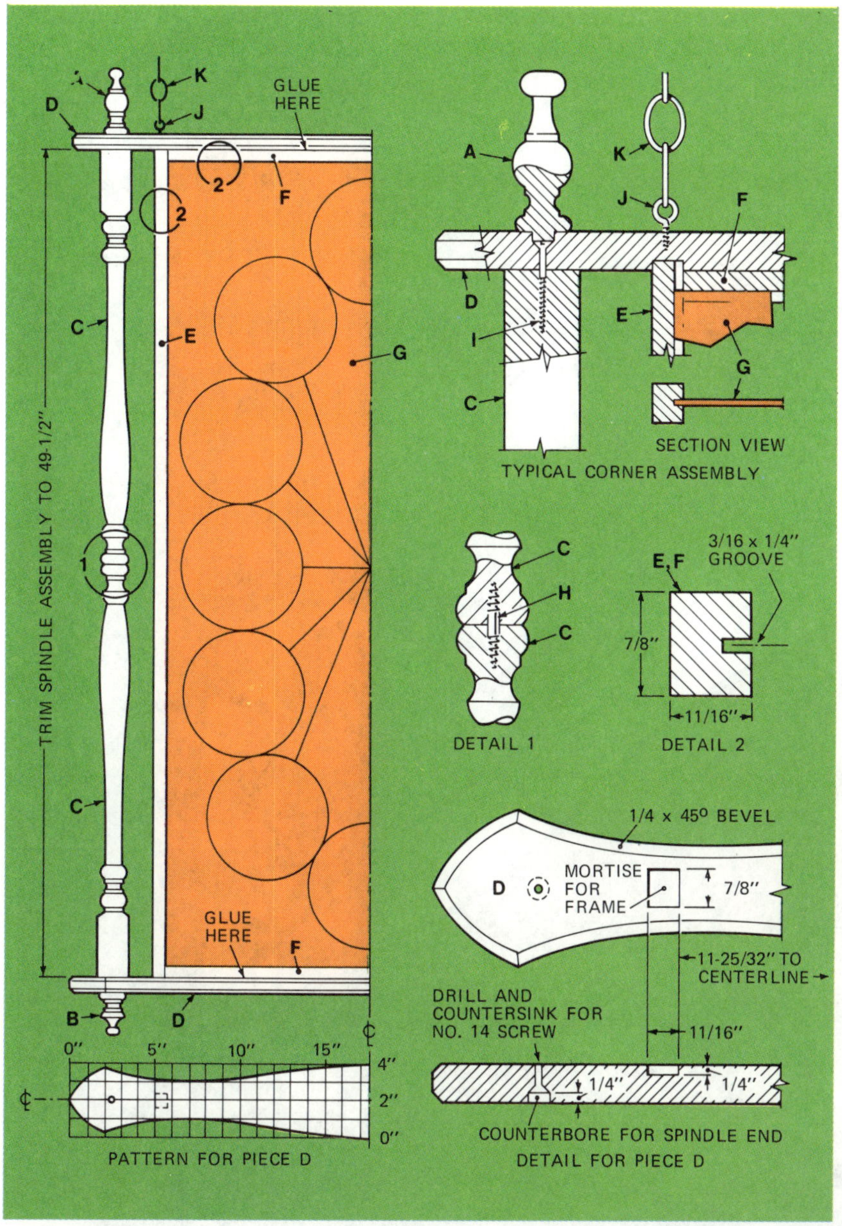

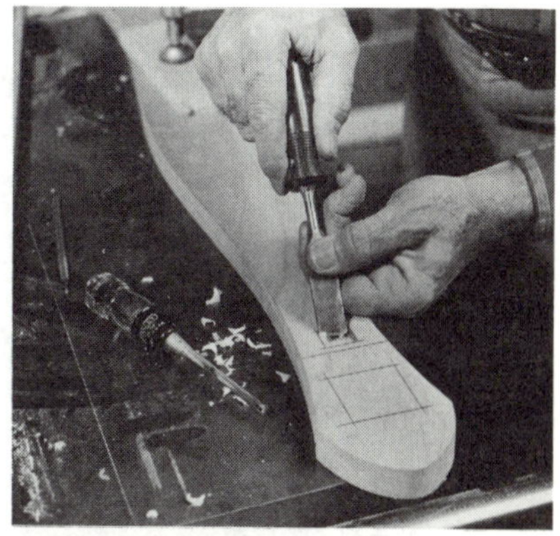

MAKE MORTISES in the cross members (D) by first boring ¼x¾-in.-dia. holes to remove much of the waste. Chisel out remaining waste to the bottom of the hole.

TRIM oversize spindles (C) to fit. Use a straightedge or square to mark cut.

clamp spindles

Clamp the spindles in place with bar clamps. Bore pilot holes for attachment screws through cross members (D) into the long spindles. Counterbore for the screwheads.

Assemble the unit without the zodiac panel. Attach screw eyes (J) and chain (K); hang to paint. Finish end spindles separately. Disassemble, keeping mating parts together; reassemble with panel.

MATERIALS LIST—ZODIAC PANEL

Key	No.	Size and description (use)
A	2	large spindle end
B	2	small spindle end
C	4	30" stock spindle turning or two 60" turnings
D	2	13/16 × 4 × 35" maple (cross member)
E	2	11/16 × 7/8 × 49½" maple (vertical frame)
F	2	11/16 × 7/8 × 29 3/16" maple (horizontal frame)
G	1	1/8 × 24 × 48" acrylic sheet (decorative panel)
H	2	dowel screw
I	4	2" No. 14 fh screw
J	2	large-size screw eye
K	2	chain as needed to suspend panel

Misc.: White glue and black Krylon semigloss spray paint. To glass-stain the panel, you'll need: full-size pattern; eye droppers; toothpick; four or five 4-oz. bottles of Titan's Liquid Pewter or Liquid Lead. Also, 2-oz. bottles of Glas Stain in the following colors: Red, 2 bottles (1)*; Amber, 2 bottles (2); Light Blue, 2 bottles (3); Turquoise 2 bottles (4); White, 1 bottle (5); Yellow, 1 bottle (6); Lemon Yellow, 2 or 3 bottles (7); Pumpkin, 1 bottle (8); Pink, 1 bottle (9); Clear Extender, 1 bottle (10); and Hot Orange, 1 bottle (11).

The art of real stained glass

By ROBERT WORTHAM

■ ESSENTIALLY, A STAINED-GLASS WINDOW is a transparent design of colored glass held together by lead strips and enclosed in a frame of wood or metal. Its design can be as complex as a jigsaw puzzle or as simple as a checkerboard.

The latter project can consist of three rows of glass panes, each measuring 2⅞x5½ in. with alternating colors of blue and amber, surrounded by a 1-in.-wide amber border. Tools required are a glass cutter, lead knife, hammer, shingle nails, square, 40 to 80-watt soldering iron, 60-40 solid-core solder and oleic acid (flux).

An inexpensive glass cutter with a steel cutting wheel is adequate for general cutting but one with a tungsten wheel will stay sharp longer. An inexpensive lead knife can be made by sharpening the opposite curve of a linoleum knife. Do not use a soldering iron of higher than recommended wattage or it may melt the lead during soldering.

Stained-glass sources are listed in your local directory under "glass, stained, & supplies." The glass can also be purchased by mail from Whittemore-Durgin, Box 2065, Hanover, MA 02339.

Cathedral glass is machine-rolled, smooth on one side and has medium to heavy texture on the other. Of uniform ⅛-in. thickness, this glass is priced from $1.95 to $3 per square foot. You cut cathedral glass on the smooth side.

Antique glass is not an old glass, but a product of modern glass chemistry. A very soft glass, it cuts easily on the smooth side and costs from $3 to $6 per square foot.

SEE ALSO
Bottle craft . . . Clay pottery . . . Glass cutting . . . Internal carving . . . Jewelry . . . Lapidary . . . Marquetry . . . Potter's wheels . . . Tin-can crafts

It's the irregularities of stained glass that enable it to refract and multiply light. In window and door installations, the smooth side of the glass faces inward.

Especially contoured strips of lead, called lead *came,* make up the skeletal component into which stained glass is fitted to compose a stained-glass window. Lead comes in 6-foot strips and must be stretched before cutting to remove crimps and twists. To straighten lead, fasten one end in a vise and grip the other with pliers and pull. A strip will increase about two inches in length after straightening, but avoid excessive stretching as it will weaken the lead. In all window and door designs the longest leads should run continuously along the greatest dimension of the design (that is, uncut from border lead to border lead).

The pattern of a leaded-glass window is drawn full-size on white paper and used as a substrate on which the components of the window are assembled. Lay out the pattern first in pencil, then ink the lines with a 1/16-in.-wide felt-tip pen. The inked lines, called "heart" lines, approximate the 1/16-in.-thickness of the lead heart on the inside leads.

Staple the pattern to 3/4-in.-thick plywood and assemble the window on it. Nail wood cleats at a 90° angle along two sides of the plywood workboard to hold the window components together and insure squareness as the window is assembled. Place three sides of the border lead in position on the pattern, leaving off the fourth side so the glass and inside leads can be fitted into place.

Beginning at the inside corner where cleats intersect, fit a 1-in. border glass into the channels of the border lead and of the inside leads across the width of the window. Now cut the shorter leads that form intersections between the full-length leads and position them across the width of the window, completing the top border. Proceed with the second row of glass and leads, tapping each glass section gently and snugly into place with a hammer and wood block.

nails hold pieces in place

Use shingle nails across the width of the window and along the border lead to hold the design together. Proceed with the third row of glass and leads. As each glass is fitted into the lead channels, remove the two nails of the preceding row and renail it at the end of the third row. After two or more glass sections have been nailed, soldering can begin.

Solder the two 45° mitered corners of the border leads, then the intersections of the inside leads. To solder an "open" glass section, use scrap glass held with nails to keep solder from running into the channels of open intersections.

After a couple of window sections have been soldered, the remainder of the window is assembled and nailed up to complete the soldering. When all joints and intersections have been soldered on one side of the design, turn the window over and solder on the opposite side.

Using 1/8-in. solid-core wire solder (rosin-core will not adhere), melt the solder onto the intersection with a tacking motion. Do not preheat the lead intersection as in regular soldering and keep the tip of the iron a fraction of an inch above the lead, dropping the solder onto the lead. If the melted solder "peaks" after soldering, the iron is not hot enough; if the solder bubbles, the iron is too hot. Let the iron cool for a few seconds; then begin again.

Use metal sash putty (gray) to fill gaps in the lead channels. With your thumb, force the putty in between the glass and the lead leaves on both sides of the window.

When puttying is completed, remove putty oils and residue from the oleic acid by scrubbing both sides of the window with dry sawdust and a stiff brush. Let putty set overnight before installing window in its frame.

BORDER LEAD is channeled along one edge to fit standard 1/8-in. glass and in section is shaped like a block Y. Flat and oval inside lead is double-channeled and in section is shaped like a capital I.

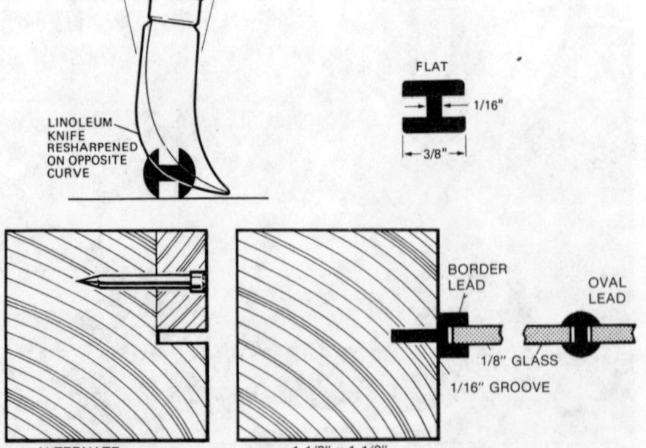

1. PATTERN for this 12x20-in. window is penciled, then inked with 1/16-in.-wide felt-tip pen. Inked lines (called "heart" lines) approximate the 1/16-in. thickness of lead hearts. Shaded double lines are the 9/16-in. border lines.

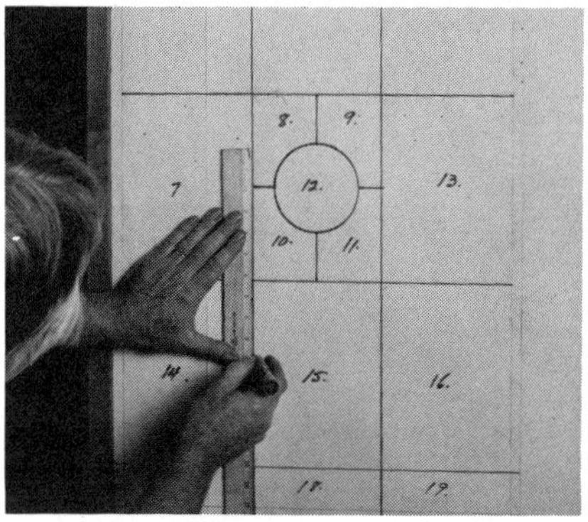

2. WHEN PATTERN IS complex like this one, number each section and corresponding glass pane as they are cut. This is important in a design where several colors of glass are used.

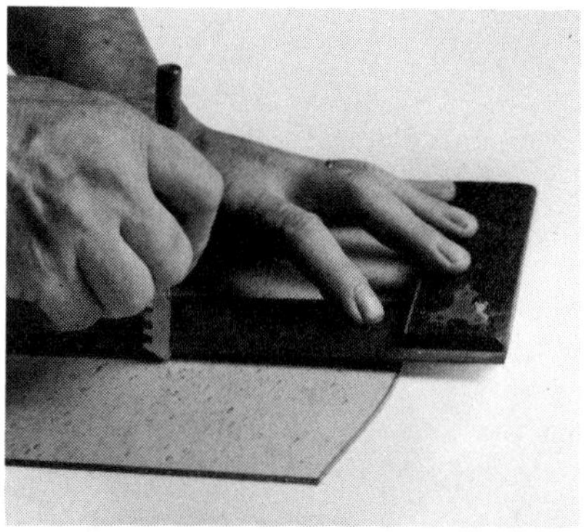

3. TO SCORE GLASS, dip the cutter in kerosene to clean the cutting wheel, hold cutter perpendicular to glass and begin scoring a fraction of an inch from edge of the glass in a continuous even stroke without lifting the cutter.

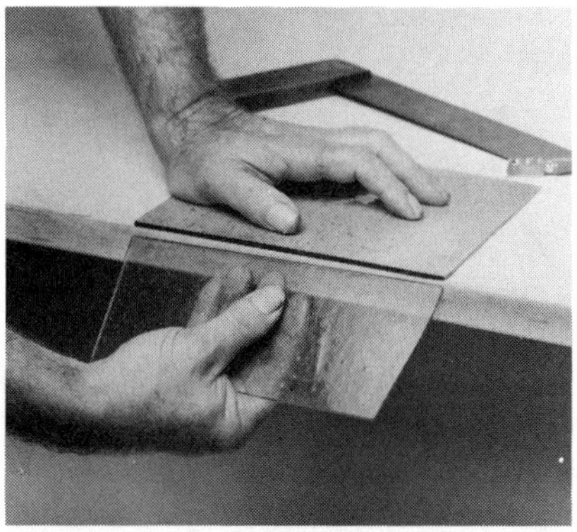

4. AFTER SCORING, place score line parallel to and beyond table edge and press down firmly on each side of line. If score is uniform its full length, glass will separate evenly and cleanly and fit channels of leads perfectly.

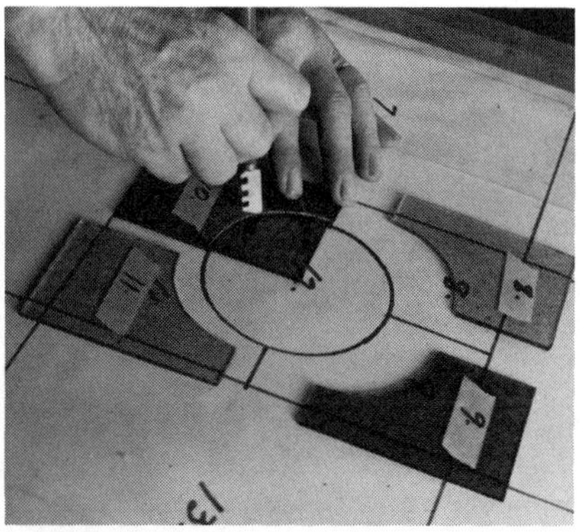

5. WHEN CUTTING out for a rondel, place the glass on top of circle pattern as shown and score glass freehand, carefully following the outside edge of the circular heart line with the cutter. Keep cutter perpendicular to the glass.

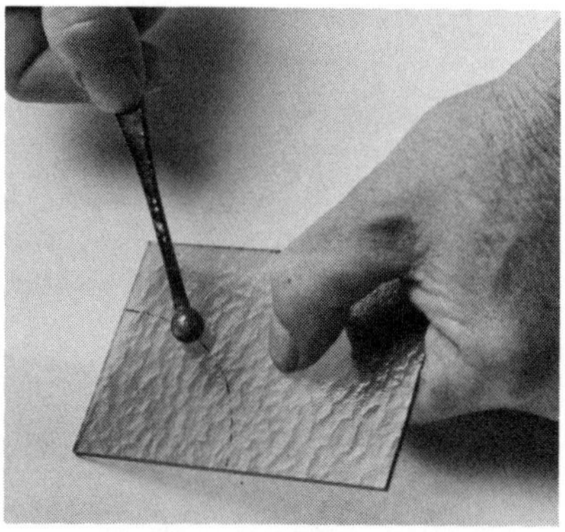

6. TURN THE SCORE line over, grip the glass as shown, press downward on glass and tap along score line with the ball end of the cutter. As you gently tap, you will see glass gradually fracture along the score line.

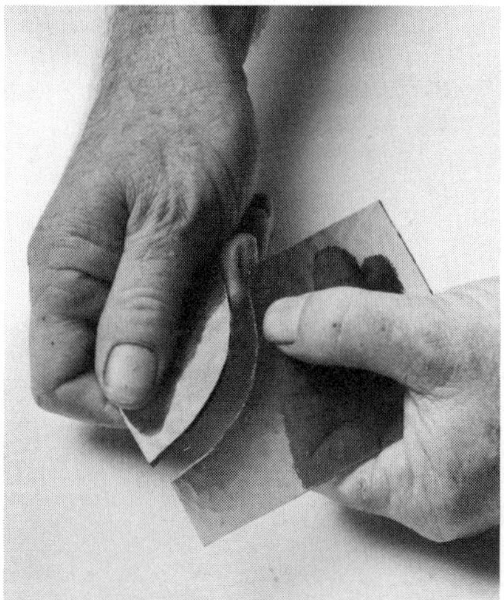

7. USING YOUR knuckles as a fulcrum, grip the glass with both hands and snap the pane by bending down and outward on both pieces. The glass will part neatly if you make the score line cleanly with the same even pressure.

8. L-SHAPED CLEATS nailed to wood workboard hold the window along two sides and assure squareness. Tap each section of glass firmly into channels of leads with hammer and wood block.

Basics of wood staining

Once you prepare the surface correctly the battle is more than half over. A pigmented oil stain is the easiest for the beginner to apply and gives immediate quality results

■ THE MOST IMPORTANT step in obtaining a quality stain job is to correctly prepare the surface even before you start to apply the stain. Though all steps in preparation are important, none is more so than the final sanding you give the raw wood. Here are tips that will save you time and labor as well as assure professional-looking results:

■ Always try to sand with the grain. If you must sand across the grain, do so with a very fine paper and use light pressure.

■ Use a rigid backup block. A chalkboard eraser is a dandy tool for this purpose—its other (soft) surface can be used later to sand between finish coats.

■ To extend an abrasive paper's useful life, tap it lightly on workbench so that dust clogging the coating will fall away.

■ Between sandings with various grits, thoroughly dust or vacuum the work. Always wipe thoroughly with a tack cloth after dusting.

Basically, there are six stains—penetrating resin, water, pigmented (oil) wiping, NGR (non-grain-raising), padding and varnish (or lacquer) stains. All of them do what they are supposed to

SEE ALSO
Finishes, wood . . . Furniture, care of . . . Sanding . . . Varnish . . . Wood finishes . . . Woods

FINAL SANDING ON raw wood is done with 180-grit paper. A chalkboard eraser is a good backup block.

A TACK CLOTH is wiped across all of the surfaces to pick up minute particles of dust.

APPLY BOILED LINSEED oil to end-grain surfaces to equalize the amount of stain absorbed.

do; the important difference is how they are worked. Pigmented oil stains are the best choice for beginning finishers, so the discussion here will be limited to that type. Though some may argue that an oil stain hides too much grain, it gives you a great deal of control and working time. In fact, any time you think too much grain has been hidden, simply wipe the still-damp stained surface with a turpentine-soaked rag. If you decide a stain is too dark after it has dried, lighten it by sanding with 180-grit or finer sandpaper.

When staining softwoods, you can assure an even color tone by first sealing the wood with a coat of one-lb.-cut white shellac (thinned 50 percent with denatured alcohol). Allow the sealer coat to dry overnight, then rub lightly with double-O steel wool; dust and wipe with a tack rag before staining.

If you would rather not use a sealer—but do not want the end grain to absorb a greater amount of stain and turn darker than the surface areas—first give the end grains only a coat of boiled linseed oil.

You can apply oil stain with rags or brush, but the latter is neater. Allow stain to set five or more minutes, then wipe off excess with clean, lint-free cloth. Make certain that final wipes are with the grain to avoid streaks.

NEXT, THOROUGHLY dust entire piece using a clean brush saved just for finishing projects.

WIPE WITH tack cloth after dusting. Replace tack cloth in envelope to make it last longer.

WORKING ONE surface at a time is a good idea. Apply oil stain with bristle brush or rags.

AFTER ALLOWING it to dry 5 to 10 minutes, wipe off excess. Last wipe should be with grain.

TYPICAL HOUSEHOLD stains can be found just about anywhere: A, brick floor; B, wood floor; C, floor tile; D, washable fabric; E, synthetic fabric; F, rug; G, wood; H, nonwashable fabric; I, laminate; J, white fabric; K, painted surface.

How to remove stains from almost anything

ALMOST ANYTHING CAN, or will, stain something. There are staining agents that can cause spots on synthetic and natural fabrics, painted surfaces, masonry, marble and other surfaces commonly found in any home. However, most stains can be classified by types—and for each type there is an effective solvent that will break down and remove the stain.

On these pages are several charts listing the most common household stains, the solvents to use on them and the best methods to use to remove them. When removing stains, it's important to remember that it is possible a spot may be a combination of more than one staining agent. (For example, a machine oil stain could include traces of metal.)

Also keep in mind that a solvent that won't harm one type of fabric may harm another. Because of this, the choice of solvent is determined by both the stain and the fabric. Generally, water or a combination of water and a second solution, can be used on washable fabrics—but will not be effective on nonwashable fabrics.

Carbon tetrachloride, and other nonwater solutions, are useful on both types of fabrics. *Caution: Regardless of the type of solution used, and with carbon tet in particular, take time to read the manufacturer's instructions for using.* Follow all safety instructions and work in a well-ventilated area. If possible, work outdoors when using carbon tet or naphtha.

How you treat stains on white or colored fabrics is important, too: Inert solvents such as carbon tet, benzol, alcohol and water can be used on both colored and white fabrics. But avoid using active solvents such as citric, tartaric acids, alkali (ammonia or borax), laundry bleaches and hydrogen peroxide on colored fabrics. These will generally change the colors of dyes. There are four ways of applying solvents to fabrics for removing stains: 1) soaking, 2) applying pressure, 3) front sponging, and 4) back sponging.

SEE ALSO
Concrete . . . Floors . . . Furniture, care of . . . Tile, floor

WHEN TO WATER-SPRAY STAINS PRIOR TO USING SOLVENT

RESPOND TO WATER SPRAY

Alcoholic beverages
Blood
Candy
Catsup
Chocolate
Cocoa
Coffee
Egg
Fruits, fruit juice
Gelatine
Glue
Grass
Ice cream
Iodine
Meat juice
Mercurochrome (may need chemical treatment)
Mildew (may need chemical treatment)
Milk
Mud (allow to dry first and brush)
Mustard (yellow stain often impossible to remove completely)
Perfume (wet immediately; may not be removable if set)
Perspiration (wet immediately; may not be removable if set; may affect dyes)
Soft drinks
Sugar
Tea (treat as soon as possible)
Tobacco
Tomato juice
Toothpaste
Wine
Writing ink

STAINS LISTED above generally will respond to a water-spray treatment before dry cleaning with a solvent. Blood must be removed before dry cleaning.

DO NOT REQUIRE WATER SPRAY

Adhesive tapes
Butter
Candle wax (scrape off first)
Carbon paper
Chewing gum (scrape off excess)
Cod liver oil
Crayon
Cream
Fats
Floor wax
Gravy (spray lightly to remove starch first)
Grease, soil and tar
Ballpoint-pen ink (may need chemical treatment)
Lead pencil
Linseed oil (if set, almost impossible to remove)
Lipstick (some stains)
Machine oil
Mascara
Mayonnaise
Petroleum jelly
Rouge
Salad dressing
Shoe polish (may require chemical treatment)
Soot

DRY CLEANING only is required by above stains. Some may call for special treatment—in some cases with chemicals (refer to the comments in parentheses).

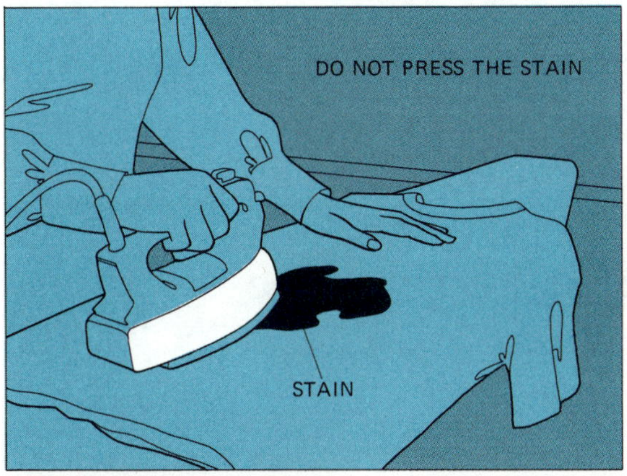

DON'T SET THE STAIN

If a stain becomes set (fixed in the fabric), it can never be removed without some damage to the fabric. Thus, there are several rules of thumb you should follow to help safeguard against setting stains inadvertently:

1. Avoid heat. If a garment or slipcover becomes stained, *do not* press the stain, because heat sets stains.
2. Sponge stained areas as quickly as possible using lukewarm water.
3. *Don't* use home-spotting agents such as cleaning or lighter fluid. Check charts on these pages to determine which solvent and method to use.
4. Don't rub stain; sponge it as shown at right.

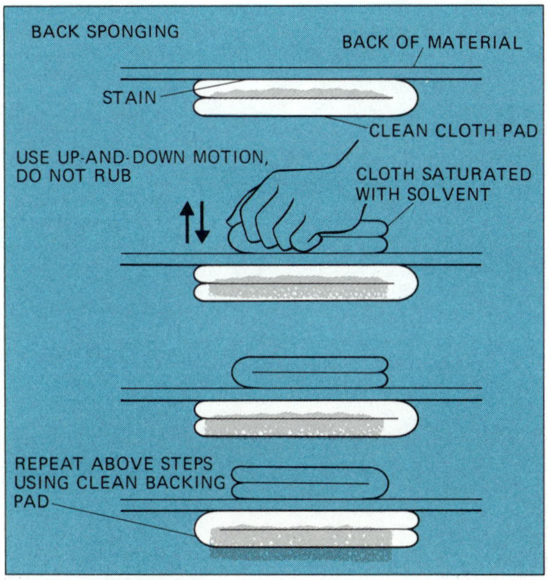

BACK SPONGING

To back sponge, place stained side face down on clean, absorbent material. Then sponge the back of the stain with a pad saturated with solvent appropriate for both material and stain. Important: Do not rub; rather, use an up-and-down padding motion. Final step is to replace the cloth pad below with a clean one and repeat the padding to remove all traces of stain from the fabric.

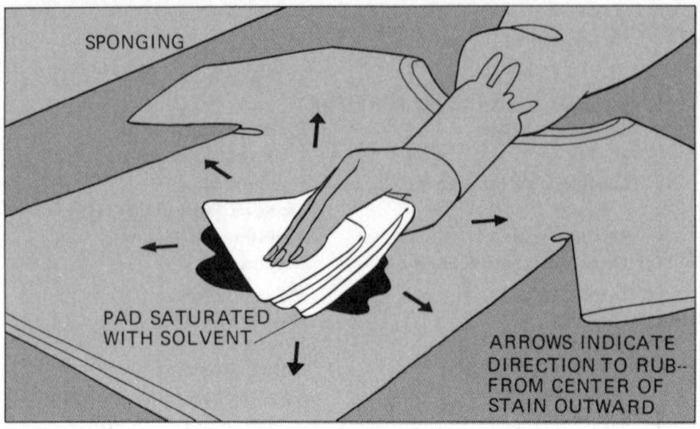

FRONT SPONGING

Sponging is probably the most frequently used method of removing stains from non-washable fabrics. Front sponging (applying solvent to the face of the fabric) works well with most grease solvents such as carbon tet. The stained fabric should be backed up with absorbent material or a blotter, and the rubbing strokes should be away from the center of the stain. Don't rub in circles over stained areas. This will only cause rings (of the stain) which will decrease in darkness as the circle, or stain, spreads.

COMMON STAINS AND THEIR TREATMENT

STAIN	HOW TO REMOVE IT
Coffee	Hot water; if stain remains, use oxidizing solvent.
Gum	Scrape off as much as possible; then use carbon tet.
Ink	Apply citric acid or oxalic acid—or apply these alternately with laundry bleach. Some colored inks can be removed with water or alcohol.
Iodine	Use hot water or alcohol; on starched material, use hypo.
Latex paint (fresh)	Use water, detergent, ammonia.
Latex paint (old)	Soak in ammonia.
Lipstick	Rub with lard or petroleum jelly; use grease solvent, detergent.
Mildew	Detergent; then use a laundry bleach or hydrogen peroxide.
Oil paint (fresh)	Remove oil with turpentine or benzol; then launder. On nonwashables, use carbon tet.
Oil paint (old)	Soak in ammonia or borax; then launder.
	NOTE: Before using any solvent on fabric, be sure it is safe. Test on scrap of same material if possible or try solvent on out-of-sight part (i.e. shirttail) of garment first.

TYPICAL SOLVENTS

SOLVENT CLASS	NAME OF SOLVENT
Hot water	
Inert solvents	Carbon tetrachloride*, benzol, turpentine and alcohol.
Oxidizing solvents	Laundry bleach and hydrogen peroxide*.
Detergents	Detergent solution, soap in alcohol.*
Acids	Citric acid, oxalic acid, tartaric acid, acetic acid (vinegar).
Alkali	Ammonia water, borax solution.
Reducing solvents	Hypo solution.
Lacquer solvents	Acetone, lacquer thinner.
	*Mildest solvent of its class; best for delicate materials.

TYPES OF STAINS

TYPE	EXAMPLES	SOLVENT Washable Material	SOLVENT Nonwashable Material
Protein*	Egg, meat, blood, milk, cream	Cold water, detergent	Cold water, inert solvent, detergent
Grease	Petroleum jelly, fats, oils motor oil tar	Grease solvent, detergent	Grease solvent
Water-soluble	Sugar, candy, syrup	Water, detergent	Cold water† inert solvent, detergent
Dye‡	Fruit, grass, dyes	Hot water, oxidizing agent	Warm water mild oxidizing agent
Starchy	Flour, starch	Hot water, detergent	Inert solvent, detergent, warm water
Iron (rust)	Rust	Acid	Acid†
Solid soil	Mud, mud particles	Brush off, detergent, inert solvent	Brush off, detergent, inert solvent

* Do not use heat in any form or hot water.
† Sometimes usable by sponging; test before using.
‡ Do not use soap or alkaline substances.

ASPHALT AND VINYL-ASBESTOS FLOOR TILES

Stain-removal methods: A. Remove or wipe from floor. **B.** If freshly spilled, take up by blotting—don't rub; let dry. **C.** Wash with water-soaked rag. **D.** If dry, scrape off with putty knife. **E.** Wash with cloth dipped in liquid cleaner; rinse. **F.** Rub lightly with cloth dipped in alcohol and rinse. **G.** Rub with 00 steel wool dipped in liquid cleaner; rinse. **H.** If G fails, apply mild household cleaner rub thoroughly. **I.** Polish surface when completely dry.

STAIN	METHOD FOR REMOVAL
Asphalt adhesive	ADGHI
Alcoholic beverages	ACI
Blood	AGHI
Butter	DEI
Catsup	AEI or AGHI
Cement (household)	DGHI
Chewing gum	DGHI
Cigaret burns	GHI
Coffee	ACI
Detergents	ACI or GI
Dye	BGHI
Eggs	ACI
Foodstuffs	ADGHI
Fruit juice	AEI
Furniture polish	ADGHI
Grass stains	GHI
Grease (vegetable)	ADGHI
Ice cream	AEI
Lacquer	BEI or DGHI
Mercurochrome	BFI or BGHI
Mildew	GHI
Milk	AEI
Mucilage	BDEGHI
Mustard	AEI
Nail polish	BEI or DGHI
Oil (vegetable or petroleum)	AEI
Paint	BEI or DGHI
Rubber heel marks	GHI
Rust stains	GHI or A
Shoe polish	AGHI
Soft drinks	ACI
Solvents	BEI
Strong soaps	ACI
Tar	ADGHI
Tea	ACI
Varnish	BEI or DGHI

BRICK AND WOOD STAINS

Many types of stains on materials other than fabric can be removed by washing with a mild detergent. Where an oily substance has penetrated a wood (or concrete) floor, a poultice consisting of an oil solvent (such as turpentine) mixed with an absorbent agent—corn meal, for example—will usually do the stain-lifting job. Stains on marble tabletops can frequently be removed using this method. If the stain is still fresh, it is best to dust on the absorbent material, then apply a pad saturated with solvent. Ordinary stains that penetrate brick and stone masonry can usually be removed with this method, but in all likelihood, some degree of rubbing will be necessary.

How to lay out and build stairs

■ CHANCES ARE, the stairs a homeowner is most likely to replace are either in the basement or on the back porch. Interior stairs are generally of the more intricate housed-stringer type (below). This type should be left to professional stairbuilders.

You can build stairs either in your shop or at their location. Generally speaking, the more intricate the stair design, the better it is to do the building in the shop. But if you do, make certain you will be able to move the finished staircase into its position.

SEE ALSO

Additions, house . . . Basement stairwells . . . Decks . . . House additions . . . Lumber . . . Measurements . . . Railings . . . Steps

Three things to keep in mind when laying out and installing a stairway are safety, adequate headroom and space for the passage of furniture. If the stair rise is too steep or too shallow, the steps are sure to be difficult to ascend and descend, and could cause missteps and falls. Poor layout may result in inadequate headroom which could lead to bumped heads (for tall persons) and inability to maneuver furniture up or down the stairs.

In most homes, there are two types of stairs. Principal stairs are designed to provide easy, comfortable access to another level; they are architecturally coordinated to the room in which they are located. The second type, service (or basement) stairs, are generally steeper and constructed of less expensive materials.

PRINCIPAL STAIRS

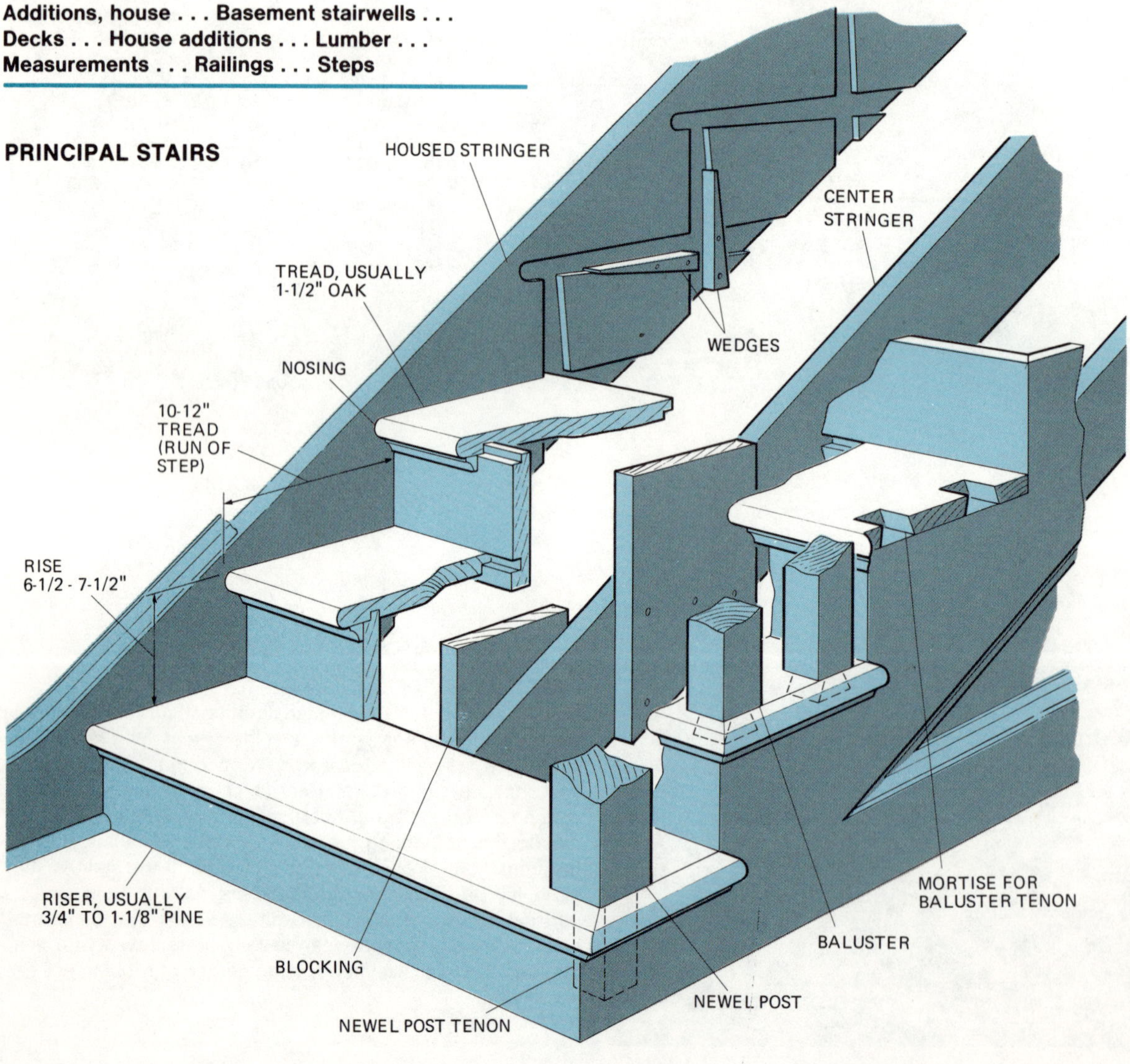

TYPES OF STAIRS

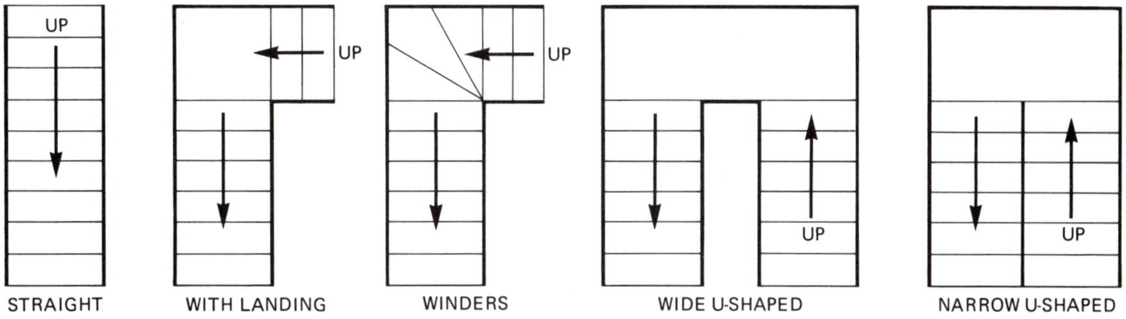

Stairways may have a straight, continuous run with or without an intermediate platform (landing), or they can consist of two or more runs at angles to each other. If your stairs must have an angle, it is at this point that the landing should be installed.

Another stair design incorporates winders—the turn is negotiated by radiating treads. For safety, if winders must be used, they should be installed at, or near the foot—not at the top—of the stairs.

Remember these points when laying out stairs:

1. Allow for minimum headroom of 80 in.
2. Generally, treads should be between 10 and 12 in. wide and risers should be 7½-in. high. The formula used by most professionals is: Twice the riser height plugs the tread width should equal 25. When you lay out your stairs, use risers that will put you close to that number.
3. Angle of the stairs should be between 30° and 36°.

STAIRWAY DESIGN

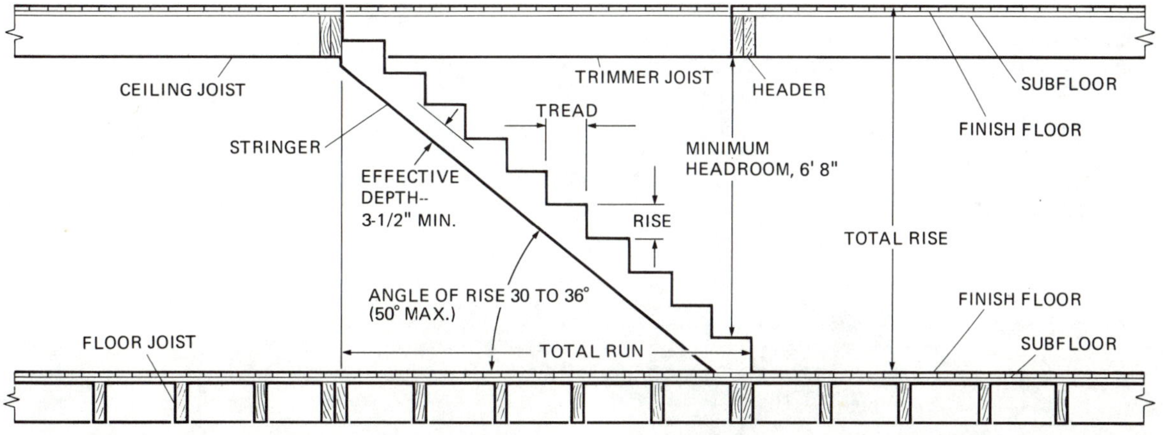

There is a definite relationship between width of treads and height of riser. All stairs should be laid out to conform with these well-established rules.

Any variance from these standards will result in awkward stairs which create a safety hazard and are tiring to use. If the treads are too short, the risers will be too high, so that your toe is likely to kick the riser on each step. But when the treads are too long, the risers will be too low, enough so that you will be making a conscientious effort to shorten your stride; this, too, is tiring.

Experience has proven that a riser of 7 to 7½ in. is about perfect. By using the formula mentioned you will find that the tread for a 7½-in. riser is 10 in. For comfort, as the riser gets shorter, the tread should be correspondingly wider. For example, a 6½-in. riser should have a 12-in. tread.

MATHEMATICS IN STAIRBUILDING

When replacing an existing stairway, you already know its location and width, but you will need to determine the correct height of the risers and width of the treads. (If a landing is to be included, consider it—for design purposes—as simply another step. Its length and width will be decided by the available space at the landing location.)

To figure the number of riser needed, you first select a suitable riser height. Then divide the total rise—distance in inches from top of the lower floor to top of the upper floor—by the riser height chosen.

If you get a full number as your answer, let it represent the amount of risers needed. Usually, however, the result will include a fraction. When this happens, divide the story (total) height by the whole number that's nearest (above or below) the fractional answer. The result of this second division will give the riser height. You can then proportion the tread by using the formula outlined on the preceding page.

In another formula to adjust riser height, you multiply the tread width by the riser height. Ideally, the answer should be as close to 75 as possible. Thus, a riser height of $7\frac{1}{2}$ in. multiplied by a tread width of 10 in. gives the perfect combination—75.

Here's an example of such calculations, assuming a story height of 9 ft. 6 in., or 114 in. and riser height of $7\frac{1}{2}$ in. When you divide the 114-in. story height by $7\frac{1}{2}$ in., you get 15-$\frac{1}{5}$ risers. Obviously, you cannot have a fifth of a riser, so the nearest whole number to use in the next calculation is 15. In other words, you can assume that 15 risers will be required, so you now divide the total story height of 114 in. by 15 in. to get 7.6 in., or approximately $7\frac{9}{16}$ in. as the height for each riser.

Next, to find the width of the treads, multiply the riser height by 2 and subtract this from 25. For example, 2 x $7\frac{9}{16}$ in. equals $15\frac{1}{8}$ in. Deduct this figure from 25, which leave $9\frac{7}{8}$ in. as the correct tread width.

Thus, the figures you should use for this example stairway are:

1. Risers: 15, each $7\frac{9}{16}$ in. high.
2. Treads: 14, each $9\frac{7}{8}$ in. wide.

Note that there is always one more riser than the number of treads.

TYPES OF STRINGER (CARRIAGES)

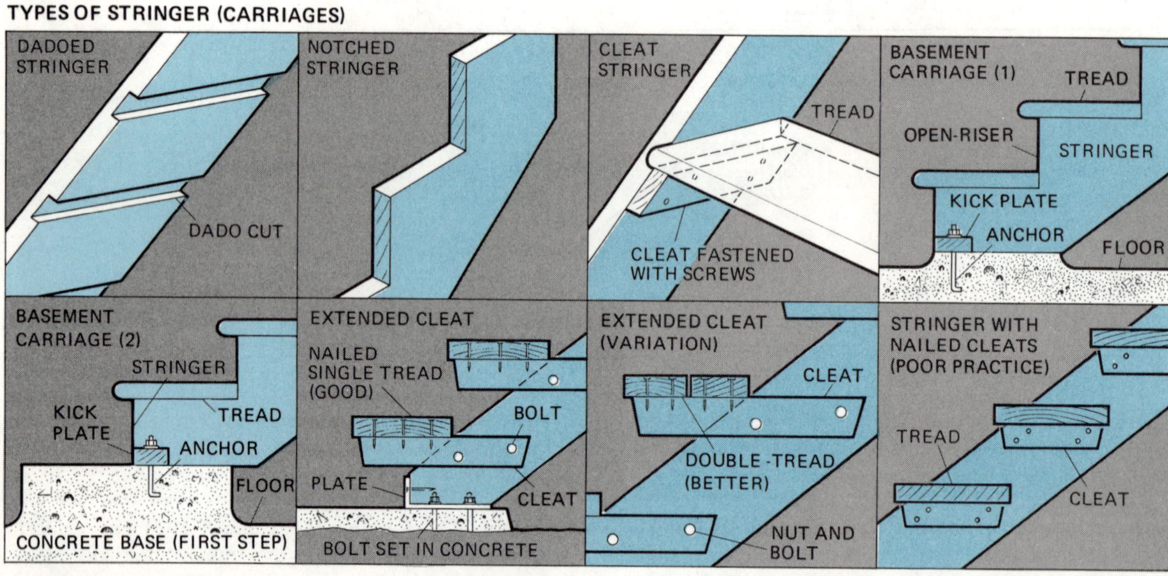

PLANNING STRINGERS

Treads and risers should be fixed solidly to stringers that are set level and plumb. Several methods for fastening treads and risers to stringers are shown above. Stringers shown here can be built by a careful do-it-yourselfer. The intricate housed stringer (page 2874) with tapered dadoes and wedges is better left in the hands of a pro.

In contemporary architecture, open stairways are frequently called for; that is, no risers are used. This type of stairway is becoming increasingly popular as modern architecture comes into greater use. However, when you contemplate replacing a stairway in an older home, the stair design should remain conventional—unless the entire home decor is being changed—in order to conform to the house style. It's safe to say that in a majority of cases a stairway should be replaced by a design that is similar to that of the original stairway.

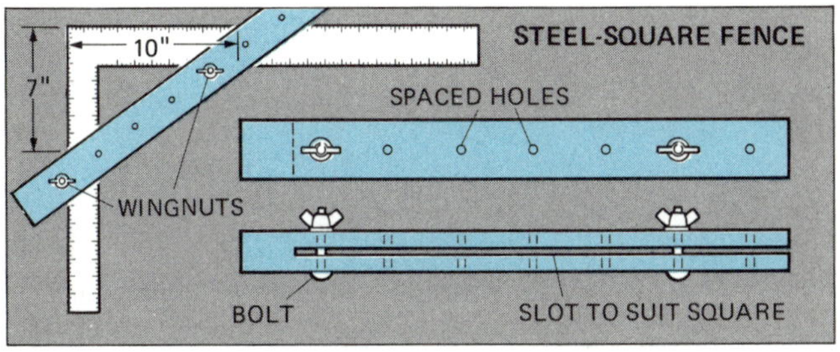

FOR ACCURACY, USE A FENCE

It is just about impossible to lay out a stringer accurately without an aid such as the fence shown at left. Use hardwood and simply bore a series of in-line holes down the center of the fence to accommodate a pair of wingnuts. Then, saw a slot through from the top to the bottom so that the fence can be used on the square as shown.

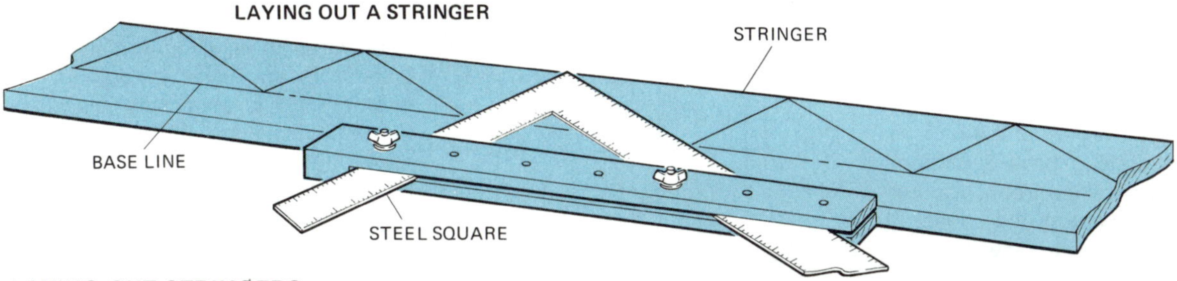

LAYING OUT STRINGERS

Since lumber shrinkage is one of the stairbuilder's worst enemies, you will be wise to use only well-seasoned lumber. If you plan to construct a principal stairway, you can purchase treads and risers of standard widths from a local lumberyard. Most yards also stock (or can quickly get) standard oak treads that are dressed to an actual thickness of 1¹/₁₆ in. These days it is not uncommon to find risers constructed of 1-in. pine (actual dimension, ¾ in.). But since there is less chance of cupping and warpage with the heftier stock, you'll find it better to use 1⅛-in. material (5/4-in. stock).

Starting steps (with curved ends), newel posts, handrails and balusters also are stock items carried by most building-supply outlets.

Secondary stairs are generally built using 2x6, 2x8 or 2x10 lumber for the stringers and treads. If risers are to be installed on such a stairway, they can be of ¾-in. stock.

After calculating the number of risers and treads required, and their respective height and width, begin by laying them out on the stringers as shown in the above sketch using a steel framing square. Your layout must be accurate.

After riser and tread positions have been indicated on the stringers, you can proceed with construction of the stairs. Stringers can be cleated, dadoed or notched, depending on your preference. If they are of the latter type, for structural reasons you must adhere to the 3½-in. minimum distance between base line and edge of stringer as shown in the drawing on page 2777.

If stringers are to be dadoed, construct a template or jig from ¼-in. plywood which can be clamped or tacked to the stringers to guide your router. When you're satisfied that the jig is accurate, make match marks on it so that it can be aligned accurately on the stringer each time it is relocated. The jig design should allow at least one riser and one tread groove to be made with each clamped setup.

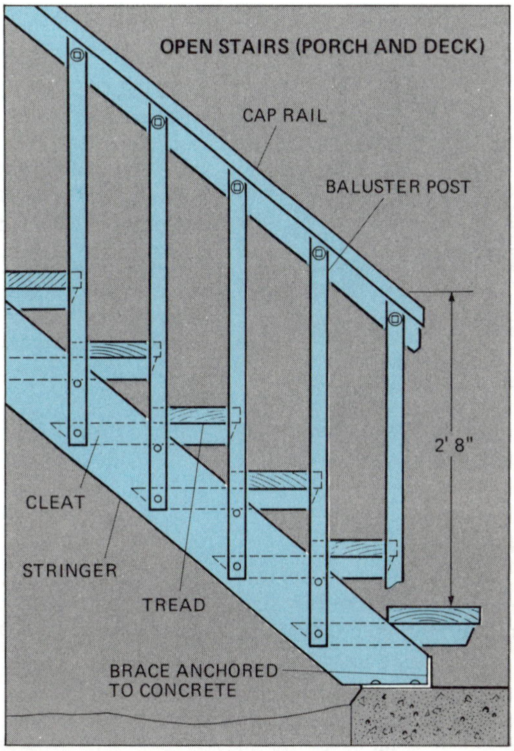

ABOUT HANDRAILS

For safety—particularly for the elderly—all stairways should have a handrail. On a closed stairway, it is simply attached to the wall using handrail brackets. On open stairs, the handrail is located atop balusters which end against a newel post at the foot of the stairs. Usually balusters are dovetailed into the treads, but they can be installed by toenailing three or four finishing nails into the tread. If you use the latter method, predrill pilot holes to prevent splitting the hardwood treads. Regardless of stair style, handrails should always be 32 in. above the tread at the riser line.

How to stop stalling

By MORT SCHULTZ

■ GONE ARE THE DAYS when practically every engine stall could be blamed on an incorrect carburetor idle speed or choke setting. Emissions controls and vacuum systems are presently giving drivers the most fits.

Eighty-five percent of the cars experiencing stalling have a malfunctioning emissions control or vacuum-related component as the cause. By stalling, I mean an engine that quits

KEEPING the choke valve working freely is basic preventive maintenance.

running at idle or while the car is moving, when the engine is cold or warmed up.

no laughing matter

Stalling can kill you. An engine that has a tendency to stall can die suddenly when the car is cruising, or when acceleration is necessary.

Stalling, therefore, should not be taken lightly. If you drive one of the cars involved in a recall or safety investigation, get it to a dealer. If you have a different make or model, find out what causes stalling and fix it.

There are many deficiencies that

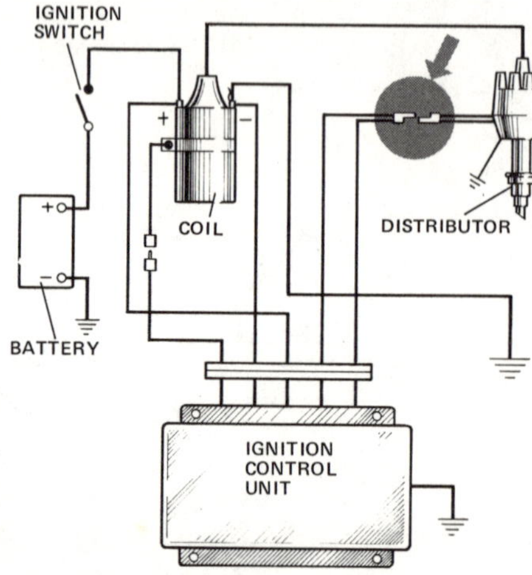

CONNECTOR (arrow) on electronic ignition systems of 1974–76 AMC vehicles loses contact and causes stalling—and it led to recall by the manufacturer. Problems like this make home troubleshooting tricky.

THERMOSTATIC air-cleaner operation when engine is cold is shown below. As engine warms up, the air valve opens, allowing cooler outside air into the carburetor. Make sure the valve is working properly.

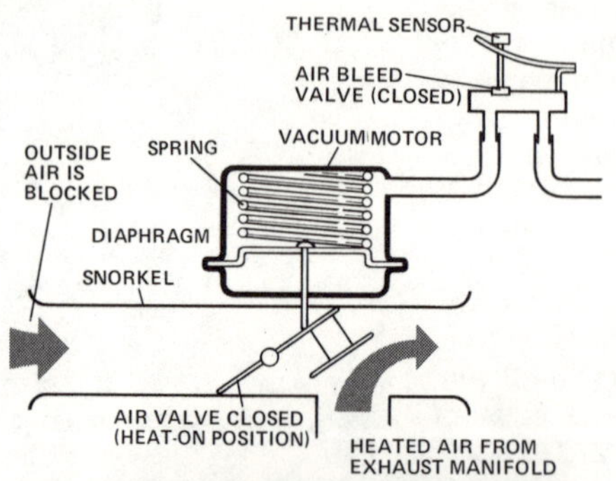

contribute. Initially, an engine tuneup should be done. Concentrate on the following:

■ A compression test with the engine warm, to establish if stalling results from excessive carbon in the engine. This is especially important for an older engine. If compression is high, indicating carbon, GM's Top Engine Cleaner may help. Try several cans before deciding to dismantle the engine.

■ Servicing sparkplugs, cables, ignition timing and distributor parts, and adjusting the point dwell of non-electronic ignition systems.

■ Testing the automatic choke to make sure it isn't sticking, and seeing that the choke is set to the manufacturer's specifications.

■ Setting slow (curb) and fast-idle speed to specification. If the carburetor has not been serviced in 30,000 miles, it probably needs overhaul. A worn accelerator pump, sticking needle valve, damaged float and clogged passages will cause stalling. Also, look for a throttle linkage that catches as the accelerator is pressed.

■ Dirty carburetor air filter element and clogged fuel filter. If water has gotten into the fuel system, stalling will occur. When you disconnect the fuel line to replace the fuel filter, let some gas drop in your hand. If globules of water remain when the gas evaporates, the fuel system, including the tank, should be drained and cleaned.

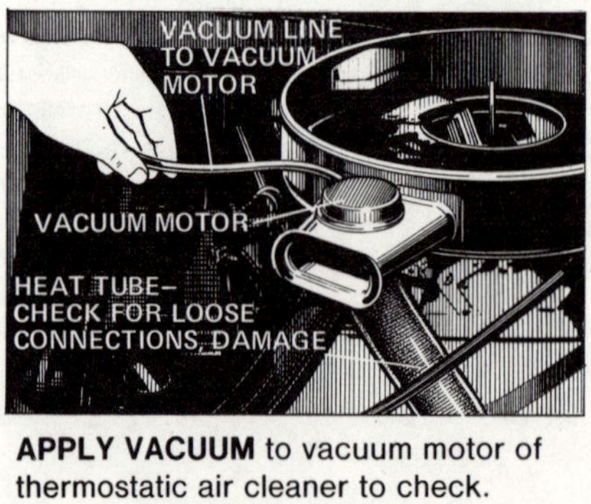

APPLY VACUUM to vacuum motor of thermostatic air cleaner to check.

SENSOR ASSEMBLY is found in air cleaner housing and is easy to replace.

SEE ALSO

Alternators, auto . . .
Carburetors, auto . . . Chokes, auto . . .
Electronic ignition, auto . . .
Engines, auto . . . Fuel systems, auto . . .
Ignition systems, auto . . .
Misfiring, auto

■ Clogged PCV valve.
■ In older cars, stalling can be caused by a weak fuel pump which is not pumping enough gas. This is especially noticeable on hills.

stalling affects cold engines

You should also keep in mind that you're inviting a stall if you start a modern engine and attempt to drive in freeway traffic, before it's properly warmed up. You can't get much speed or acceleration from a cold engine. On the other hand, you should avoid excessive idling to warm up the engine, especially one having a catalytic converter. Moderation is needed. Start the engine and drive the car slowly for a few minutes.

If the tune-up suggested above doesn't prevent stalling, the trouble is probably caused by:
■ An inoperative thermostatic air cleaner.
■ Vacuum loss around the carburetor and intake manifold.
■ Split, kinked or loose vacuum hoses.
■ Damaged vacuum break.
■ Inoperative manifold heat-control valve or vacuum-controlled fuel vaporization valve.
■ Leaking exhaust-gas recirculation (EGR) valve.
■ Cracked or loosely connected ignition wires.

thermostatic air cleaner

The thermostatic air cleaner reduces the production of carbon monoxide by regulating air temperature at the air cleaner inlet. A door in the inlet (snorkel) closes when the engine

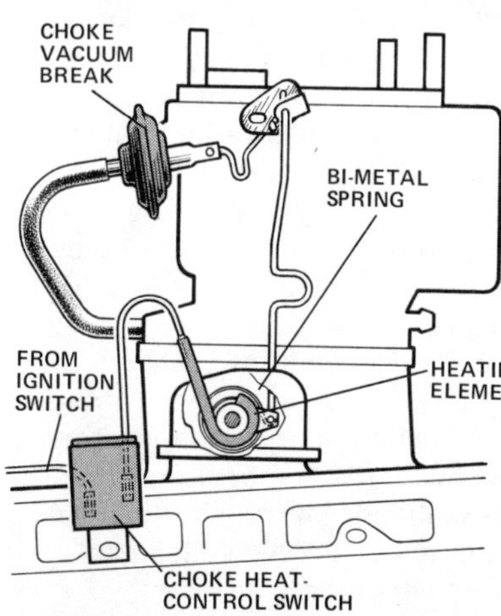

CHOKE vacuum break and control switch must work properly.

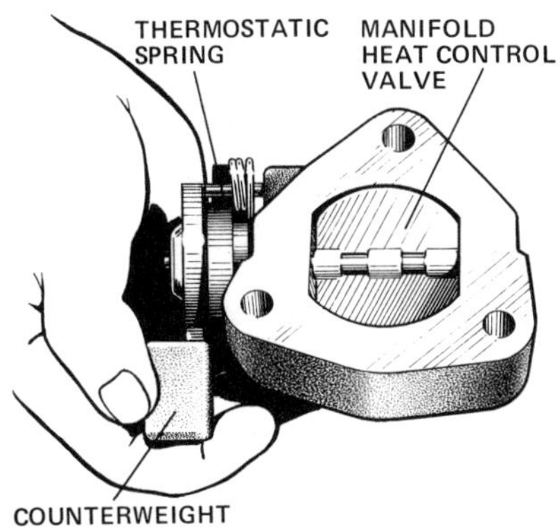

MANIFOLD heat-control valve must work freely; be sure to check it regularly.

is cold to let hot air, diverted from the exhaust manifold, enter the carburetor. Carbon monoxide levels are reduced as the temperature of the fuel mixture, which includes incoming air, increases.

When the engine is cold, the damper door in the snorkel of the thermostatic air cleaner should be closed. Stalling can occur if it isn't, since the engine is calibrated to run when cold on the air/gas ratio provided by a closed damper door.

If you cannot see the door by looking into the nose of the snorkel, remove the air cleaner cover and filter, and check the door operation from the backside. Start the engine after it has been shut down for several hours or, if the engine is warm, place a damp rag over sensor in the air cleaner. The door should close.

If the damper door isn't closed when the engine is cold, the hot-air tube to the air cleaner may be split or loose, or the temperature sensor or vacuum motor is shot. Check the hot-air tube. Replace it if it's damaged. Make sure the tube is secure.

Disconnect the hose of the vacuum motor at the engine end and apply vacuum. This may be done with a vacuum pump, or by putting the end of the hose in your mouth and drawing in.

If the damper door stays open, replace the vacuum motor. If the door closes, replace the sensor.

When the engine is warm, the damper door should open. If it stays closed, the fuel mixture will be affected and stalling can occur.

If the door is not open, replace the sensor, which usually solves the problem. But if not, the damper door is sticking and the mechanism will have to be replaced.

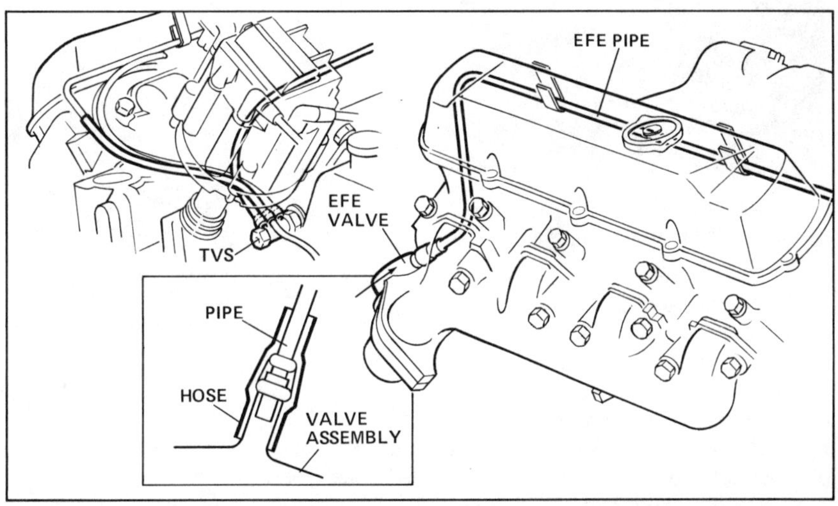

EARLY FUEL EVAPORATION (EFE) valve installation is shown here on late-model Cadillac. EFE system, along with thermostatic vacuum switch (TVS), heats fuel before burning.

tracking down vacuum loss

Vacuum may be leaking from the carburetor and intake manifold, or from a damaged or loose vacuum hose. Among the components that need vacuum to function are the air-conditioning and heating systems, EGR system, distributor-advance mechanism, power-brake booster, speed control, headlamp covers and automatic transmission modulator.

Maintaining adequate vacuum, which the engine needs to run at maximum efficiency, depends on vacuum hoses remaining intact.

The quickest way to determine if a vacuum leak exists is with a vacuum gauge. Connect the gauge to a vacuum port on the engine and let the engine idle.

If the gauge shows a reading below the normal vacuum specification for the engine, examine each vacuum hose for a loose connection or split. Then, check for vacuum loss around the carburetor and intake manifold.

Let the engine idle as you apply a mixture of engine oil and kerosene to the crack around joining surfaces. Keep your eye on the vacuum gauge. If it shows an increase in vacuum caused by the oil-kerosene mixture sealing the leak, carburetor bolts are loose or a gasket is bad.

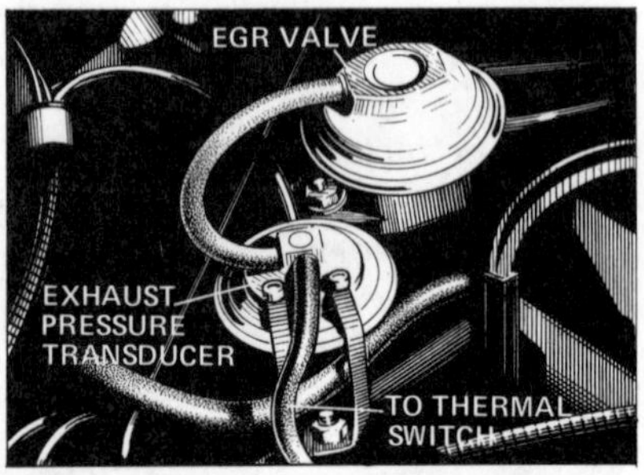

BACK PRESSURE transducer, if car has one, will be in tandem with the EGR valve.

The purpose of a vacuum break is to prevent overchoking. When a cold engine is started, engine vacuum is transmitted to the vacuum break, causing the choke plate to open partially. If this did not happen, an engine would stall.

Check the vacuum break, which is on the carburetor, by starting the engine when cold. Alternately install and remove the hose from the vacuum break. The linkage should move. If not, replace the vacuum break. Its diaphragm has a hole.

about those heat valves

Some engines have a manifold heat-control valve which is operated by a thermostatic spring. Other engines have a vaporization valve which operates by vacuum. GM, for example, uses a vaporization valve it calls EFE for "Early Fuel Evaporation."

Both mechanisms direct heat to the intake manifold to permit fuel vaporization as an engine warms up. If

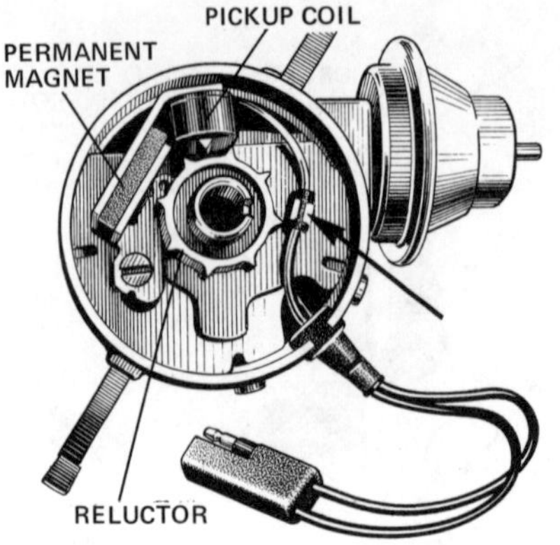

IGNITION CHECK should include wires in the distributor.

vaporization did not take place, the engine would stall.

To determine if a manifold heat-control valve is working, operate the valve's counterweight, *with the engine cold.* The counterweight is under the exhaust manifold, which gets skin-searing hot when the engine is warmed up.

If the counterweight doesn't move, the valve is stuck. Try freeing the valve by lubricating the valve shaft

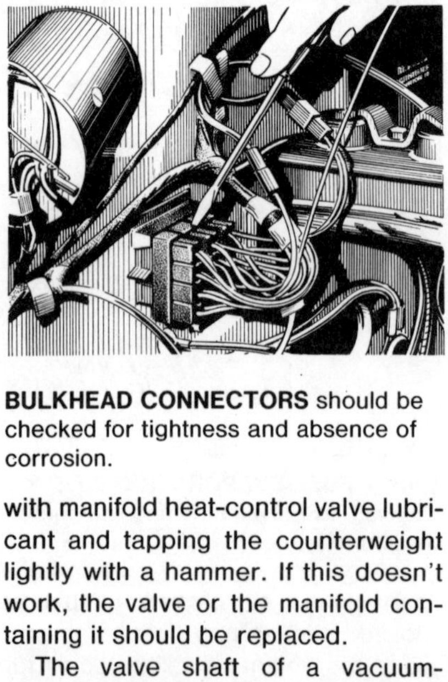

BULKHEAD CONNECTORS should be checked for tightness and absence of corrosion.

with manifold heat-control valve lubricant and tapping the counterweight lightly with a hammer. If this doesn't work, the valve or the manifold containing it should be replaced.

The valve shaft of a vacuum-operated vaporization valve should also be lubricated with manifold heat lube. This valve is controlled by a thermostatic vacuum switch (TVS).

The TVS closes the vaporization valve when the coolant temperature is below 120° F. This forces exhaust gases into the intake manifold to concentrate some heat on the fuel mixture and allow vaporization. The TVS switches off and the valve opens to permit normal exhausting of gases when the engine temperature reaches 120° F.

If lubricating the valve fails to bring free movement, check hoses for damage and connections for looseness. If this doesn't restore vacuum to the valve, replace the TVS, which may be damaged, or the valve, which may be stuck.

If an EGR valve leaks, a loss of vacuum causes the engine to stall at idle and low speeds. Many of the bugs affecting EGR have been eliminated, but the part still deserves attention when stalling occurs.

EGR valves, except those with back pressure transducers, are tested in this way:

1. Set the transmission in PARK and run the engine at 1400 to 1600 rpm. Let engine warm up to 120° F.

2. Place a finger under the EGR valve and disconnect the vacuum hose. The valve's diaphragm should move down and engine speed should increase. Reconnect the hose. The diaphragm should move up and engine speed should decrease.

3. If this doesn't happen, feel the end of the hose for vacuum. If none is present, the hose or carburetor port may be plugged or leaking, or the EGR's thermostatic vacuum switch (TVS) may be shot.

Back-pressure models should be removed from the engine for testing with an external constant vacuum source.

One of the most devious stalls results when an engine on-the-drive suddenly cuts out, then starts right up. This should make you suspect a loose or bare primary ignition wire. Check connections at ignition and inside distributor for tightness.

Carefully look over the coil-to-distributor wire, especially inside the distributor. If insulation has worn away, a bare spot may be touching the metal housing. This will short the ignition system.

If the procedures outlined here don't solve your stalling problem, your best bet is to check the service bulletins for your model. Ask the service manager who handles your make of car to consult his bulletin index. If he is unresponsive, direct your inquiry to the manufacturer or zone office nearest you.

AN INVERTED ROLLER SKATE will make it a lot easier the next time you have to handle a large drum or cylindrical object. Simply place the skate so that it supports the drum near one end, and position wooden blocks at the other end of the barrel to keep it level. Another arrangement would be to use a pair of skates and eliminate the blocks.—*W. B. Ervin.*

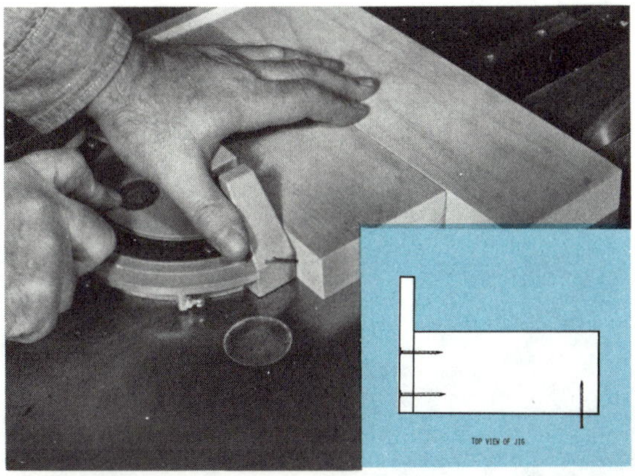

THERE'S NO NEED to screw-fasten a stop to your miter gauge when you have a lot of same-size cuts to make on your table saw. Make an L-shaped jig as shown in the drawing from shop scrap and drive a 6d or 8d finishing nail in the edge. In use, simply hook the jig against the end of the miter gauge and hold it there while work is being cut.—*Raymond Bried.*

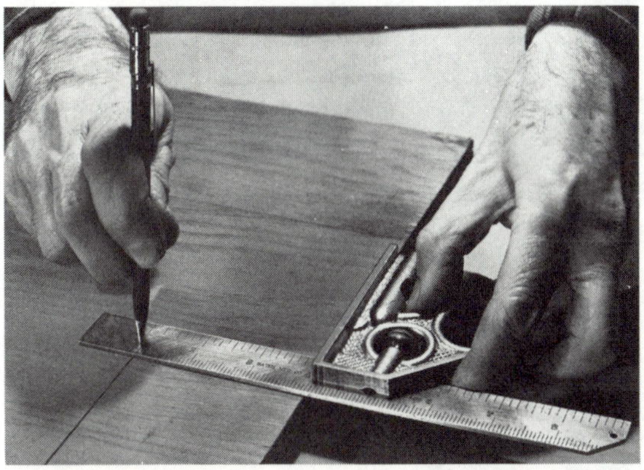

AFTER DRILLING a small hole in the end of the tongue in my combination square, I found that with a pencil point inserted I could scribe lines quickly and without any chance of the pencil moving. It sure beats the old method of holding the pencil on the end of the tongue where it easily—and often—slips off.—*Robert Finch.*

WHILE ASSEMBLING a picture frame recently, I ran short of clamps. Then I hit upon the idea of using masking tape to hold the joints securely. Close the joint by making contact at the outer edge first, then spot several pieces of the masking tape at strategic points. Apply glue to the point and close it; the tape will then hold the work in place until the glue is dry.—*Sterling Ruark.*

Bench-saw dolly rolls where you want it

By HARRY WICKS

This smooth-rolling stand, adaptable to any table saw built on a pedestal, increases shop mobility and working comfort without causing any wobbling or inaccurate cutting

FROM TIME TO TIME my table saw appears in photos accompanying workshop stories. Each time it does, I receive letters from readers requesting information about the dolly beneath the saw. Because of this interest in a shop-built accessory, we are publishing the construction details for readers who want to duplicate the setup.

Designed to suit the 10-in. Delta Unisaw shown below, the frame can be altered to accept any make of table saw that rests on a pedestal rather than on a four-legged stand. The dolly rolls on four casters with minimum effort. Yet, because of the saw and frame weight, you will not need to use lock-type casters. Regardless of the material being cut, the saw does not move. In the 18 years the dolly has been in use in my shop, I haven't noticed any wobbling or inaccurate cutting as a result of movement.

THIS RUGGEDLY BUILT dolly rolls on four bed casters with minimum effort and easily supports the author's 10-in. Delta Unisaw.

SEE ALSO

Bandsaws . . . Motors, shop . . . Power-tool stands . . . Table saws . . . Workbenches . . . Workshops

Before you begin to construct the dolly, measure your saw's pedestal and, if necessary, alter the dimensions shown on the drawing. If you lack welding equipment, have the frame made by a local ironworks shop. (Note: The price for such a frame made in the New York area is about $20. That's for all angle-iron, welding and bolt-hole cutting.)

Start the assembly by clamping the 2x6s to the frame and boring the holes for the 12 4½-in. bolts. Next, attach the casters. The ¼-in.-plywood bottom is not a must, but it does keep sawdust from piling up under the casters.

For looks, the stand shown was finished by spraying the iron frame with flat black enamel; the 2x6s were sprayed with clear varnish. If you plan to spray-paint your saw dolly, do it after boring all necessary holes, but before final assembly.

UPSIDE-DOWN view of the dolly (above) shows how the frame and casters are positioned on the underside of a pair of 2x6s. The closeup photo (right) shows how the bed casters are fastened. The stand puts the saw-table height at about 36½ in.

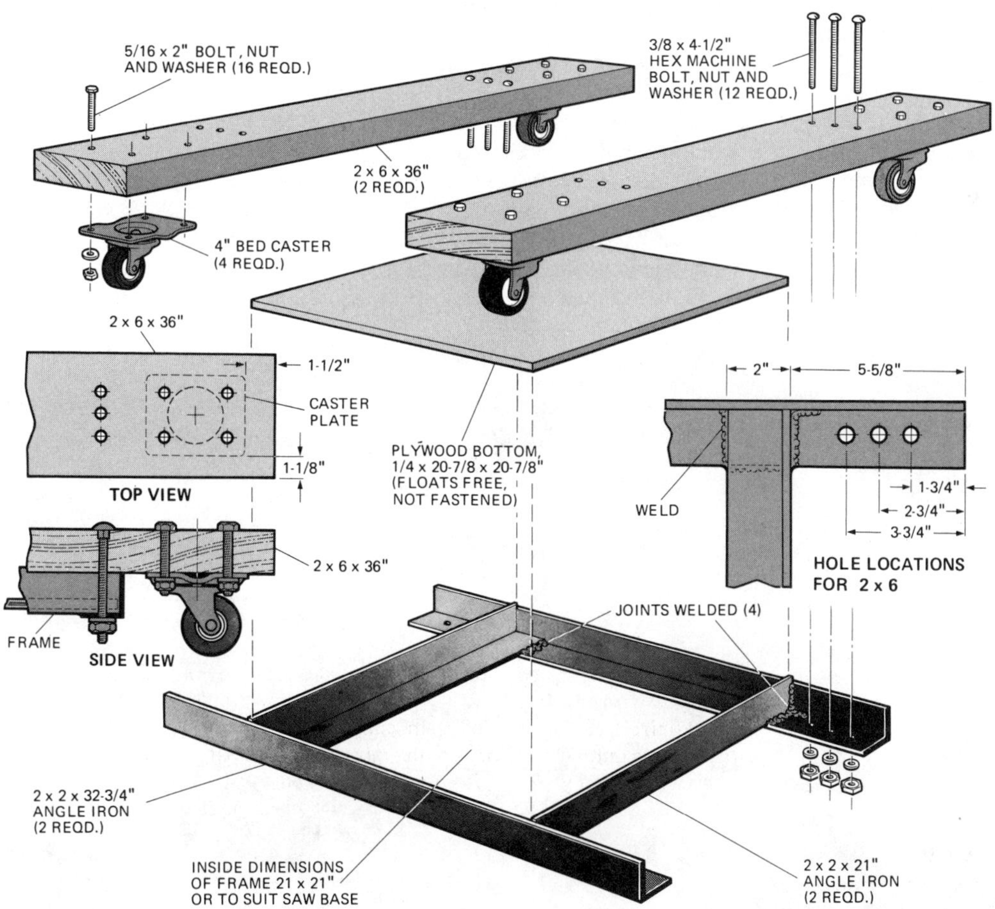

Keep your steering and suspension systems working

Nothing can be more elusive than a shimmy or thump which only shows up at particular highway speeds. When you stop or slow down, the problem disappears, making it extremely difficult to find. If you have suspension or steering problems, here are some things you can investigate to pin down the problem

■ WHEN CAR OWNERS get together to trade complaints, one topic that always turns up is suspension problems. The usual problems are shimmy (vibration) and wheel tramp conditions. Noisy steering is also a frequent complaint, followed by problems with shock absorbers, springs, front-end alignment and wheel bearings.

Some suspension problems are better left to professionals, but you can frequently diagnose problems yourself. In some cases the cure may be as simple as inflating your tires to the proper pressure. Here are some tips on running down suspension and steering problems.

shaking things up

The terms shimmy, vibration and quiver are synonymous. None, however, is the same as wheel tramp (thump).

Shimmy is the continuous shaking sensation you feel in the steering wheel (most often), floor or seat while driving on a paved highway at a set speed usually between 50 and 70 mph. It continues as long as you maintain that speed, but disappears or diminishes when the speed is increased or decreased.

Front-wheel tramp is a cyclical thumping sensation that's transmitted through the steering wheel, floor or seat at a speed of about 25 mph.

Some malfunctions that cause vibration may also cause wheel tramp, but usually what creates one sensation will not produce the other.

Wheel and tire unbalance is often blamed for vibration, and yet it's just one of 11 possible reasons—not even the most common. Here's a list of all usual causes of vibration. An asterisk means that the particular reason should be tackled before others since testing is easier and can be made without costing money.

- Improper tire pressure*
- Tire bulge*
- Loose wheel nuts*
- Worn shock absorbers*

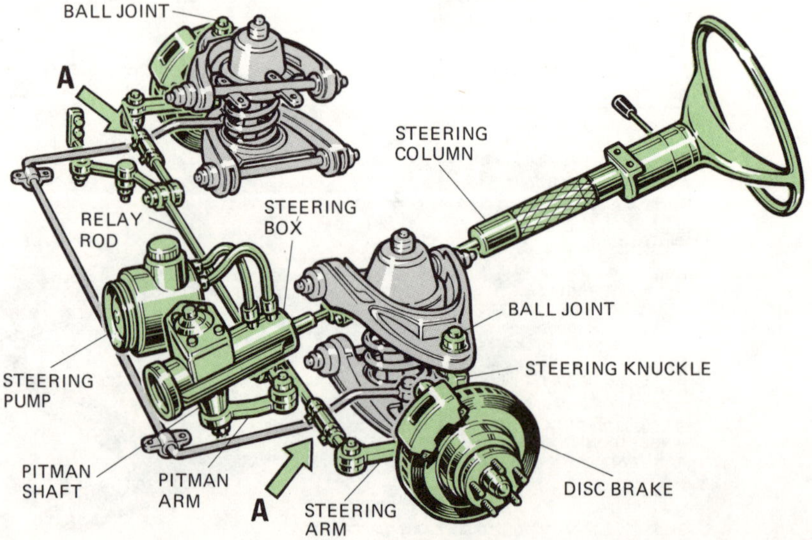

STEERING LINKAGE can be tested for looseness at tie-rod adjustment sleeves (A).

SEE ALSO
Bottle craft . . . Clay pottery . . . Glass cutting . . . Internal carving . . . Jewelry . . . Lapidary . . . Marquetry . . Potter's wheels . . . Tin-can crafts

- Loose steering linkage*
- Worn or loose front wheel bearings*
- Loose engine mount*
- Incorrect driveshaft angularity*
- Worn ball joints
- Unbalanced wheel and tire assemblies
- Improper front-end alignment

eliminating shimmy

Proceed as follows:

1. See that tire pressure is neither low nor uneven, and examine tire sidewalls for bulges that can cause shimmy. Discard a bulging tire—it's unsafe.

2. Tighten wheel nuts with a hand wrench, preferably a torque wrench, to manufacturer specification. Tighten nuts in a crisscross manner to equalize pressure around the wheel. Tighten each nut, in turn, to half its torque value—then go back and tighten each to full value.

Caution: Avoid having wheel nuts tightened with pneumatic power wrenches, which can enlarge wheel-nut holes, preventing nuts from securing the wheel. This would cause the wheel to wobble. Pneumatic tools can also distort brake drums and discs.

3. Test shock absorbers by pushing up and down on the bumper or fender at each corner of the car in turn. Increase the length of the stroke with each push until the car is rocking really well. Then release your grasp on the bumper or fender at the bottom of a downstroke. If the car continues to rock up and down two or more times, the shock absorber in that corner is probably worn and should be removed from the car for further testing. Replace if necessary.

Other ways of discovering a bad shock include examining the shock's case for fluid. A leaking shock absorber should be replaced. You should also grasp each shock and try shaking it. If the shock is loose, tighten fasteners and retest. If still loose, the bushing is probably worn and should be replaced, if possible. If not, replace the shock.

Important: If one shock absorber has to be replaced, replace the other shock on the same axle. It is not necessary, however, to replace shocks at the other end of the car, assuming both are still in good condition.

4. Examine steering linkage, consisting of tie rods, pitman arm, idler arm and relay rod. Look for bent components. Grasp each and try shaking. If any rod is bent and/or demonstrates looseness, replace that part. A damaged or worn steering linkage component results in vibration and also loose steering control, jerky steering and side-to-side wander of the car.

5. To determine if front wheel bearings are causing vibration, feel wheels or hubcaps after driving the car several miles. Friction could heat the wheels, signifying a worn or improperly adjusted wheel bearing. You should also jack up the front of the car and spin each wheel by hand. If you hear clicking, grinding or scraping, remove the wheel, inspect bearings for damage, and adjust bearings properly before replacing the wheel.

Important: With cars having front-wheel drive only, inspect rear wheel bearings as we described. If a vehicle is equipped with both front and rear-wheel drive (that is, four-wheel drive), the inspection is unnecessary. Wheel bearings on an axle with a drive system seldom fail because they are being treated constantly with lubricant from the differential or transfer case.

6. One of the most serious conditions that causes vibration is a loose engine mount. Reports have reached us of mounts loosening so badly that engines have actually rocked forward, smashing radiators. In more severe cases, loosened engine mounts have caused throttles to jam, leading to runaway cars.

At the first indication of shimmy, engine mounts should be tested. Vibration is the initial indication of looseness.

If a car has a manual transmission, let the engine idle. Set the hand brake tightly, place the transmission in gear and have someone watch the engine as you let the clutch out. If an engine mount is loose or defective, the engine will give a violent upward jerk as it stalls out.

If the car is equipped with automatic transmission, place a hydraulic jack under the oil pan or some other accessible section of the engine block. Put a 2x4 wood block between the jack and engine to prevent dam-

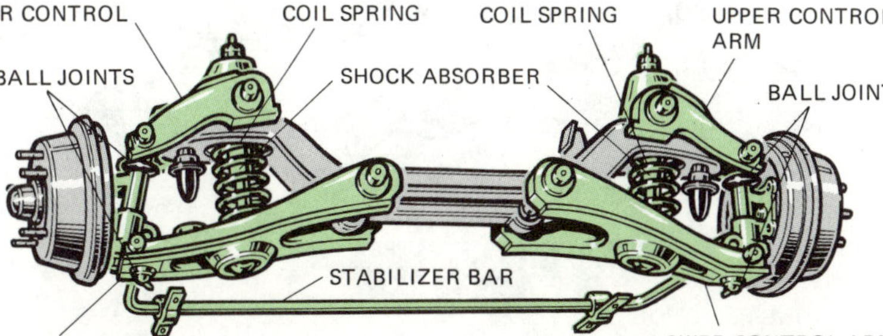

FRONT SUSPENSION components for typical rear-wheel drive car are shown here.

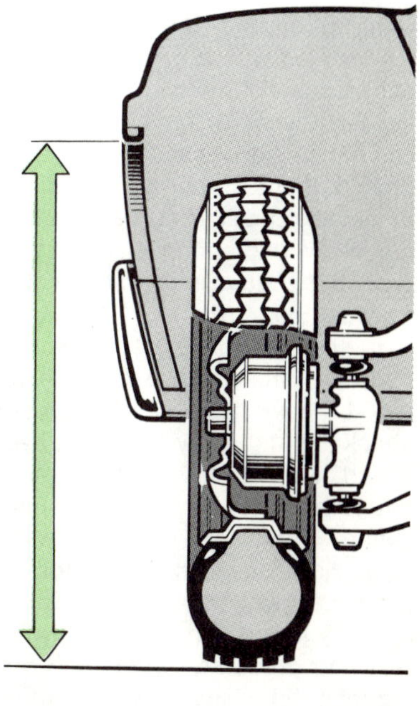

WEAK or broken springs can be detected by comparing height of sides.

age, and lift up carefully on the engine. If the engine mount is loose, the engine will lift far enough off the mount for you to see daylight between the two.

Caution: Don't put too much pressure on the oil pan. You may cause damage.

If an engine mount is loose, it should be tightened with a torque wrench to manufacturer specification. If damaged, or if it won't tighten up, it should be replaced.

7. Check universal joints as discussed in the section on transmission and drive train. With the car on a two-post lift so wheels hang free and the driveshaft is not obstructed, have someone start the engine and place the transmission in gear as you watch the action of the driveshaft.

Driveshaft motion should be smooth. If the shaft is out of alignment, it will whip. Edges of the shaft will look blurry.

Wash the shaft with cleaning solvent on the chance that a cake of mud or some other foreign matter is throwing the shaft out of balance. Look for damage to the shaft. A shaft that's bent or dented should be replaced.

Now, bring the car down to the ground. See that it's resting on level pavement and measure the distance from the ground to the center of the fender well with a gauge. Do this at each corner of the car. You are looking for a weak or broken spring that can cause a driveshaft to whip during driving. If one corner measures lower than the opposing corner, the existence of a bad spring is verified. This procedure can also be used to check for weak springs.

If shimmy still exists after other possible causes have been investigated, have driveshaft angularity checked. Angularity has to be determined with a driveshaft alignment gauge against manufacturer specification.

8. Have ball joints tested for axial (up-and-down) movement. This is done by jacking up each front wheel, relieving pressure on the load-bearing joint, attaching a dial indicator to the wheel assembly and prying up on the wheel assembly. See if movement falls within manufacturer requirements. If it exceeds this specification, ball joints should be replaced.

Ball joints in some cars since 1974 (GM in particular) have indicators that allow you to make this check yourself. Just wipe off the base of the joint and scrape a screwdriver or your fingernail across it. If you can feel a nub, the ball joint is not worn beyond limits. If you can't, replace the joint.

9. If vibration started right after you put new tires on the car, replaced a brake drum or disc, rotated tires, or upset the original setting of wheel assemblies in some way, have wheel-assembly balance tested dynamically and statically—that is, with wheel assemblies in motion and at rest, respectively. Correct an unbalanced condition with balancing weights.

10. Finally, a misaligned front end may be causing the vibration, and the car's camber, caster and toe should be checked against manufacturer specification and corrected. Besides vibration, front-end misalignment can cause pulling of the car to one side on a level roadway when you remove your hands from the steering wheel, instability (wander and weaving), tire squeal on turns and uneven tire wear.

tramp, tramp, tramp

There are only three reasons for wheel tramp—weak shock absorbers, unbalanced wheel assemblies and out-of-round tires. We've discussed how to check out the first two.

To verify the existence of an out-of-round tire, inflate all tires to 50 pounds and drive the car. If a tire is causing tramp, you will not feel the sensation. To uncover the offender, reduce inflation in one tire to normal pressure and drive the car. Follow the procedure for each of the tires until tramp reappears, revealing the eccentric tire.

steering problems

Other than vibration already discussed, the most common complaint relative to steering is noise when the steering wheel is turned sharply.

Start by seeing to it that the power-steering-pump drive belt is properly tightened. Loose drive belts cause more power steering difficulties, including noise, than anything else. Noise may also be caused by a glazed belt or pump pulley.

If noise continues, the job becomes one for a steering technician. The noise may not be coming from the booster, but from the steering itself. Maybe the cross shaft has to be adjusted or is damaged.

Another frequent steering-related complaint is a rattle which seems to be coming from the steering wheel itself. This is most frequently caused by a worn or loose steering column coupling. To test for this condition, give the steering wheel a couple of good shakes while the car is at rest. If the noise occurs, check out the coupling. Either tighten it to manufacturer specification or, if worn, replace it.

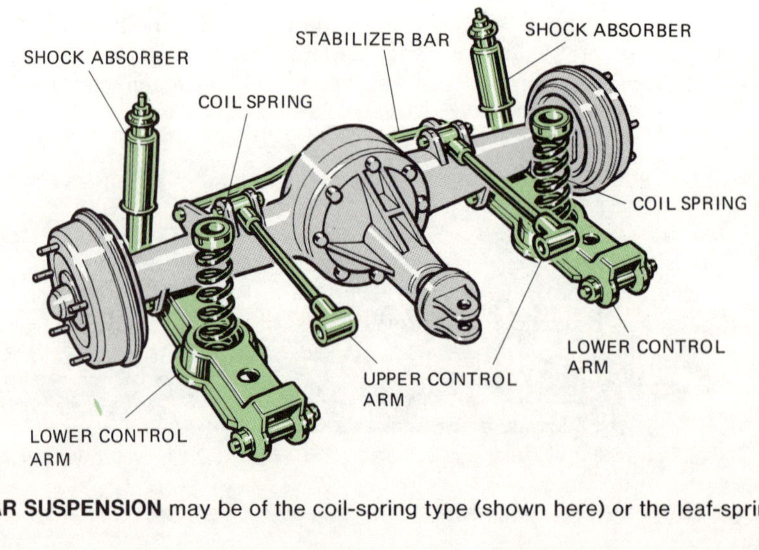

REAR SUSPENSION may be of the coil-spring type (shown here) or the leaf-spring.

1 USE POINTED trowel to trim back overgrown grass and expose the stone. Save the sod for finishing after the stones are raised to new level.

2 USE BACK of the shovel to force sod away from edge of the stone. Carefully expose all of the edges so that the stone can be raised easily.

3 TIP STONE on edge and pour in sand needed to raise it to the proper grade. Next, level the sand with a shovel and reposition the stone.

4 USE A 6-FT. straightedge to check the elevation and slope of the raised stones. The tops of the stones should conform to the grade of the lawn.

5 TAMP THE SOD back into place around the raised stones. The finished job provides a dry, clearly-defined walkway.

How to level stepping stones

By JAMES McMAHON

PLAN TO BRING stones up to grade after it rains, when the ground is easily worked. The best approach is to raise every third stone and then bring the intermediate stones up to grade, using your straightedge between those previously set. Use the trowel to trim overgrown grass as shown, and expose the outline of the stone. Push sod back until the stone's bottom edge is exposed before trying to raise the stone.

Use a straightedge and a carpenter's level to help judge how much sand you'll need. The top of the stone should be about 1 in. above ground level. Pry up one side and stand stone on edge (there's no need to lift and remove it). Hold stone with one hand, then pour and spread sand with the other. Lay stone back in position. Check again with straightedge and level. Repeat process, adding or removing sand as needed to attain proper level. Be sure to stand on the stone and check for "rocking" before you press the sod back around the edges. Tamp sod with a 2x4. Clean dirt off newly exposed edges of stones with trowel.

SEE ALSO

Grass . . . Landscaping . . . Lawns . . . Paths, garden . . . Patios . . . Retaining walls

How to build brick and masonry steps

Exterior stairs made of either concrete or brick must be built on a good, solid foundation. You can do the calculations and the work yourself if you follow these instructions

EXTERIOR STAIRS should be designed and built as carefully as interior stairs. Their riser-to-tread ratios vary somewhat from interior-stair standards: Riser height on principal exterior stairs should be between 6 and 7 in., with a minimum tread of 12 in. In most outdoor situations, you'll have room to meet these specifications without going through complicated calculations. Good support for the weight of materials is essential to make steps that will be stable and won't crack through settling. If located over backfill, their footings must rest on undisturbed ground.

Common (building) bricks come in many colors and three grades; unless frost is extremely infrequent in your area, SW, for severe weathering, is the grade you'll want. Used brick is attractive in many applications, but it is necessary to check each individual brick for cracks. Even the smallest cracks can open up and cause problems. What comes closest to a standard size for common brick is 2¾ x 4½ x 8½ in. nominal. Actual size is ½ in. smaller in each dimension—the space taken up by ½-in. mortar joints between bricks. By using the nominal size in estimating the number of bricks needed, you get an automatic allowance for joint space—but check on the sizes stocked locally before estimating. Otherwise you may waste your time on computations and then find that what you need is not in stock at your supplier.

The space between your finished steps and house foundation must be sealed to prevent moisture from entering this area. This is done by filling the joint with oakum (a fibrous material), then applying tar or mortar caulk.

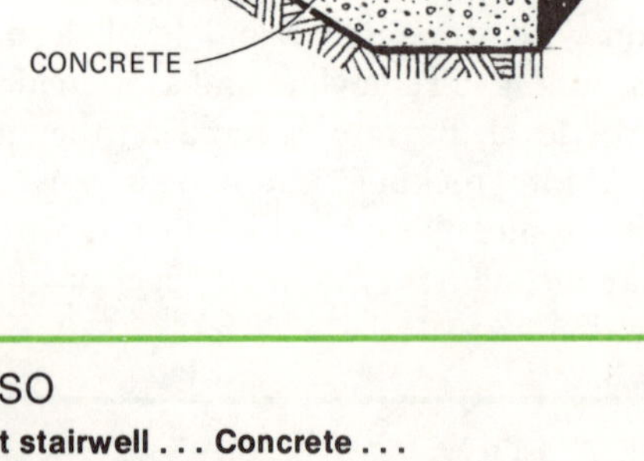

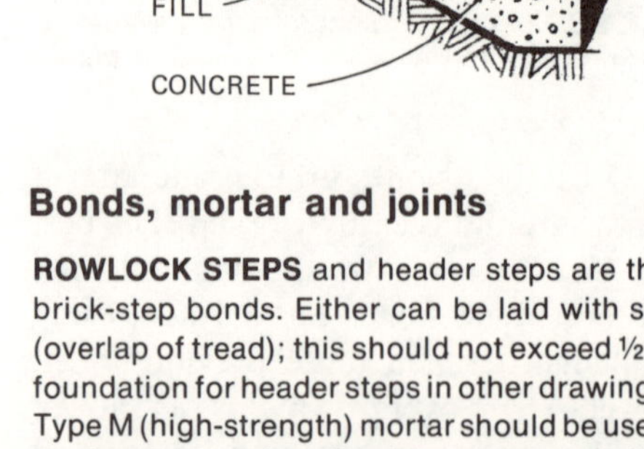

Bonds, mortar and joints

ROWLOCK STEPS and header steps are the two basic brick-step bonds. Either can be laid with slight nosing (overlap of tread); this should not exceed ½ in. Note that foundation for header steps in other drawings is simpler. Type M (high-strength) mortar should be used according to directions; mix only what you can use in 2½ hours. Mortar can be colored with lampblack or pigments. Work from the bottom up, laying bricks on a ⅜-in. mortar bed and checking with a level as you go. Flush mortar joints made with trowel edge will weather best. When mortar has set, rub with a clean brick to remove excess.

SEE ALSO

**Basement stairwell . . . Concrete . . .
Home improvement . . . House additions . . .
Measurements . . . Railings . . .
Remodeling, exterior . . . Stairs**

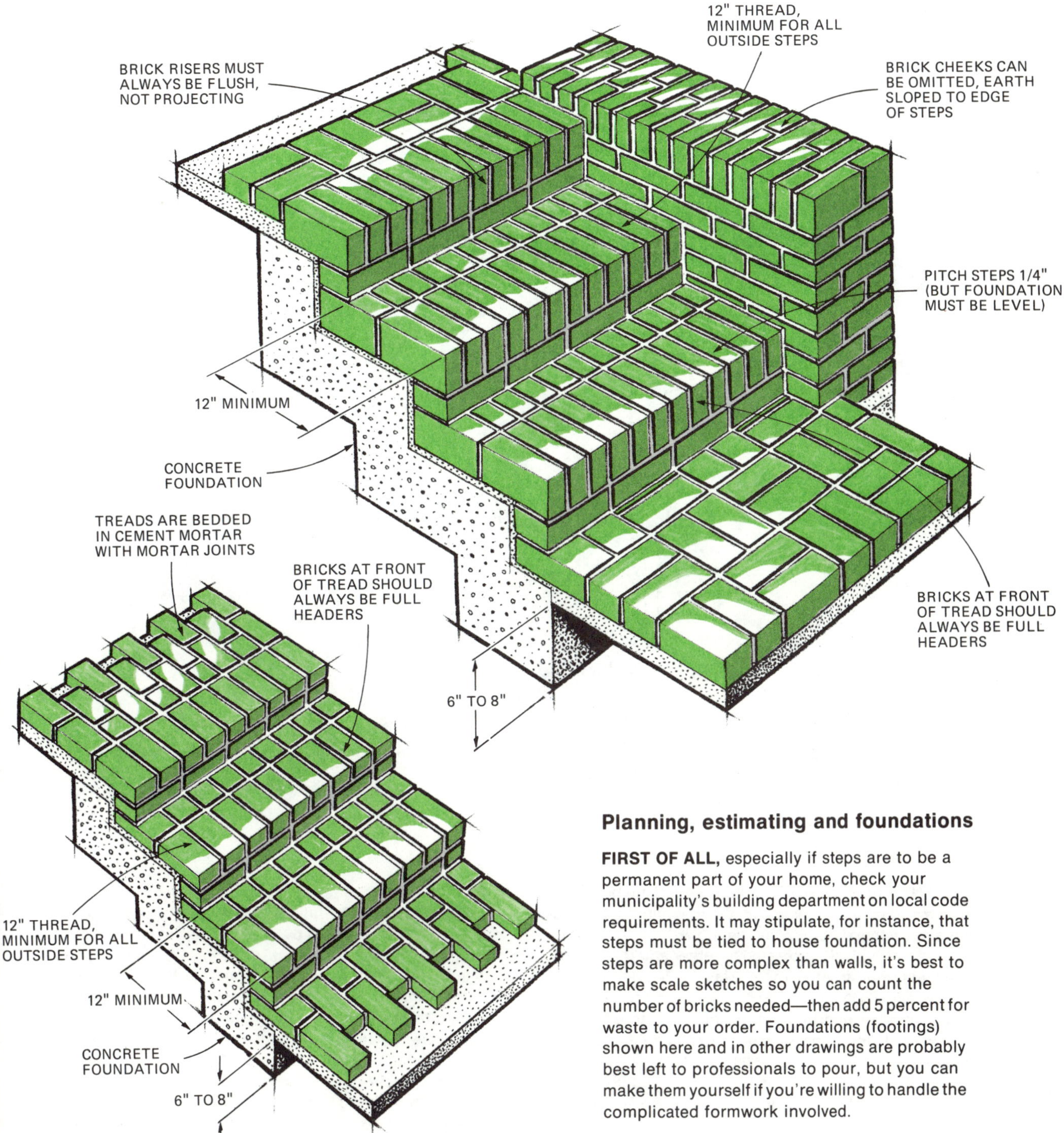

Planning, estimating and foundations

FIRST OF ALL, especially if steps are to be a permanent part of your home, check your municipality's building department on local code requirements. It may stipulate, for instance, that steps must be tied to house foundation. Since steps are more complex than walls, it's best to make scale sketches so you can count the number of bricks needed—then add 5 percent for waste to your order. Foundations (footings) shown here and in other drawings are probably best left to professionals to pour, but you can make them yourself if you're willing to handle the complicated formwork involved.

continued

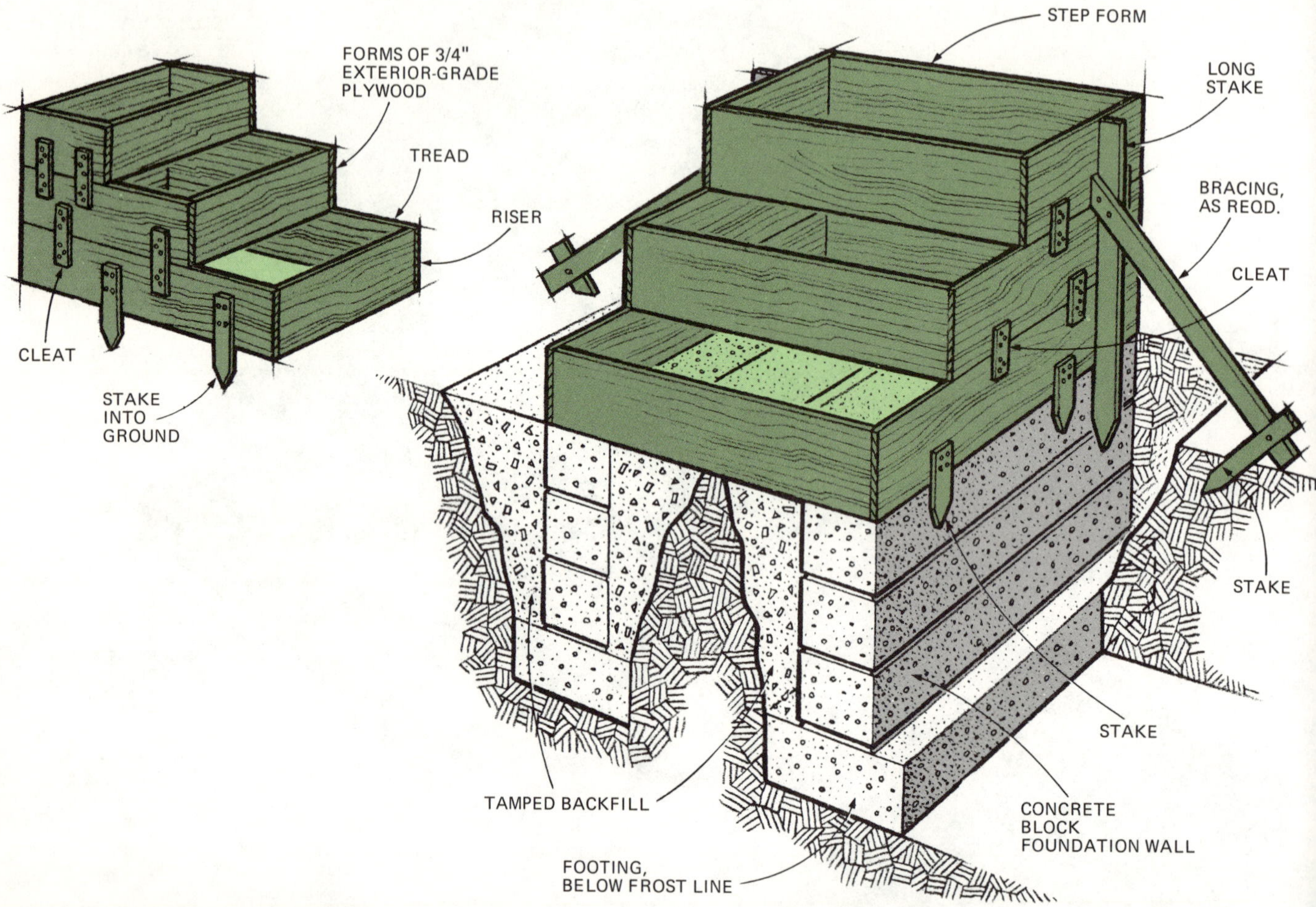

Formwork, pouring, finishing for concrete steps

FOOTINGS FOR CONCRETE steps should be below the area frost line and at least 8 in. thick. When the footing has set, a concrete-block foundation wall can be built up to grade with blocks mortared together and their cores filled with mortar. After the mortar has set (about 24 hours), backfill the soil around the wall, carefully tamping each 6-in. layer, until tamped backfill is at grade. The site is now ready for forms, which should be built as shown above with ¾-in. plywood for batter boards and 1-in. and 2-in. nominal stock for bracing. Forms must be well nailed and solid, so that pressure of concrete will not force them apart.

Since steps of this type require a large amount of concrete, you are well advised to use transit-mix (truck-mixed) concrete, pouring the steps monolithically (as a single unit); the stiffness of the mix should make it unnecessary to close in lower-step treads. You *can* hand-mix and pour one layer at a time, but this is not really worth the extra effort, as it raises the problem of tying the layers together. Estimate the amount of concrete needed by finding the volume of the steps in cubic feet and dividing by 27 to convert to cubic yards, and add 5 percent for waste. One cu. yd. is usually the minimum order for transit-mix concrete. Before pouring, give the inside of the forms a thin coat of form oil to keep concrete from adhering to wood. When the pour is complete, rap forms vigorously all over with a hammer; this helps the mix to settle and fill voids (honeycombs) that may occur next to the form boards. You should *not* pour if the temperature is below 40°F. or if it is raining. Use a wood float to finish the steps—a steel trowel would give too slick a surface. When concrete has set for at least 36 hours, carefully remove forms. Rough spots can be rubbed smooth with a carborundum stone and water. Fill any voids at this time with a cement-and-sand mix, troweled and rubbed smooth with the stone while still wet. To cure, keep steps moist and covered (to retain moisture) for five to seven days.

Rustic slab stool

By ELMA and WILLARD WALTNER

■ THIS ROUGH-HEWN STOOL will be right at home in an early American setting. It's made of 2-in. pine (actually 1⅝ in.) and assembled without nails or screws.

Rough-carving the edges of the top and legs with a hatchet gives the stool rustic look. To save time, saw the legs to shape; then chop them for texture. Work from bottom to top to avoid splitting. Finish by lightly sanding the burrs that are left from chopping.

Notice that the wedge slots in the stretcher extend into the leg openings so that the pegs draw the stretcher tight. The pegs should taper slightly from end to end.

Give the stool a coat of natural wood filler, followed by two coats of fruitwood stain. Then apply a coat of clear satin finish, sand lightly and rub with a cloth to give the stool a well-used look.

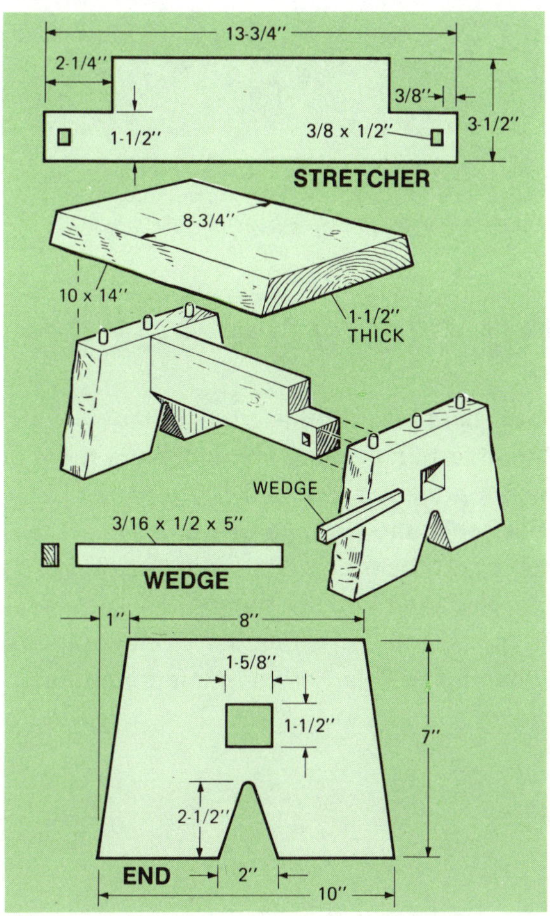

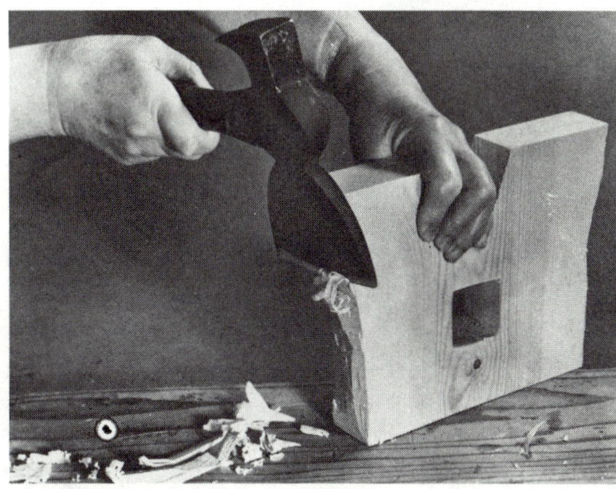

HAND-HEWN LOOK is produced by lightly chopping edges of the legs and top with a hatchet, then sanding.

LIGHT SANDING with a flap abrasive wheel gives a worn look to "adzed" edges. It can be done by hand.

SEE ALSO

Gifts, Christmas . . . Sanding . . . Staining, wood

GARAGE-WALL storage unit is a double-duty built-in that provides both work and storage space. It doesn't take as much space as it looks, and can be made to take only two feet off the end of a garage. The long workbench is especially handy for car and yard-tool fix-it jobs that require a long layout area. There's a great deal of storage space both above and below.

Great ideas for finding storage space

Looking for more storage space? Today, the answer isn't just another trunk in the attic. In the modern equipment-packed home, you need to hide things away and still have them at your fingertips, ready for instant use. There's the movie projector, the hi-fi rig, your prized fishing, hunting and photographic gear, countless tools and toys, games and hobby supplies, skis and tennis rackets and baseball bats, kitchen and laundry appliances, a model train or road-race set—all must have their place yet be kept handy if you're going to use and enjoy them. On these pages you will find a number of clever ideas for versatile, space-saving storage arrangements that can make living more efficient and fun

SEE ALSO
**Closets . . . Garage remodeling . . .
Garages, storage . . . Hi-fi centers . . .
Hobby centers . . . Kitchens . . . Mudrooms . . .
Privacy screens . . . Room dividers . . .
Storage walls . . . Study centers . . . Theaters, home**

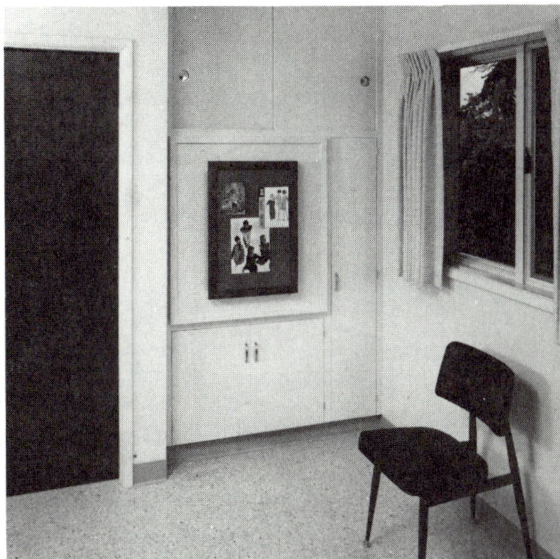

HIDDEN NEATLY in the wall, this fold-out work center is ready in an instant for sewing or family hobbies. Shelves and drawers behind the drop-down worktable store supplies. Tall cupboard at right end is big enough to take an ironing board or guns and fishing rods. Hinged leg, designed to look like a decorative wall panel, swings out to support the table's outer end.

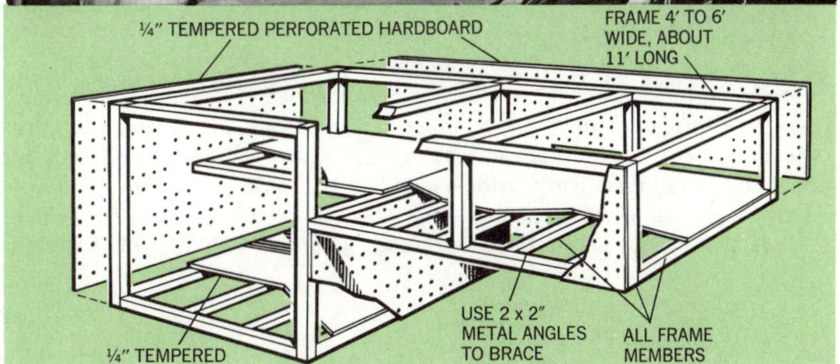

DESIGNED TO HANG over the hood of a car, this L-shaped storage unit takes advantage of normally wasted garage space. It's perfect for garden supplies, extra tires, folding patio chairs and similar items. Side panels of Masonite perforated hardboard (Pegboard) provide additional space on the outside for hanging tools. If ceiling is low enough, you can fasten the unit directly to it. If not, suspend the outer end on chains or cables anchored to the ceiling with screw hooks. Inner end of unit is fastened to wall, either with screws into studs or expansion anchors into masonry.

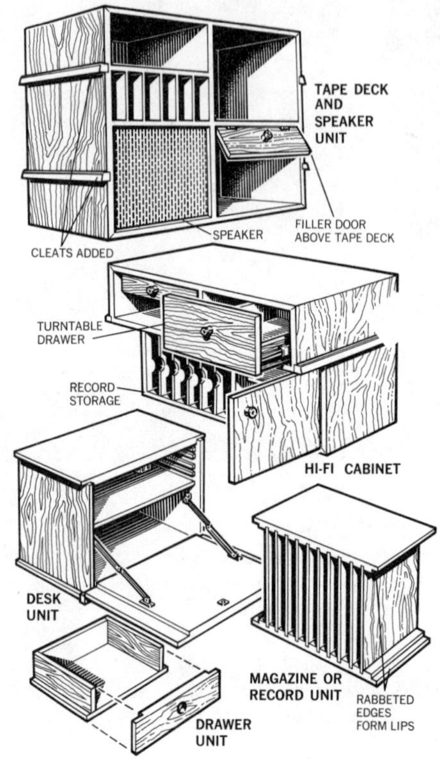

INTERCHANGEABLE STORAGE units slide in and out on tracks in two clever walls above. At left, strips of grooved Texture 1-11 plywood provide ready-made slots. Right, bevel siding nailed upside down forms support ledges. Drawings show units that can be built to slide into place.

HIGH OFF the floor, wall-hung cupboards don't block car, leave parking space underneath for bikes and other bulky gear. Each 3-foot-wide section is a different color for handsome appearance. Doors of perforated hardboard cost little and help to provide needed ventilation to prevent any mildew from forming inside. The front half of an old stepladder rested against the cabinets is especially handy for reaching the upper shelves. If even more storage is desired, full-length cabinets (right) can be added to line the side walls of the garage.

LOW-HEADROOM NOOKS under the eaves can be put to good use for storage. Scallop-topped "fence" at left, above conceals a row of shelves and clothes poles. Leaving the top part open to the ceiling makes the room seem larger than if it were closed in. Tree branches painted on the wall behind give illusion of a distant garden scene to increase the feeling of space.

SLOPING BUILT-IN at right packs a lot of storage in a little space, even has a drop-down desk. Side doors give access to rear compartments.

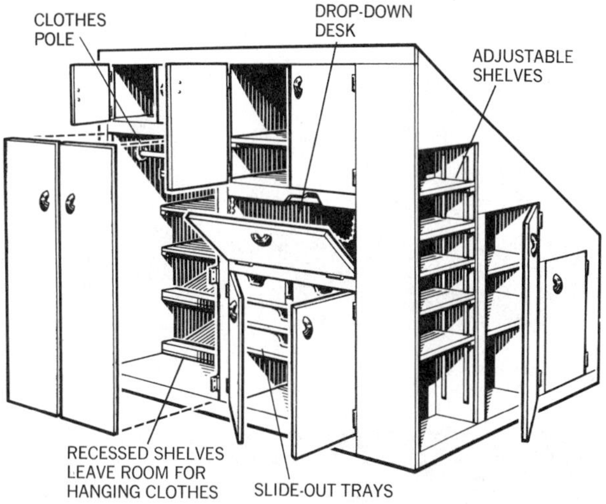

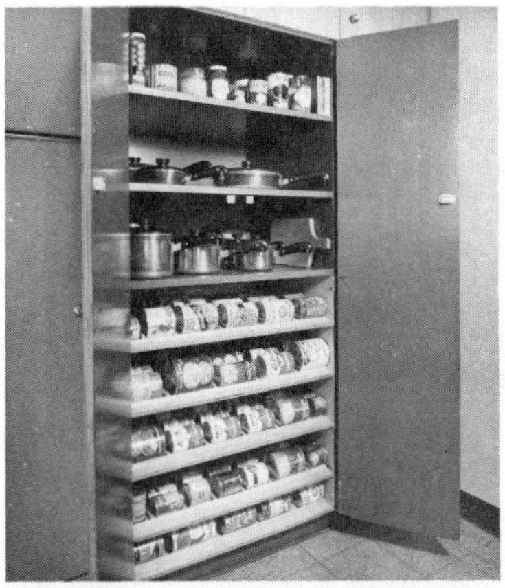

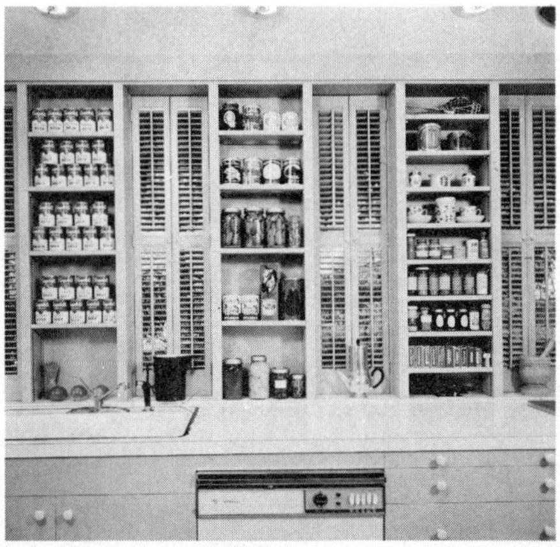

SLANTED SHELVES in cupboard at left work like supermarket racks. Cans, stored on their sides, roll conveniently down to you as you lift the front ones out. In the center photo, shallow shelves are used in place of conventional overhead cabinets. Cans and jars are easy to see and can be reached without necessity of removing the items from the front to get at those in back. In the cupboard at right, closely spaced shelves and vertical dividers keep thin objects such as trays, platters and flat pans neatly sorted.

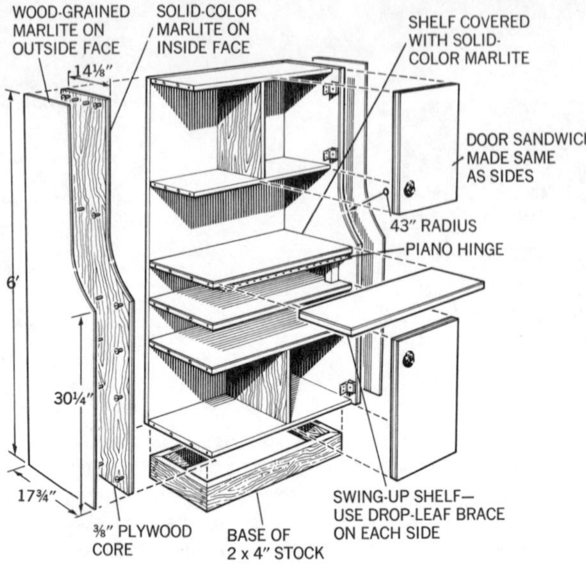

THIS MODERN HUTCH stores appliances and lets you use them at the same time. Outlets at the back enable you to keep toaster, percolator, food blender and other electrical appliances plugged in, ready for use. A hinged panel swings up to form a serving counter. Doors and sides are a clever sandwich of ⅜-in. plywood with two kinds of Marlite paneling cemented to it—wood grained outside, solid color inside.

STORAGE CAN BE handsome as well as functional. These open shelves at the foot of a stairway display decorative objects, while the larger base cabinet conceals less-showy items behind louvered doors. Such a unit not only adds storage space, but can also serve as an attractive room divider, in this case helping to screen off the stairway from a dining room.

HOLLOW SPACES behind false walls can hide hard-to-store items like the table tennis table at left, above. If you're paneling a wall, especially in a basement, it's often a good idea to locate your framing so it leaves a few inches between it and the old wall. This will provide room for recessed shelves, built-in hi-fi equipment or storage compartments such as the one here. In the wall shown, one four-foot-wide sheet of hardboard paneling is removable, creating a big opening so the table can easily be slipped in and out. Magnetized catches hold the paneling so there's nothing to show from the outside.

MULTIPURPOSE BUILT-IN is room divider, storage wall, hi-fi center and worktable all rolled into one. Front panels house a tape deck, amplifier, stereo speakers and a TV set. Surrounding counter adds workspace for editing tapes, doing school homework and similar chores. Wood-grained panels give wall a handsome appearance.

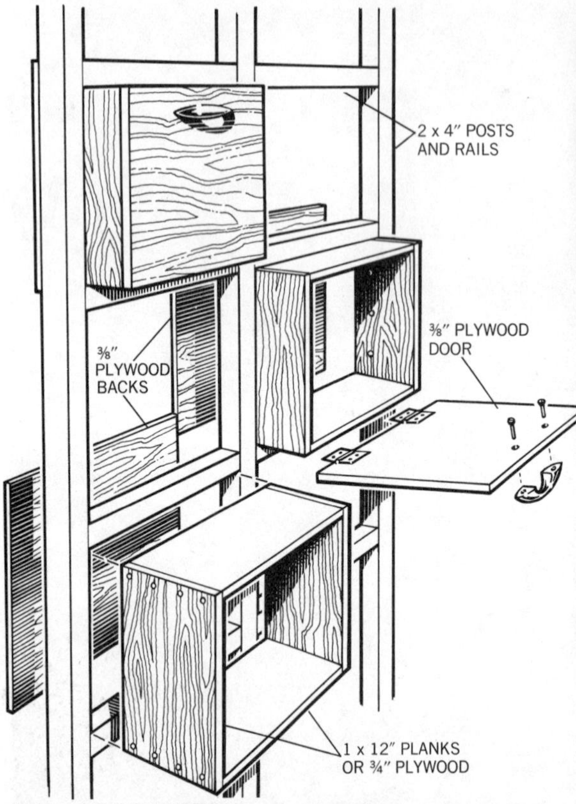

WALL OF CABINETS in a pleasing staggered arrangement gives shade and privacy and at the same time stores garden supplies, barbecue utensils and other outdoor items. Cabinets can be built under an existing structure, such as along the open side of a carport or porch, or they can be part of a garden shelter, as here. If the wall is load bearing, use four-by-four posts instead of two-by-fours shown in the drawing. Note that backs of cabinets are extended to overlap posts and cross rails. This adds extra bracing and helps to strengthen the wall. Redwood is a good choice for this type of unit.

MINIATURE PROJECTION BOOTH—actually an unused cellar alcove closed in with pine paneling—not only stores photo equipment out of the way, but lets you leave it set up for quick use. Swiveling projector platform holds a Kodak Instamatic Super-8 machine alongside a 16-mm model so either can be run without disturbing the other. A slide and movie projector could be paired in the same way. Left-hand photo on opposite page shows projection window and smaller viewing port for operator to see. The screen is mounted behind doors at the far end of the cellar (photo, far right).

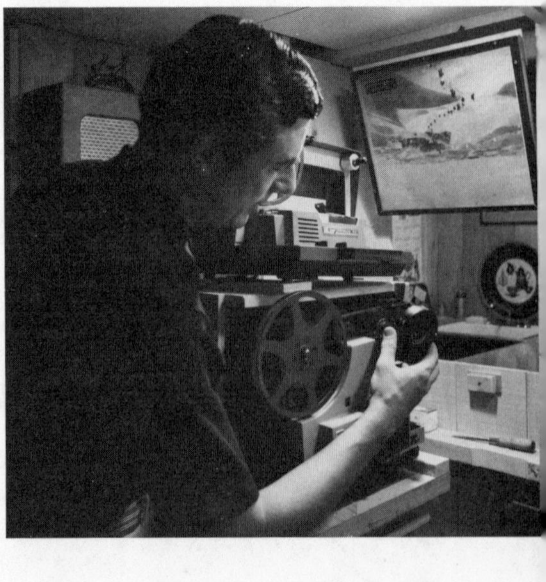

MOUNTED ON casters, this mobile cart for a TV set can be turned to give best viewing angle, depending on where the viewers are seated, or even rolled from room to room. When not in use, TV can be turned to face the wall, as at far left, to conceal its blank screen. Casters, mounted underneath a recessed bottom, are fixed in front and swivel at back for easy maneuvering. The cart is made of plywood and covered with painted burlap.

HOME LAUNDRY center like one at left designed by Maytag combines washer and dryer with shelves and a work counter for easing washday chores and storing supplies attractively. Wall of perforated hardboard at back supports shelf brackets and other hook-in fixtures. Three-section tilt-out bin under counter makes it easy to sort soiled clothes.

HANDY BOOT cupboard above keeps wet and muddy overshoes out of sight, lets them drain harmlessly into bottom drip pan. Boots rest on a slide-out rack of perforated hardboard. A removable baking tin below catches drips.

FACING OPPOSITE ways, these over-under bunkbeds help to divide a room for youngsters of different ages and interests. On one side, lower bunk doubles as couch when area is used for teenage get-togethers. On other side, a train board drops down. Study desk swings out from the end. Celotex V-grooved panels cover bunks.

SLIDE-OUT TRAIN board goes to bed along with its owner, storing neatly away underneath. Its sloping design lets it fill the opening under the bed when pushed in for a trim appearance, while leaving the sides and back unobstructed for reaching the trains easily. Extra train equipment is kept in cupboard that forms bed's headboard.

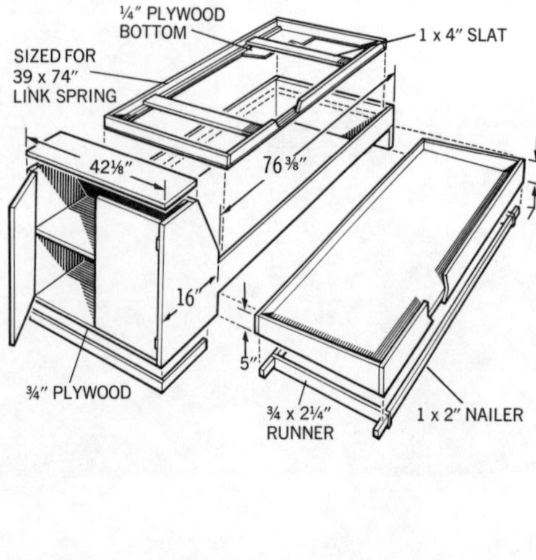

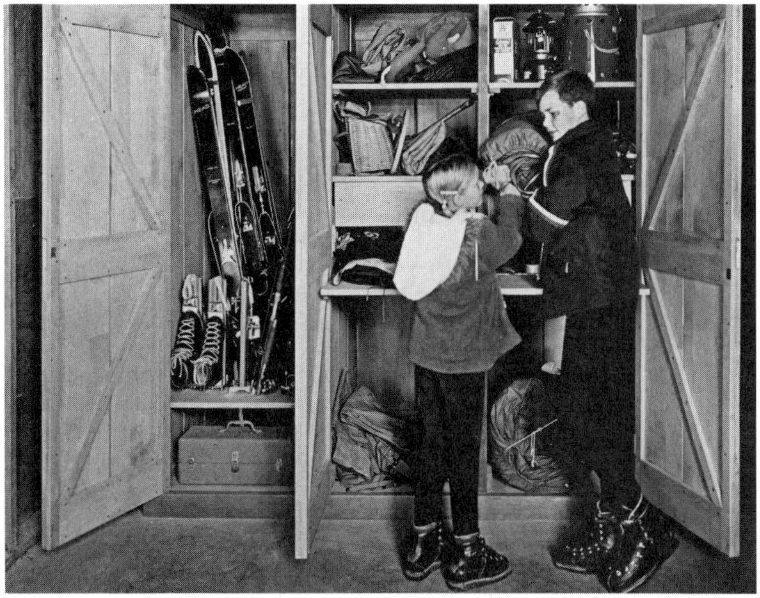

SPECIAL COMPARTMENTS in this roomy storage unit take all the bulky things that never seem to fit anywhere—campstoves, sleeping bags, fishing-tackle boxes, ski boots, life jackets and similar outdoor gear. The tall section on the left side lets you slip skis, fishing poles, boat oars and other long items down behind a shelf where they're kept out of the way at the back. A hinged shelf swings out to provide space for working on equipment. Above this are two drawers for small items such as fishing reels and ski goggles.

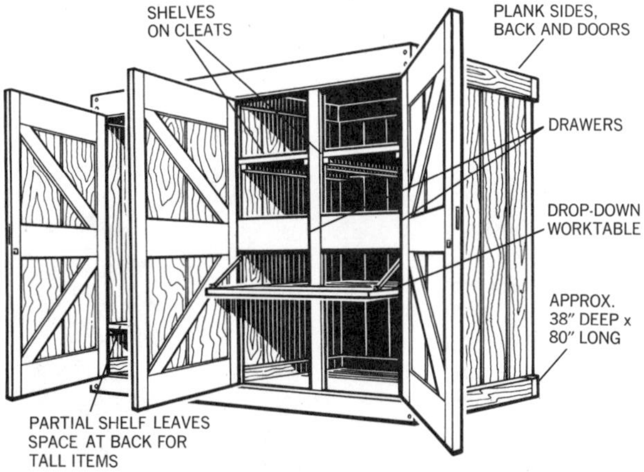

A COMBINATION of perforated paneling and floor-to-ceiling poles creates this unusual storage arrangement for a playroom, den or child's bedroom. The square two-by-two poles, spaced about a foot away from the wall support the front edges of shelves, while the rear edges rest on shelf brackets hooked into the paneling's holes. A small desk is also suspended between the poles. Special Georgia-Pacific V-grooved hardboard paneling has perforations in upper two-thirds and is solid at bottom for a wainscot look.

AN UNUSED DOUBLE closet becomes a small home office at left. Lined with bright checkered wallpaper, it provides enough room for a typing table and file cabinet. With doors closed, it's quickly hidden from view. A similar closet is converted into an attractive vanity alcove in left-hand photo on opposite page. Shallow shelves and drawers at back hold toiletries, yet still leave space for hanging clothes. Inset photo shows handy sloping shoe rack under drawers. Makeup mirror is indirectly lighted from recessed fixture above. At far right, single closet with doors removed becomes a bookcase helping to make a small room seem much bigger.

PADDED BENCHES along a wall are an easy way to gain extra seating space and at the same time add storage room inside. Bench at right makes use of space at one end as a bin for fireplace logs. Additional compartments along the bench hide assorted household items behind cupboard doors. Lift-up seat-tops are another good way to get at space inside a bench and save the framing and fitting required for doors. Such under-bench bins are ideal for holding a slide or movie projector, musical instruments, record collections and stacks of sheet music or old magazines. Slide-out drawers can also house a phonograph and other hi-fi equipment. Bench can be sized to take cushions in 18, 20 and 24-inch squares.

SWING-UP TOP on this versatile hobby bench opens to provide a convenient work area underneath for building models, electronic kits and other small projects. With the top closed, delicate parts and partially assembled projects are protected from damage between sessions. Upper surface also serves as a desk top for doing homework. The design permits quick cleanup since tools and parts don't have to be put away—you just close the lid down over them. Sides around the work area keep tiny pieces from getting lost. Adjustable shelf standards on the walls store supplies and display completed projects handsomely. They can be put up in various arrangements.

STEALING A SMALL slice off an existing room can often give you needed space for special activities. A sliding partition like one above can hide a sewing nook, a hobby bench, a desk, a bar for parties and equipment that must be readily available yet out of sight. It's also useful for screening off a TV set or airconditioner, as at night. Wall shown here is made of framed plywood panels, wallpapered, that slide in floor and ceiling tracks.

OCCUPYING NO MORE than 6 feet of space, the island clothes sorting cabinet (above) can add a world of convenience and efficiency to a home laundry. The pretreatment sink doubles as a member of your laundry team and a clean-up area for messy fingers. The island's many drawers make it a fine companion for any washer/dryer. A wall-supported counter fitted with drawers and equipped with bar stools (upper right) provides a work/study area for the whole family. Each youngster can have his own "desk" for homework or craft activity. It's an excellent place to budget the family paycheck and plan menus. The shelf is solidly supported by protruding 2x4s anchored to wall studs. The counter is covered with Formica and each area is complete with drawer. Low-bridge areas (right) back under sloping roof of attic rooms are waiting to store countless items such as luggage, Christmas decorations, seasonal wearing apparel and the like. Standard window shutters, hinged and held shut with magnetic catches are used to make attractive and inexpensive doors.

New look for a tired wall

SEE ALSO

Bookcases . . . Cabinet furniture . . . Hi-fi centers . . . Room dividers . . Shelves . . . Study centers

SETTLING CAUSED the outside wall to crack and the ceiling joists to sag in one of the upstair's bedrooms of James Cherry's 80-year-old house in Minneapolis. While repairing the wall, Mr. Cherry got the idea to convert the seldom-used guest room into a den-sitting-room-library where he could relax, read and listen to music.

Because the room is large with a high ceiling,

the owner wanted to create a feeling of intimacy. After considering the options, he achieved this effect by filling the window wall from floor to ceiling and corner to corner with the bookshelf system shown on these pages. Visually, the change reduces the room in size; practically, it hides the cracked wall and gives support to those sagging ceiling joists.

The wall system designed by Mr. Cherry is based on plasterboard-covered 2x4 frames with shelving in between. For visual uniformity, the dropped soffit was built-in. The design can easily be adapted to any size wall with a little careful planning. Desk-level and floor-level shelves project slightly more than bookshelves to lessen the dominance of the vertical fins.

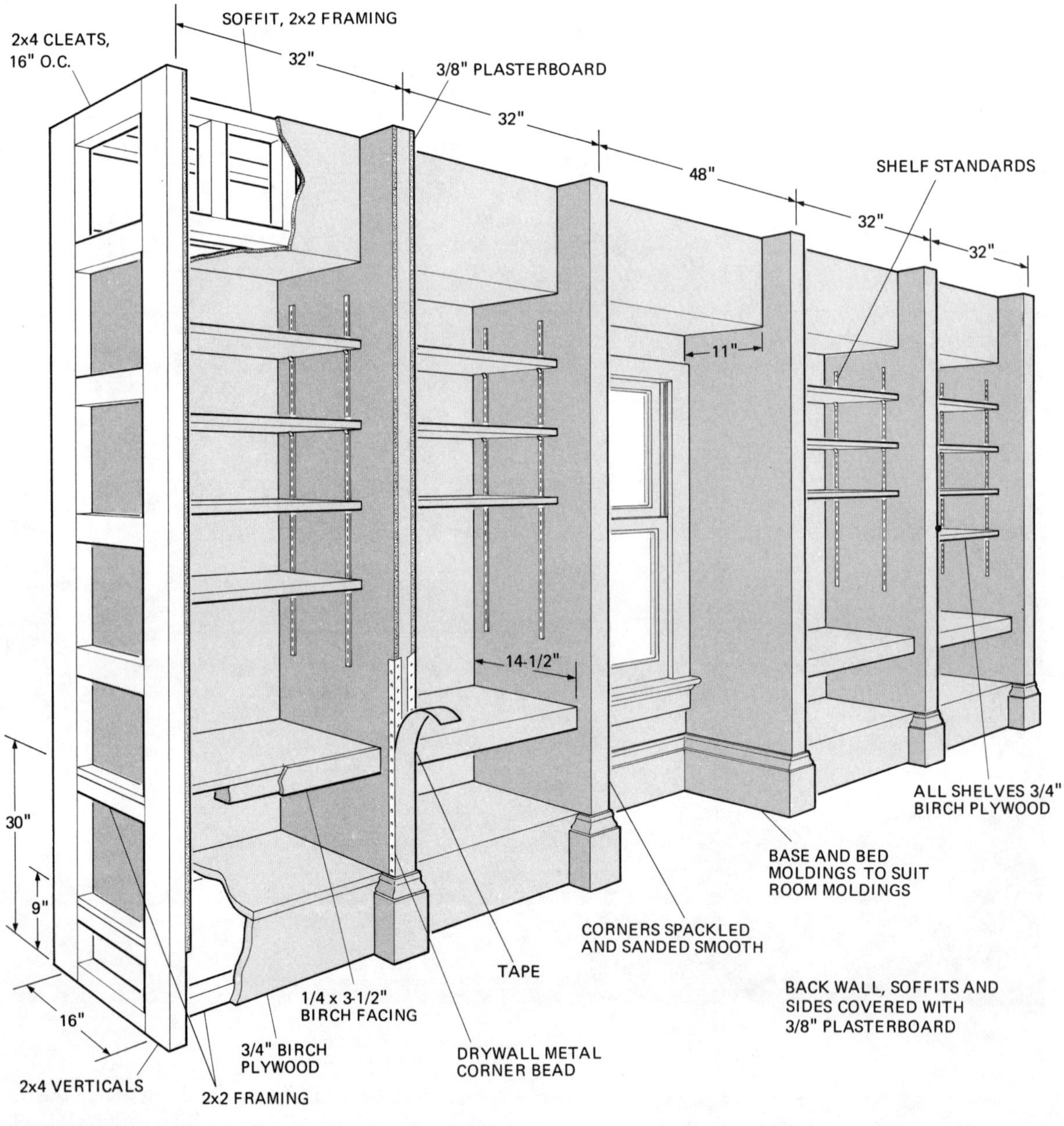

AN UNUSED BEDROOM was converted to the combination den-sitting-room-library at the left. This sturdy wall unit has several shelves for books and speakers, four desk-level shelves for lamp and decorations, and four floor-level shelves for the stereo receiver and more books. It makes the room feel more intimate while supporting sagging ceiling joists.

Concrete patch didn't hold

Last summer I patched a step on my concrete stoop, a corner that broke away. It didn't hold; just fell out of place. I'd like to try again, as I don't want to replace the stoop. Can you tell me the right procedure?—C.T., R.I.

Did you use a concrete patcher especially prepared for the purpose? New concrete won't always bond to old, even though you may have cleaned out all dirt and loose material. Obtain a concrete-patching material which comes as a dry mix and add water in a measured proportion. Again clean the area to be patched thoroughly and make an L-shaped form, bracing or staking the form so it will stay in place until the concrete mix sets. When mixing, be sure to follow instructions on the container in *all* details. After troweling the mix in place, cover with burlap or coarse cloth and keep damp several days.

Painting basement floor

I want to paint part of my basement floor, but I'm confused about the paints and methods. My floor is in good condition, smooth and with no cracks. Can you start me in the right direction?—E.J. Long, Fort Worth, Tex.

Manufacturers generally recommend a latex-alkyd paint (water- emulsion) for concrete floors. Follow the rather detailed instructions for application on the container. In all cases, the floor should be thoroughly washed and scrubbed beforehand to remove all dust and debris. You can use a brush, but a roller with a stand-up handle is better and faster, with less chance of laps showing. Provide adequate ventilation, using a fan if necessary to move air and blow out fumes.

If your floor has a near glass-smooth finish, the instructions may recommend that the surface be etched before applying paint. This is done with a muriatic acid solution; follow directions to the letter.

Painting steel basement sashes

I want to paint the steel sashes and frames of my basement windows. To paint the frames I must take out the sashes, but how? The frames are welded at the corners and so far I don't have the "combination."—R. Masters, Birmingham, Ala.

All basement metal sashes I know of are designed to be lifted out of their frames. I have such windows and to get them out they must be tilted inward about halfway, then one end is raised until one "ear," or lug, clears the frame. This requires a careful, controlled maneuver, but once the lug is clear, the sash is easily lifted out.

'Numbered' roof

My house is to be reroofed. The contractor says he will use a No. 235 asphalt shingle, that this is a standard shingle and that he would not recommend a heavier covering on my "roof deck." What's he talking about?—N.H., Wis.

If you have the number correct, he means he's installing a shingle that weighs 235 pounds for each 100 square feet of roof area, that is, an area 10x10 feet. I assume that the new shingles are to be laid over the old. Your contractor has undoubtedly examined the roofing and checked the deck and the rafter size and he feels that this is the heaviest shingle he can use as an "overroofing." This weight shingle is expected to give at least 15 years' service, usually more except under extreme conditions. The term "roof deck" refers to the boards that are laid over the rafters.

You might ask the contractor if he intends to use a shingle of the self-sealing type. It's recommended because the undersides of its tabs are coated with a self-sealing adhesive to keep them from being turned up and torn during high winds.

'Cold' siding

I want to cover my old wood siding with new aluminum siding, but I've been told that this siding is "cold"—that my old house will be cold and difficult to heat. Right or wrong?—D.F., Kans.

To me, "cold" is a new term applied to house siding. Much would depend on what your informant meant by it. Perhaps he is right in what he meant to say. But I don't think application of aluminum siding will make your home colder temperaturewise, or more difficult to heat, provided that it is installed according to accepted practice and that your heating installation is adequate to cope with winter temperatures in your locality.

Remover doesn't

I always work with paint and varnish removers outdoors. Often the remover doesn't "remove." The residues seem to harden and dry up on the surface and won't strip off easily. I must be doing something wrong, but what?—Jerry Bates, Canton, Ohio.

You may be brushing the remover too thinly. It works best when laid on in a one-direction stroke, using a full brush at each sweep. Also, in the open on a dry day, remover tends to evaporate more rapidly, even though a retarder is included in its formulation. Try laying a thickness of waxed paper over the surface immediately after applying remover.

How to repair aluminum storms and screens

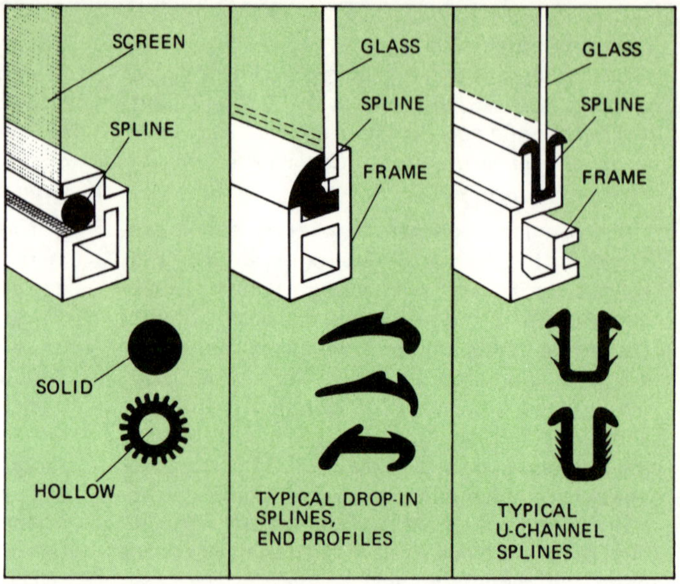

2. Splines for aluminum storms and screens

Splines are made in a variety of shapes. At left above are round splines, solid or hollow, used to secure screens to frames. There are two kinds of storm-sash frame, each with its own type of spline. Drop-in type, center, is easier to handle as it does not require disassembly of frame for re-glazing. Take-apart type, right, using U-channel splines, must be disassembled. Frame and spline designs vary considerably, depending upon the maker, but correct spline shape and size is available by the package or the roll

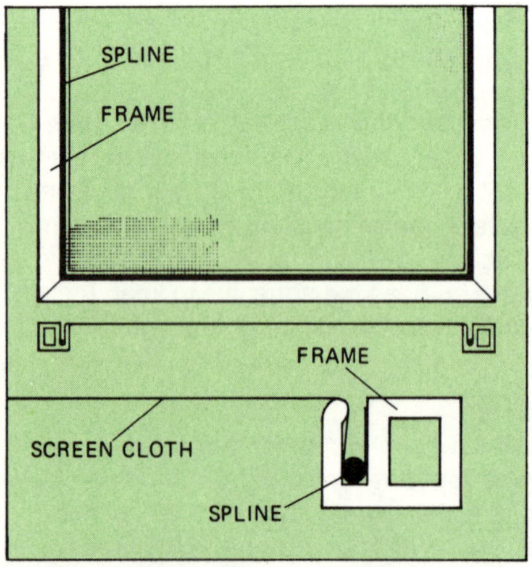

1. Typical aluminum screen

The screen cloth is secured by a plastic spline in frame groove. Replacing a torn window screen is simple if proper technique and tools are used. Begin by locating the ends of the spline in groove, lift them with an awl or screwdriver blade and pull the spline out of groove on all four sides of the frame. If the spline breaks, it must be replaced. In that event, save a sample of the old spline in order to purchase the correct replacement

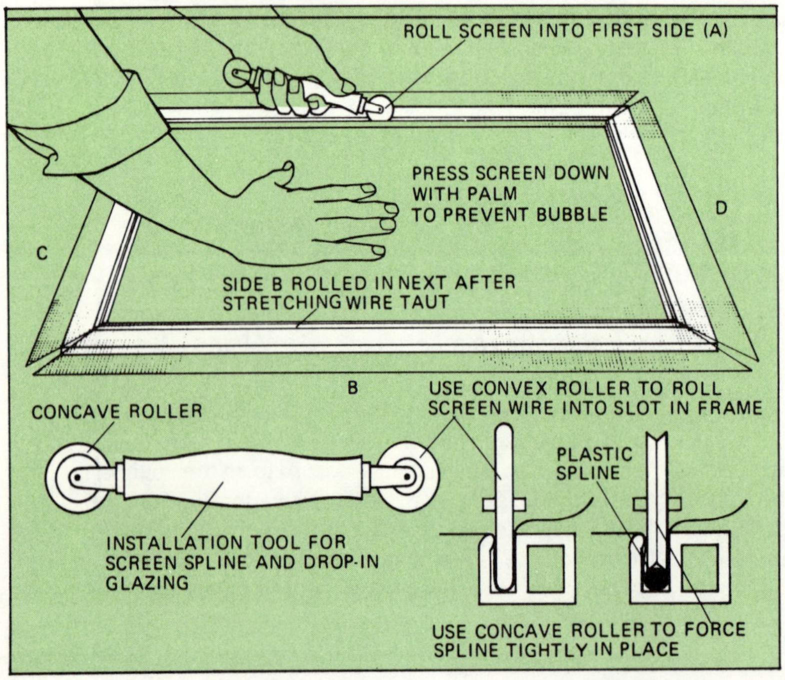

3. Reinstalling screen wire

Push old screen out from the back of frame. Measure outside length and width of frame and cut new screen at least 2 in. over-size in all directions. Holding screen down on frame, use installation tool's convex roller to force into groove with five or six passes—don't try it with one pass or screen will rip. Place spline on groove, force it in place with concave roller. Turn frame, repeat on opposite side, pulling screen tight and working convex roller down and to outside of frame. If frame bows, start over with new screen. If not, place spline with concave roller. Screen should now feel tight. Using scissors, make V-cuts in screen at corners to relieve tension; then finish the last two sides in the same way

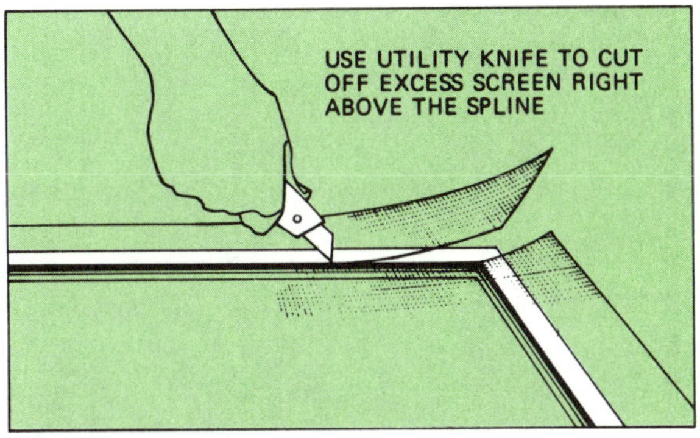

4. Trimming the wire

After screen has been grooved and locked in with spline on all four sides, insert tip of a utility knife just above spline in groove's outer side. Hold frame and run knife along inside edge. Excess screen can now be pulled away and discarded. Take care when cutting to avoid splines

SEE ALSO

Doors . . . Glass cutting . . . Locks, door . . . Screens . . . Sliding glass doors . . . Windows . . . Winterizing, homes

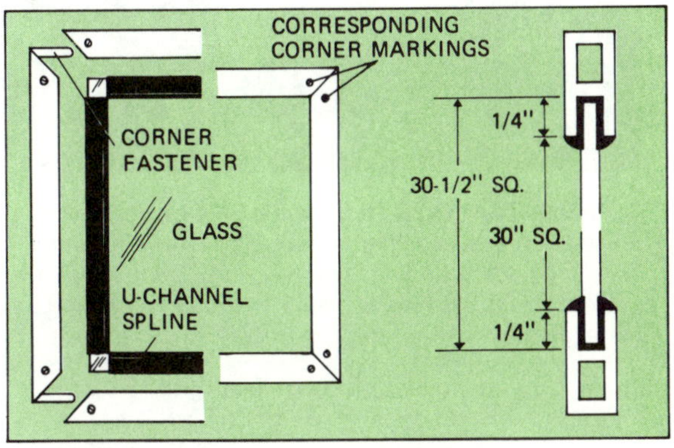

6. Assuring accurate reassembly

Take-apart frame, above, should be matched at three corners to assure accurate reassembly. For width and height of frame for glass, take distances between opposite U-channel bottoms. Be sure to allow (subtract) for spline. Fit U-channel spline over all four edges of the pane. Then using a wood or plastic mallet, gently tap on a section of the frame—one without corner fasteners—into place over the spline on the glass edge. Repeat on opposite edge, then line up frame sections to which corner fasteners are attached with corresponding holes on first two sides. After gently tapping frame together, replace corner screws or the clips as is seen at the sketch on the right

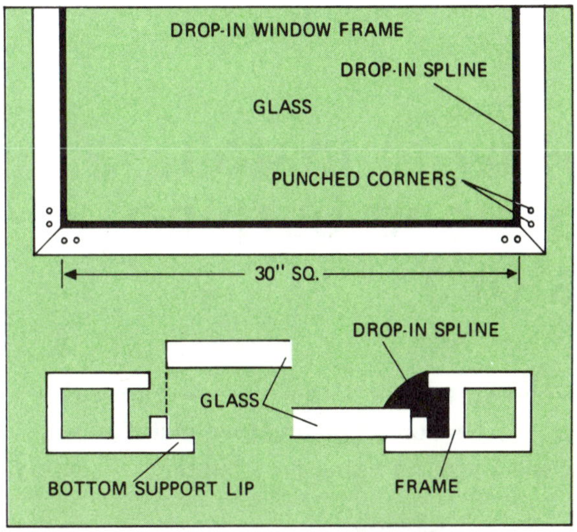

5. Reglazing aluminum storm sash

Replacement of glass in aluminum storm sash requires precaution of wearing gloves and safety goggles. To remove glued-in glass, brush the pieces with paint remover; save a scrap piece to assure you buy the right thickness for your replacement pane. Frame above, a drop-in type, does not come apart. Measure inside dimensions including support lips. Cut window glass to size and carefully lay it inside the frame so that it rests on the lips. Insert drop-in spline by laying it on the window beveled side up and pushing it into the frame with your fingers. Repeat the procedure for the other three sides and the window is finished. Here, too, if the old spline breaks, replace it with a new one

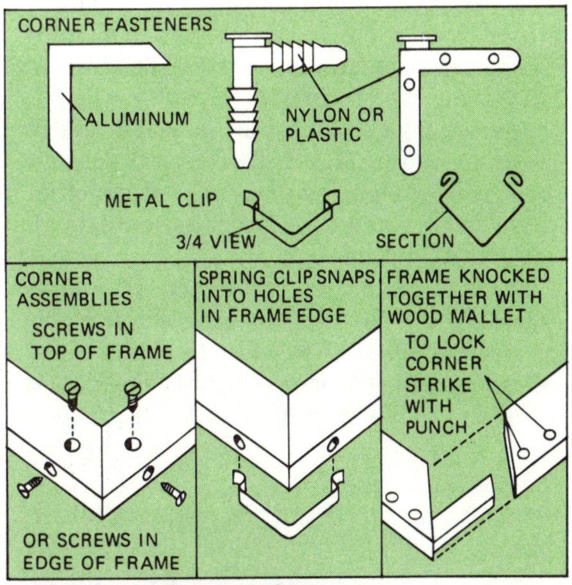

7. For smooth operation

Keep window tracks clean and spray with silicone lubricant. A mild cleaner and water will remove discoloration; avoid using abrasives

How to install a wood-burning stove

Wood stoves don't cause fires—careless people do. Here's some tips on stove installation that will keep the home fires burning . . . safely

By JOHN E. GAYNOR

IN A RECENT YEAR, 14,000 home fires were started by wood or coal stoves, according to the National Fire Protection Assn. (NFPA). More than 150 occupants lost their lives, and some 4600 were injured.

Frightening statistics? Yes, but they don't tell the real story. First, stove fires are fortunately rare compared to the number of stoves in use. Those 14,000 cases, as tragic as they were, represent only 0.2 percent of stoves installed in U.S. homes.

More importantly, studies by the NFPA and other consumer-safety agencies all indicate that most stove-related fires actually result from improper installation or careless use, *not* faulty equipment. In other words, stoves themselves do not cause fires—people do.

The best location for a wood stove is in a fairly large, open area. Most bedrooms and dens are too small and cluttered to make good use of the considerable heat a stove generates, and safe use could be a problem.

Don't be lulled into a false sense of security because your walls are of noncombustible plaster or plasterboard. The fact that the plaster itself can't burn is not the point. The real danger lies in a curious and little-known characteristic of wood:

SEE ALSO

Boilers . . . Energy, saving . . . Fireplaces . . . Furnaces . . . Heat pumps . . . Heating systems, home . . . Heating systems, solar . . . Solar energy . . . Winterizing, homes

COMBINATION stove/fireplace unit is by Jotul. It is correctly placed against a non-combustible masonry wall. A masonry base is also placed under the unit to protect any joists below. Under the masonry base is a metal shield.

When it's subjected even to moderate heat over a long period, its normal flash point (ignition temperature) of 700° F. can be drastically lowered—some researchers think to as little as 200° F.—less than the boiling point of water!

"Wood studs, even though covered by noncombustible plasterboard, can burn at abnormally low temperatures if exposed to constant heat from a wood stove," says the Engineering Experiment Station of the Georgia Institute of Technology. The same is true of floor joists, even when under brick, slate or tile.

This is why it is essential to maintain the recommended clearances around a stove and its

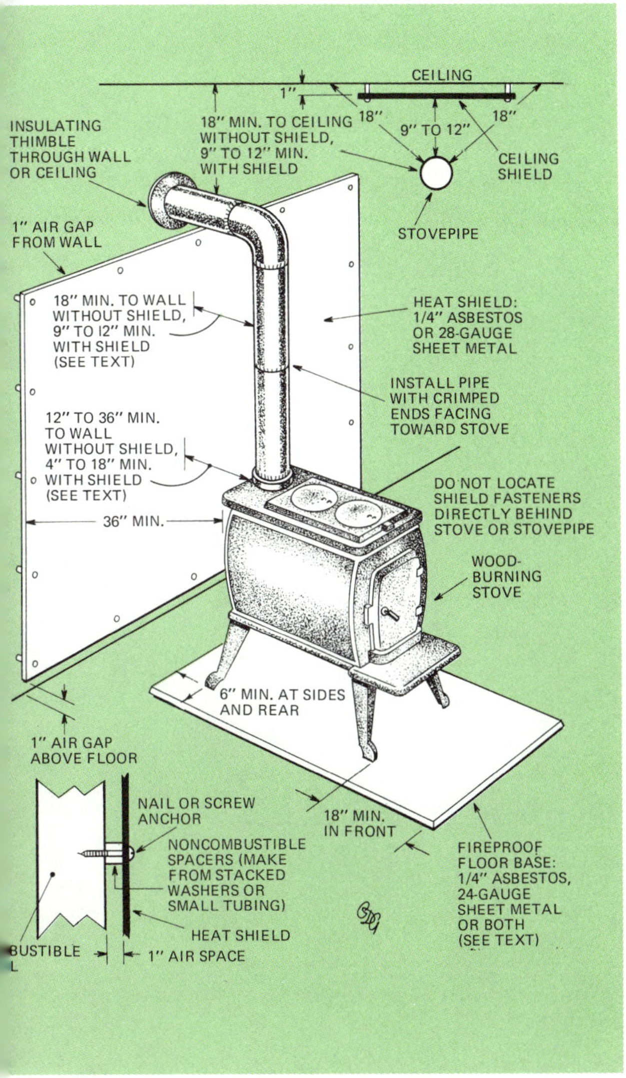

PROPERLY installed heat shield permits safe operation near a combustible wall, reducing normally required clearance by 50 percent or more. It should be spaced at least 1 in. from wall. Fireproof base must extend 18 in. front., 6 in. at sides and rear.

flue. The clearances given here were established by the NFPA. However, they are *minimums.* If a particular stove maker recommends a greater clearance, heed his advice. Freestanding fireplaces give off less heat than a stove and usually require less clearance. Follow the manufacturer's instructions.

A radiant-type stove, the kind that discharges heat directly though a single-wall firebox, must be placed no less than 36 in. from a combustible wall (any wood-stud wall regardless of its facing). A double-wall circulator stove with an outer shell doesn't get as hot and can be placed as near as 12 in. to a wall.

With a heat shield on the wall behind the stove, you can reduce these clearances. It must be of noncombustible material, either 28-gauge sheet metal or ¼-in.-thick asbestos millboard. It must be installed with metal spacers, so that it is held 1 in. away from the wall and 1 in. off the floor. This is to allow air to flow up behind the shield and keep the wall cool. Don't locate any fasteners directly behind the stove or stovepipe—they could transmit heat through the shield to the wall.

With the shield in place, stove-to-wall clearances are now as follows: For a radiant stove, 18 in. with asbestos-millboard backing, 12 in. with sheet metal; for a circulator stove, 6 in. with asbestos, 4 in. with sheet metal.

stovepipe clearances

There is an important exception to the clearances given above. Your stovepipe, which also gives off considerable heat, must adhere to its own minimum wall clearances. These are: 18 in. with no shield, 12 in. with asbestos shield, 9 in. with metal shield. If the stovepipe comes out at the rear of the stove, as it does on many models, the pipe itself, not the stove, may control the installation. This is especially true in the case of circulator stoves, which normally require less clearance than the pipe. Whatever the situation, be sure *both* stove and pipe meet minimum clearance requirements.

The size of the shield is determined by how far away the stove and pipe are located. It must be wide enough so that the diagonal distance from each rear corner of the stove to its side edge measures a minimum of 36 in. for a radiant and 12 in. for a circulator. The easiest way to do this is to swing a yardstick from each stove corner to the wall and mark the wall where it touches. The two marks on the wall will then represent the width of the shield.

The shield that runs up behind the stovepipe can be narrower—18 in. on either side, also measured on the diagonal. However, it generally is simpler, and looks better, to carry the same-width shield all the way up the wall. If your stovepipe comes to within less than 18 in. of the ceiling before passing through the wall, you'll also need a shield above it to protect ceiling joists.

If the wall behind your stove is solid masonry with no wood studding behind it, it's not considered a combustible wall and you can eliminate the shield.

As already noted, not even a base of brick, slate or tile is considered adequate by itself to

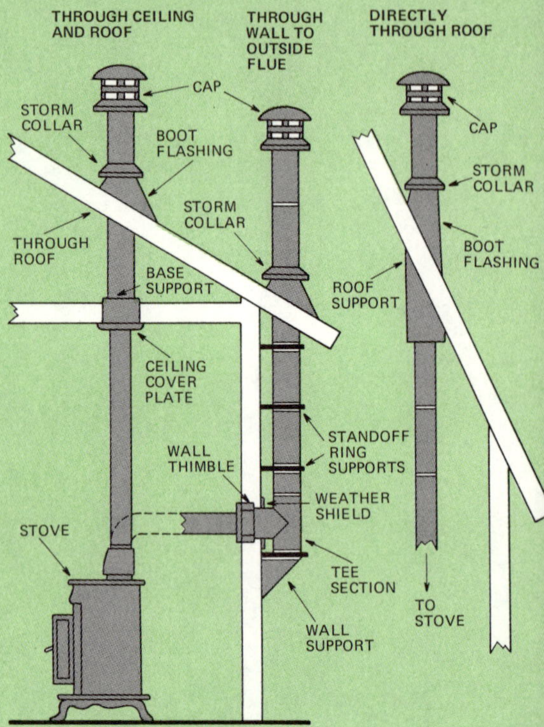

AFTERMATH of a stove fire that didn't have to happen: Photo dramatically illustrates how poorly installed heater, with no shield behind or under it, led to tragedy. Drawing at right shows three ways to correctly vent a stove to the outside. Ordinary stovepipe can be used only for short run from stove to nearest wall or ceiling. Beyond that point you need an approved prefab chimney flue to do the job right.

protect a wood floor under a stove. If the bottom of the stove stands 18 in. or more above the floor, you need a base of 24-gauge sheet metal underneath. If it's less than 18 in. from the floor, put down ¼-in. asbestos millboard first and top it with 24-gauge sheet metal. (For stoves with less than 6-in. bottom clearance, see manufacturer instructions for building up a fireproof platform.)

The base must extend a minimum of 18 in. beyond the stove in front and 6 in. on the other three sides. And remember—if you want the decorative appearance of a brick, slate or tile surface, this must go *over* the sheet-metal sub-base.

For average stovepipe diameters (6 to 10 in.), use 24-gauge corrosion-resistant steel. Some experts advise against using galvanized pipe because the zinc used in the galvanizing may vaporize at high temperatures and give off toxic fumes.

Keep the run from stove to flue as short as possible, preferably no more than 5 to 9 ft., and use no more than two 90° bends. Excessive turns impede good draft flow. Pitch horizontal runs ¼ in. to the foot *up* from stove to flue, and assemble the pipe sections so the crimped or male ends face toward the stove. This encourages creosote and moisture condensation to run back into the stove, instead of collecting in the flue. Fasten the sections together with three sheet-metal screws equally spaced around each joint.

When passing through a wall, the stovepipe must be fed through an insulating collar called a thimble. This is a double-wall ring that allows air to circulate around the hot inner pipe and dissipate heat. If the pipe feeds into an existing chimney flue, the flue must be at least 25 percent larger for proper draft.

Connecting the pipe to an existing fireplace flue is an excellent way to avoid the cost of a new chimney. In this case, the fireplace opening must be sealed with sheet metal and the stovepipe extended a short way up the chimney throat, usually the length of one pipe section. Assemble all joints with furnace cement, as well as with screws.

Ordinary single-wall stovepipe can be used only for the short run from stove to flue. It can't be run between floors or in any other enclosed areas. For this, you need insulated flue pipe.

If there is no existing flue to tie into, you can use a prefabricated metal flue. This is relatively inexpensive and easy to install. Be sure, however, that you buy only a UL-listed "Class A" metal chimney. This comes in two styles—a triple-wall type insulated by air circulation and a double-wall type packed with solid insulation.

Whatever the type, a chimney must extend a minimum height above the roofline to insure adequate draft. It must project at least 3 ft. above the point where it passes through the roof and stand 2 ft. higher than any surrounding portion of roof within 10 ft. Heed manufacturer instructions for bracing a chimney, especially if it projects more than the minimum 3 ft. In heavy storms, prefab metal chimneys are more vulnerable to wind damage than masonry and may need extra support.

Along with proper installation, a wood or coal stove must be operated carefully to avoid the chance of fire. Some people go to elaborate lengths to see that a stove is fully shielded, then do something silly like placing a cardboard carton of dry kindling right next to it. Keep your wood supply, as well as all rugs, drapes, pillows, furniture and other flammables, well away from the stove.

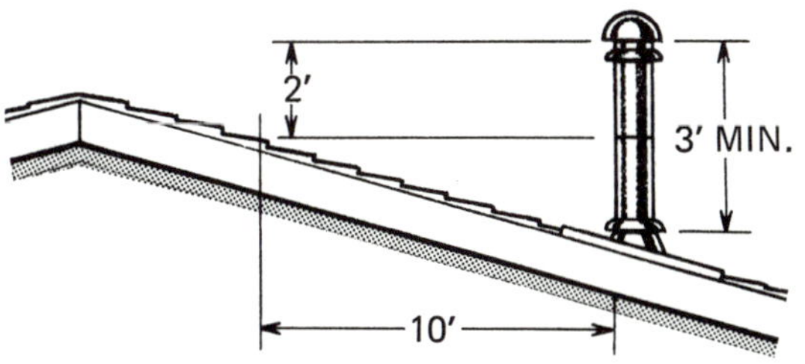

HOW HIGH must your chimney be? It must extend at least 3 ft. above the point where flue passes through roof and 2 ft. above any portion of roof within 10 ft.

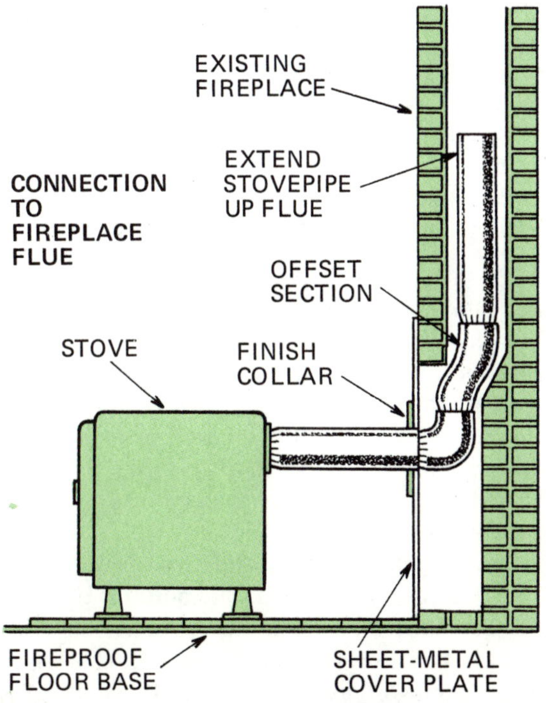

TYING STOVE into fireplace chimney saves money, can be safe. A hearth must be extended beyond the stove and stovepipe must be run short way up flue.

If you buy an old, secondhand stove, examine it closely for cracks, missing parts and other defects. Never burn coal in a wood stove unless the manufacturer specifically recommends the use of coal. And never overfire a stove to see how hot you can get it.

If you have the type of stove that also serves as an open fireplace, don't leave it unattended with the doors open. Never use flammable liquids to start or rekindle a fire. These can flare up explosively if hot coals are present. Don't use a stove for trash disposal. Flaming bits of paper can fly up the chimney and fall on the roof or start a flue fire. Keep a window open slightly to allow fresh air to circulate. This is especially important when operating a stove continuously over long periods or when burning coal. Clean out ashes regularly and store them in a covered metal container.

Check regularly for creosote buildup in the stovepipe and chimney. Creosote is a highly flammable by-product of wood combustion and can cause a violent and frightening flue fire. A yearly inspection is the recommended minimum, but more cleaning may be necessary.

No matter what kind of installation you make, most local codes require that the finished job be inspected and approved. This is actually to your own benefit as it will help to insure the safety of your family and home.

Advise your building department that you are making an installation and ask for its recommendations. In most areas, building permits are required for installing chimneys and stoves. Also notify your insurance company, or your policy may be voided in the event of fire—any fire.

Strawberries by the barrel

By WAYNE C. LECKEY

Grow strawberries in a barrel? Why not? The barrel keeps them off the ground so they grow faster and cleaner. This one's even equipped with wheels, so the strawberries follow the sun! Just follow these simple directions for a bumper crop

AN OLD BARREL can be painted, a new one stained and varnished. Treat the inside with wood preservative.

PLUCKING STRAWBERRIES from a barrel on your patio may sound crazy, but what a treat! Like fruit on a bush, berries grown in a barrel are a lot cleaner than when grown in a strawberry patch—and a lot handier. And as a center of attraction, a strawberry barrel is sure to make conversation.

A strawberry barrel doesn't have to be on a patio, of course. It can be located anywhere as long as there is plenty of sunshine. It should be placed, however, on a level concrete slab and fitted with casters so the barrel can be turned occasionally to expose all plants to direct sun. Two husky chest handles attached to opposite sides near the top will facilitate turning it.

SEE ALSO
Decks . . . Garden shelters . . . Gardening . . . House plants . . . Patios . . . Planters . . . Transplanting

Everbearing varieties of strawberry plants, considered best suited for barrel growing, produce fruit from 60 to 90 days after planting. Strawberries can be planted as soon as danger of frost has passed.

Any 50-gal. wooden barrel, new or used, will do as long as it has a good solid bottom. Holes in the side should be 1½ in. in diameter and 6 in. apart in 4 or 5 rows. You can bore 8 to 9 holes per row, which will provide for 32 to 45 plants, plus 10 more on top. The rows should be reasonably even on a horizontal plane and staggered vertically. A hole saw in an electric drill will bore the holes quickly.

PLANTS ARE WATERED through a perforated pipe in the center. Rows of holes let water seep out.

FOUR TRUCK CASTERS are attached securely to the bottom of the barrel with short lagscrews or bolts.

FIVE DRAIN HOLES are bored through the bottom of the barrel and later covered with broken clay pots.

The plants are watered through a standpipe placed in the center of the barrel. It's a section of common aluminum downspout cut to stand an inch or so above the top of the barrel. One end is closed and rows of small holes are drilled at random along its length. When in place, the pipe is filled with vermiculite or coarse gravel to allow the water to seep slowly out the holes. When filled, the barrel will weigh a good 500 lbs. so use heavy-duty swivel-type truck casters to support it.

Use a soil mixture of well-rotted cow manure, garden loam and sand—$^1/_5$ each of sand and manure by volume and the balance loam. Place a layer of broken clay flowerpots in the bottom of the barrel first. Then start adding the soil mixture up to the first row of holes and water to firm it. Now carefully insert the plants in the holes, spread the roots, fill with more soil and wet down gently. Continue until all the holes are planted. The plants in the top of the barrel are spaced about 4 in. apart. After the plants are established and actively growing, they can be forced to grow more rapidly by adding nutrients to the water. Watch, of course, that you don't overwater. When berries start to ripen, you may have to cover your barrel with cloth netting to keep the birds from eating them. This can be in the form of a lift-off cage made of wood strips with the netting stapled to it.

THE STANDPIPE IS CLOSED at the bottom with an aluminum scrap "welded" to the pipe with a glue gun.

PANELING provides appropriate backdrop when given a wipe-off coat of thin oil paint.

A wall-hung study center

These off-the-floor desk and storage units save space in your kids' room. They're relatively inexpensive and easy to build with ordinary hand tools from your shop

AFTER HORIZONTAL boards are nailed to verticals, all permanent shelves are installed with screws.

SEE ALSO

Cabinet furniture . . . Children's furniture . . . Desks . . . Modular furniture . . . Room dividers . . . Storage walls

■ IF YOU CAN SAW a board, you can build this wall-hung study center, for that's just about all you have to do to make it. You start out with plain flat boards and simply saw them to length, without even touching the width. The important thing is to saw the ends square.

In designing the project around standard-size boards which any lumberyard sells, David Blair, West Coast architect, not only has reached the ultimate in simplified construction, but has created a handsome, functional piece that any school boy (or girl) would be glad to have.

It provides an off-the-floor desk with shelf below, a cork pinup board for displaying star-studded papers, roomy shelves for reference books and a cupboard for storing all the wonderful treasures a boy collects. Pegs provide a place for a young cowboy to hang his six-shooter. There's even a bin to corral stray toys.

Remember that a 1 x 12 board, for example, is not a full 1 in. thick and 12 in. wide, but actually measures ¾ x 11½-in. This is true of all dimensioned lumber. Actual measurement is less than stock size.

Any solid lumber of the western pine species, such as ponderosa pine, larch or white fir, is appropriate. A natural finish (protected by a clear sealer) combined with painted cupboard doors, plus a colorful plastic desktop, will give it eye appeal.

Nails are used to fasten the 9-ft. 1 x 12s to the vertical members, and they are also used when nailing the desk compartment together. All the rest of the members are joined with 1½-in., No. 10, oval-head screws which are first seated in chrome cup washers and inserted in predrilled holes in the wood. The three adjustable cupboard shelves rest on regular shelf standards and supports. Six 2½-in. toggle bolts are used to hang the unit.

Depending on the grade selected (common grades of lumber cost considerably less than clear) the wood for the complete project will run from $20 to $40. Hardware will come to about $4.50, the cork, $3.25 and the plastic laminate, $2.75. To this you'll add the cost of glue, contact cement, paint and sealer. Total cost will vary and you may find that you can build it for under $40.

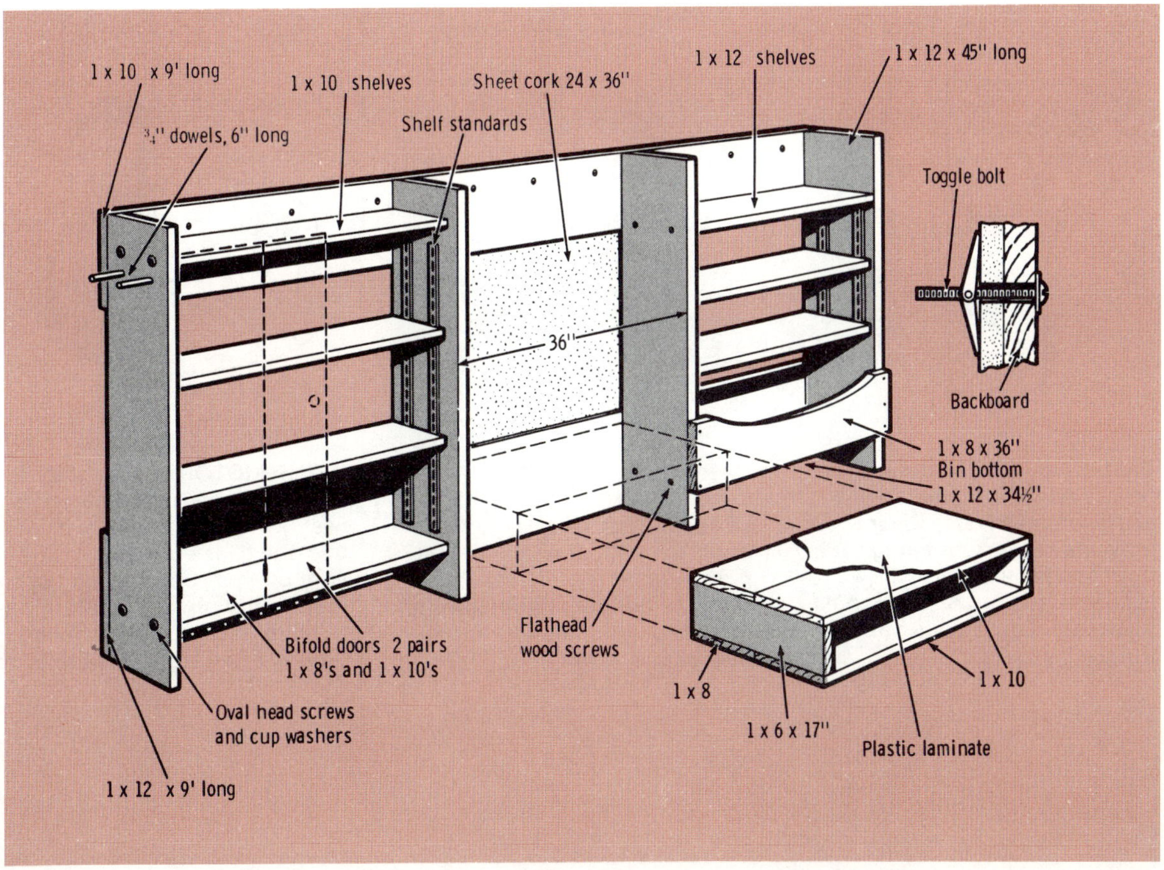

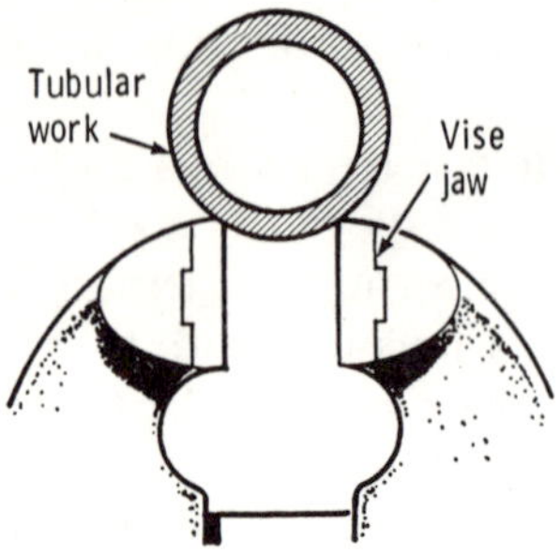

WHEN hacksawing metal tubing, don't risk crushing it out of round by clamping it in a vise. Instead, open the vise just enough so that the jaws act as a V-block. Then you can hold the tubing in the slot and rotate it slowly as the saw cuts through it.

ONE SIMPLE WAY to keep a paintbrush soft overnight without cleaning it is to stand it in a jar containing a small amount of thinner. Slip a polyethylene freezer bag over the top and secure it with a rubber band to seal in all of the fumes from the thinner.

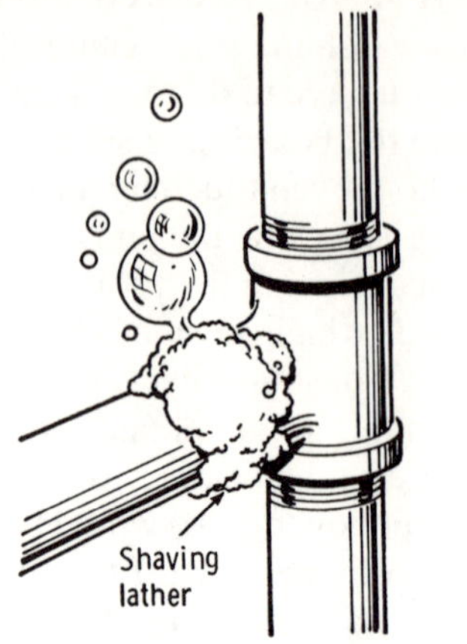

MOST PLUMBERS still use a bubbly soap solution to test connections in a home gas system. However, a much more modern material for the job is shaving cream packaged in aerosol cans. It's dense, long-lasting and excellent for use in hard-to-reach spots.

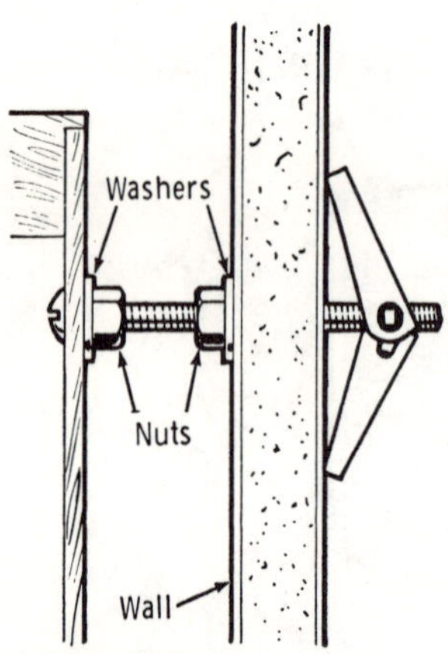

TALL CABINETS or bookcases have a tendency to wobble in cases where the baseboard prevents them from being set flush against the wall. If the wall is hollow, you can easily anchor them with toggle bolts through the back panels.

CARRYING FISHHOOKS loose in your pocket is normally not advisable. To make it safe, use a book of matches. Just slip the points under the matches and wrap the leaders around to hold them in place; then close the matchbook cover.

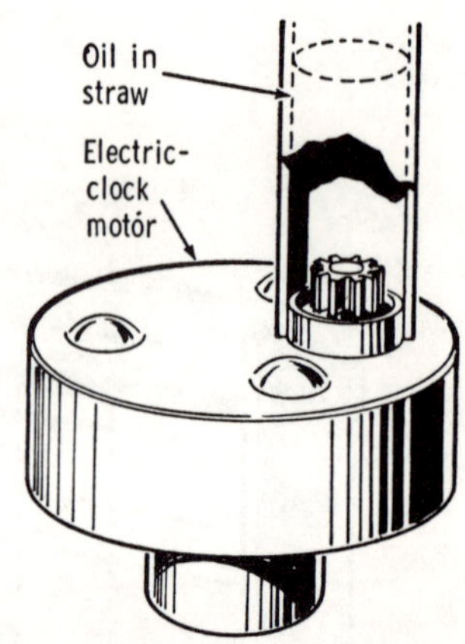

IF THE MOTOR in your electric clock becomes noisy, here's an easy way to oil it. Slip a straw over the gear shaft, pour a little light oil into it, then heat the motor enough so that air bubbles escape. Let it cool and oil will enter around the shaft.

Screen house: Pilings are used to support this structure in a unique setting by the water. The design of a screen house beats mosquitoes in back yards, too

Garden gazebo: This back-yard house is so versatile that it can be elegant for entertaining, informal or used strictly by the gardener with the green thumb

Canopy gazebo: This simple canopy has lines which are perfectly elegant and simple. The construction blends in beautifully on a wooded site

Three gracious summer houses

By MIKE MCCLINTOCK

These versatile buildings will make summer more fun around your house and may help you recall the "good old days" when families used to enjoy relaxing on a large porch

■ MANY HOUSES used to be built with a huge porch in front or off the side. On warm summer evenings you'd be likely to find a family sitting out there rather than inside a hot, stuffy house. Unfortunately, this is a thing of the past. There's another feature of the American homestead that's disappearing and that's the barn. As the car replaced the horse, garages and carports were built to shelter the new vehicles. Without a large porch or a barn, the modern American home has lost its outdoor living and working space. One of these garden houses, or a combination of some of their features could be the answer.

keep off the grass

All three have one thing in common—a wood floor. This gets you up off the ground, provides a dance floor, and means that you don't have to balance a drink between two dandelions. But in each case, the floor has been taken a crucial step further. The most common pitfall of outdoor structures is that they frequently look as if they were dropped out of a plane onto your back yard. They just don't look as though they belong there. All these gazebos have extended flooring, as deck platforms, a balcony, or a ramp, past the structural lines of the building. This softens the look of the structure and makes it more a part of the ground it's on.

SCREEN HOUSE

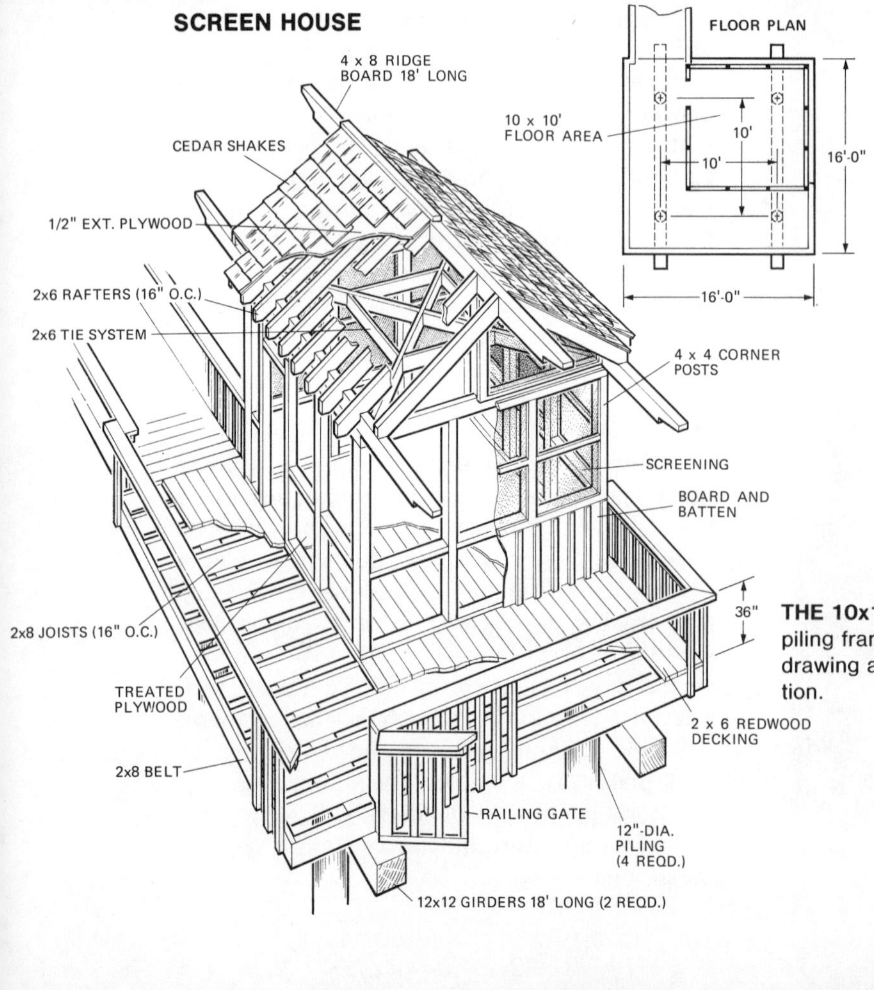

GARDEN GAZEBO

WORKING garden center is at the rear of the garden gazebo. Lattice doors on rubber wheels slide away to reveal a solid potting counter and plenty of storage space.

THE 10x10-FT. screen house is offset on the 16x16-ft. piling frame, thus creating pleasant deck space. The drawing at left gives good bird's-eye view of construction.

YOU CAN EVEN plant your garden around the gazebo. The 3x10-ft. deck units can be built to use as ramps or a walkway which leads through the garden.

THE TRELLIS roof is made up of 2x2s in frames. This puts filtered light on the deck of the gazebo or you can use plywood for shade.

turn the page

ONE SECTION of deck was not completed so the lawnmower could be wheeled into the "closet." More storage area for pots is located under the bench.

HOW ABOUT piling up some pillows and settling back on one of the benches for a sunbath? This corner deck is great to use for flowering plants too.

CANOPY GAZEBO

ONCE YOU'VE SUNK the four poles in the ground, construction can move quickly. Double girders, supported through the poles, are used to support conventional 2x8 joists. Single upper carriers support the roof. Construction techniques are simple but yield a strong and sturdy structure.

Aside from the design considerations, another tool that will make a good-looking site is landscaping. This is most obvious in the location of the canopy gazebo. The roof line, which might have looked quite severe if it were out in an open area, is successfully nestled in a stand of trees. The simplicity of the construction, using treated poles, is totally harmonious with the surroundings. On a smaller scale, the lines of the deck on the garden gazebo can be muted with shrubs or planter boxes.

All the deck platforms outside the 4x4 posts on the garden gazebo are made up from 2x8 structural-grade redwood. The interior of each box is framed 16 inches on center with short lengths, and 2x4s are face-nailed to form the deck. The dimensions are all modular (4x8, 3x12 and so forth) so there is absolutely no material waste. These platforms are so dimensionally stable that they don't need footings. They can rest securely on level ground and you can arrange them in any way you prefer. A few well-placed toenails will hold one in place as a bridge that rests on two other decks to create different levels.

The roof of the garden gazebo is designed for a dry climate; 2x4-ft. panels are made up using 2x2s to form a lattice. This will cut the direct sun but still keep the light, airy feeling you want outside. Depending on the climate where you live, part of the roof could be solid. The lattice panels fit into the roof framing system and can be removed for a piece of plywood if you want more protection. Although the plans don't include wir-

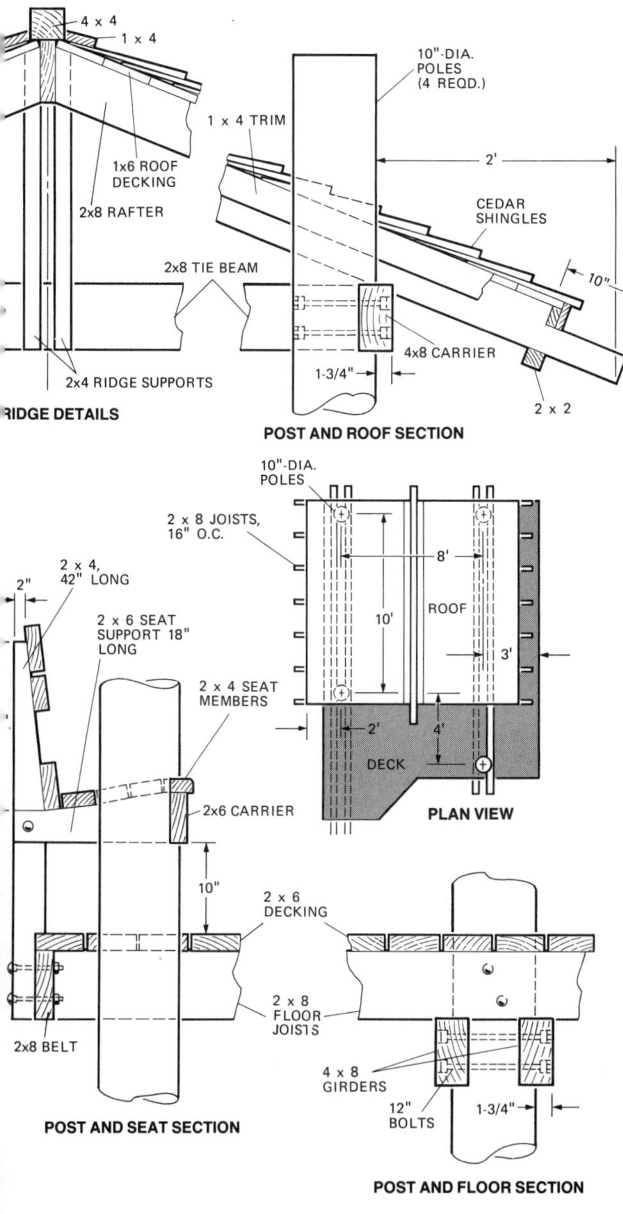

ing diagrams, I urge you to run a code-approved line from your house out to the shelter. A few simple boxes with floodlights will make it look like a dream house at night and let the party keep going well after dark. I'd also install at least one duplex receptacle (grounded) for a radio, TV, warming tray or coffeemaker.

select your location

To get the most use from your garden house, it has to be located close enough to the main house so you can easily bring out food and drink. It can't be far away from the garden or you'll spend too much time going back and forth with a wheelbarrow. It makes sense to try for a site in between. Check these guidelines.

sighting-in on a site

■ **Don't sink a pole** or pier over any underground piping or septic tank.
■ **Don't build in a natural grade depression** that collects ground water.
■ **Don't build too close** to your property line. Check local codes.
■ **Do look for a natural rise.** To get good drainage and minimum settling.
■ **Do plan ahead for access,** walkways, ramps and any electric lines.
■ **Do consult local building codes.** Make sure your site is legal.

good sense and good cents

If possible, try to keep construction time to a minimum. A smart move is to cover the surrounding lawn area with polyethylene for the few days needed, or build yourself a simple gangway into the construction area. On most jobs, the surrounding area takes such a beating that it needs major "renovating" after the building is done. The more foliage you can preserve during the job, the more natural the garden house will look on its site. Keeping the area reasonably clean can avoid reseeding or buying new sod.

keep a long-range point of view

■ **Don't** leave materials stacked on the lawn or you won't have one when you're done.
■ **Don't cut** through major roots of adjacent trees. Try a few test holes.
■ **Don't underbuild** the frame or leave it unsealed. It's outside all year round.
■ **Do protect trees and foliage** while building. They will be intact when you're done.
■ **Do use** preservative-treated timbers for all framing in contact with the ground.
■ **Do install** ground fault indicator fused circuits. It's national code for exteriors.

Don't be what I call a fair-weather carpenter. Make those toenails count. Use galvanized nails to avoid rust streaks on the wood. Try 10d nails on face-nailed decking instead of 8s. The extra bite will help minimize warping and cupping. In short, build your garden house to withstand the worst storm in 20 years. In the end, you'll save on maintenance and repairs and be able to see the results of your labors on a good-looking job.

ACCURATE SUNDIAL is easy to build from scrap wood and sheet metal. The clip-on strip, which is shown partially removed, is used to change the dial to read Daylight Saving Time.

Build a polar sundial

This unusual sundial is fun to make and use. With the instructions given here it will also be extremely accurate

By JOHN S. LORR

■ OF THE MANY sundial types used today, one of the most interesting is the polar dial, so called because the dial plate and the gnomon are parallel to the axis of the Earth and in line with the celestial pole.

To make this sundial, you should first ascertain the latitude of the area in which you live. This information is available from the local chamber of commerce, the nearest airport or from an almanac or atlas found in any library. The latitude provides the angle of the dial plate and also of the gnomon.

two ways to mark hours

For the most accurate way to locate hours (see plans), first draw a horizontal line on the dial 1½ in. from the bottom. At the midpoint, draw a 3-in.-long segment perpendicular to the horizontal line. From the top of the segment draw lines at 15° intervals, extending to either side. At each intersection, erect a line perpendicular to the horizontal line. These perpendiculars represent the hour lines, with 12:00 noon in the center. Bisect the 15° angles to locate the half-hour markings, and bisect the resulting 7½° angles to mark positions of the quarter hours.

For another way to lay out hour lines (which sacrifices some accuracy for ease), reproduce the markings by enlarging the grid in the plans and plotting the points. The grid method can also be used to reproduce various clock illustrations.

If you are a stickler for accuracy, consider two more factors. A sundial gives you the apparent solar time. To convert this approximation to mean solar or standard time, use the correction table.

The longitude of your residence should also be considered. This can be found in the same sources from which you obtained the latitude. Add four minutes for every degree of longitude that you live west of the center meridian in your time zone; subtract four minutes for every degree that you are east of this line. The center meridian for Eastern Standard Time is west longitude 75°; CST, west longitude 90°; MST, 105°, and PST, 120°.

Your sundial should be placed on a level table or stand. Point the gnomon true north by rotating the dial until the edge of the gnomon shadow points to your watch time. Then shift the shadow reading to compensate for the date and longitude corrections given above.

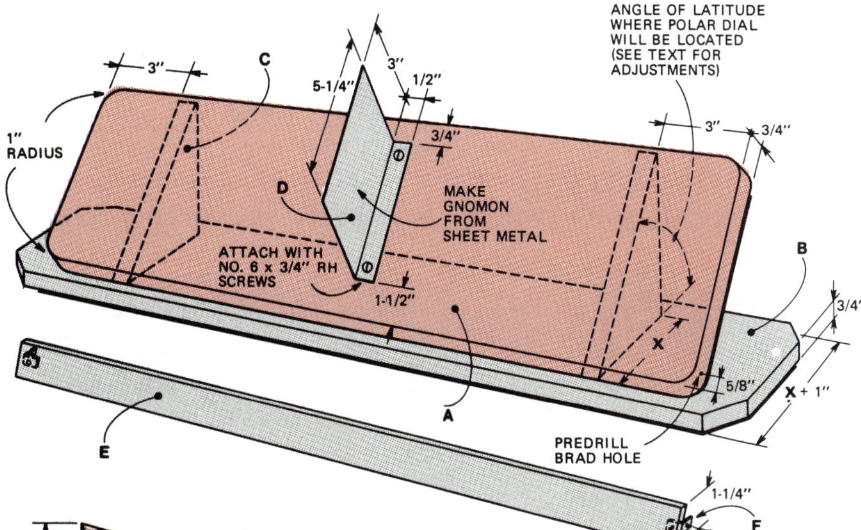

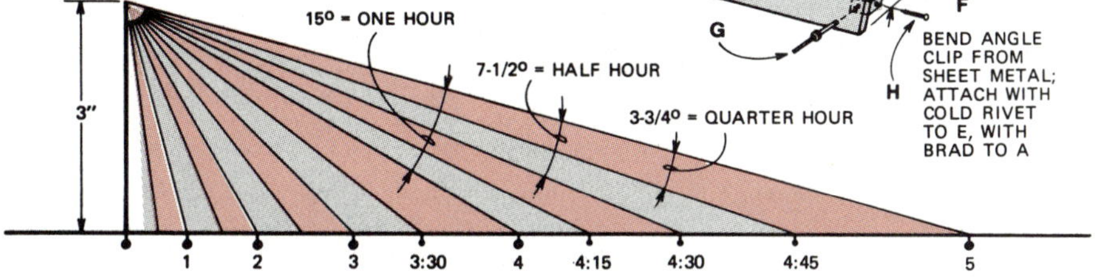

METHOD I FOR MARKING HOURS ON DIAL FACE (SEE TEXT)
(ONLY RIGHT SECTION IS SHOWN; LEFT SECTION IS A DUPLICATE IN REVERSE)

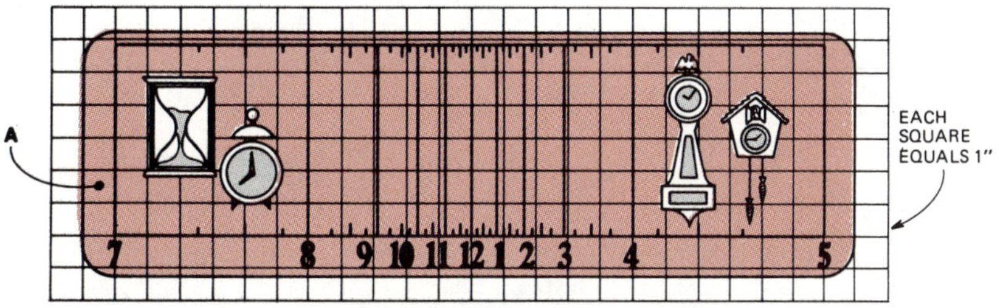

METHOD II FOR MARKING HOURS ON DIAL FACE (SEE TEXT)

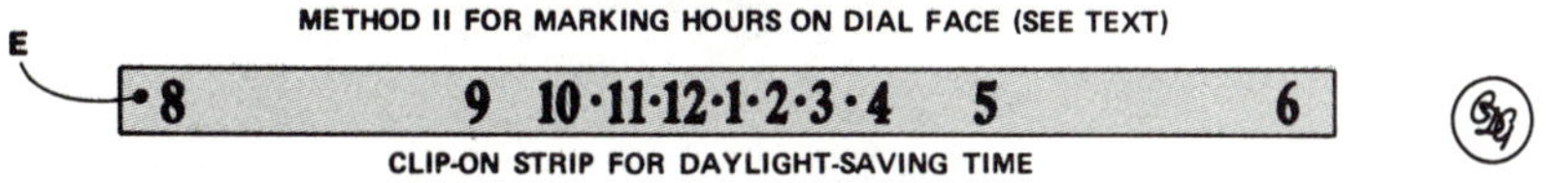

CLIP-ON STRIP FOR DAYLIGHT-SAVING TIME

SUNDIAL CORRECTION

Here are the number of minutes that must be added or subtracted from sundial time to arrive at standard time on dates given.

DAY	MIN.	DAY	MIN.	DAY	MIN.
Jan.		**May**		**Sept.**	
1	+3.5	1	−3.0	1	0.0
10	+7.5	10	−3.7	10	−3.0
20	+11.0	20	−3.6	20	−6.5
Feb.		**June**		**Oct.**	
1	+13.5	1	−2.5	1	−10.0
10	+14.5	10	−0.8	10	−13.0
20	+14.0	20	+1.3	20	−15.0
March		**July**		**Nov.**	
1	+12.5	1	+3.5	1	−16.3
10	+10.5	10	+5.0	10	−16.0
20	+7.5	20	+6.2	20	−14.4
April		**Aug.**		**Dec.**	
1	+4.0	1	+6.2	1	−11.0
10	+1.4	10	+5.3	10	−7.2
20	−1.0	20	+3.4	20	−2.5

MATERIALS LIST—POLAR SUNDIAL

Key	No.	Size and description (use)
A	1	¾ × 7½ × 24" pine (dial)
B	1	¾ × 28" long pine base (width can vary; see plans)
C	1	¾" pine (width and height can vary; see plans)
D	1	3½ × 5¼" sheet metal (gnomon)
E	1	⅛ × 1¼ × 24" plywood (clip-on strip*)
F	2	½ × 1" sheet metal bent into clip*
G	2	cold rivet*
H	2	1" brad (pin for clip-on strip)

*Clip-on strip for Daylight Saving Time can also be made from a 1¼ × 26" strip of sheet metal. Bend ends to form clips.

10 steps to a sparkling pool

To get the maximum enjoyment from your pool, you'll want to start a regular program of maintenance. Here are 10 things to consider when setting up your program

National Spa and Pool Institute, Washington, DC

■ AN EFFICIENT pool-maintenance routine is required if family and friends are to enjoy clean, healthy, sparkling water throughout the pool season. Here are 10 things to do to keep your pool—be it in-ground or above-ground—clean.

1. Determine your pool's capacity. Though pool water may appear clean and clear, if neglected, it can quickly become a breeding place for microscopic bacteria and tiny plant life called algae. Bacteria, viruses and algae cannot multiply in pool water properly treated with an inorganic chlorine sanitizer. Before you can start the chemical treatment of your pool water, you must determine the pool's capacity in gallons to give correct dosages.

If pool is rectangular or square, multiply length x width x average depth (feet) x 7.5 = total gallons (7.5 represents the number of gallons in a cubic foot of water).

If circular, multiply diameter x diameter x average depth x 5.9 = total gallons.

If oval-shape, multiply long diameter x short diameter x average depth x 5.9 = total gallons.

2. Maintain the proper pH level. If your pool contains more than 1000 gallons of water, it's essential that you test the pH level of your water at least once a week. Chlorine effectiveness is closely related to the pH level of the water. The pH scale (it runs from zero to 14) is a measure of the acidity-alkalinity level of water.

Water having a pH level between zero and seven is acidic; water having a pH level between seven and 14 is alkaline. The ideal pH range for pool water is between 7.2 and 7.6—a point where the water is slightly alkaline.

To get the pH level between 7.2 and 7.6 you should buy a reliable pool-test kit available at any pool-supply store. The test kit uses a phenol red indicator solution that changes color at different pH levels. It also should have an OTD (orthotoluidine solution) test involving color changes for chlorine residual.

3. Maintain an effective chlorine level. To satisfy the initial chlorine demand and establish a free available chlorine residual, you must treat your pool water with daily dosages of the correct amounts of chlorine sanitizer. At times, additional dosages will be required to overcome special problems such as heavy use of the pool, long periods of rain, or winds bringing in debris and pollen.

Use your pool test kit to check the level of available chlorine in the water. This should be done every day. This chlorine residual should be kept at between 0.6 and 1.0 parts per million (ppm) for unstabilized pools, and between 1.0 and 1.5 ppm for stabilized pools (these terms are explained in the following step).

4. Stabilized water could be for you. Since the sun's ultraviolet energy tends to dissipate available chlorine in pool water, pool owners who live in areas experiencing long periods of sunshine and heat may find that the chlorine residual in their pool water is being consumed quickly.

This problem can be overcome by stabilizing pool water with a chemical called cyanuric acid. Cyanuric acid protects the chlorine residual in pool water, yet it is nontoxic, does not affect the disinfection process and does not decompose.

5. Watch out for chlorine lock. If you decide to stabilize your pool water, even though you may have followed the manufacturer's directions to the letter, an excessive amount of cyanuric acid in the water can reduce the effectiveness of your chlorine sanitizer.

To remedy this condition, use a test kit that

SEE ALSO
Cabanas . . . Carpeting, outdoor . . . Poolhouses . . . Yard lighting

Target pH levels for pool water

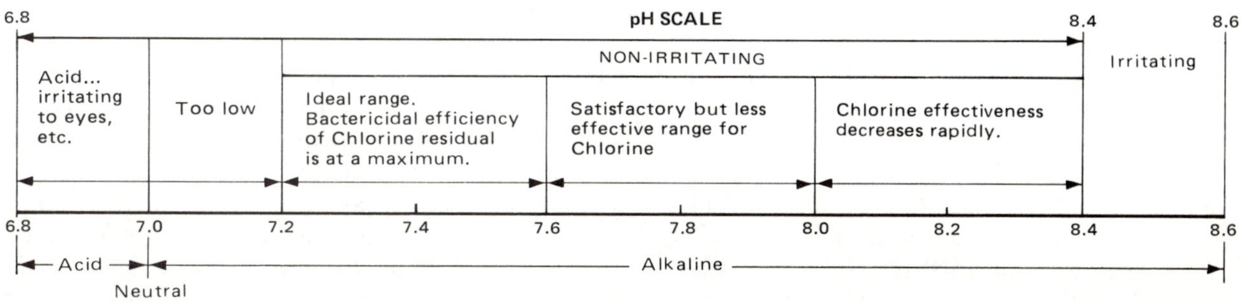

THE SECRET to a beautiful pool, such as the one shown here, is regular maintenance.

checks levels of cyanuric acid. If the level is too high, remove enough water from the pool so that the 25 to 50 ppm stabilizer level is achieved when the pool is refilled.

6. *Quick cures for warm-weather problems.* If your chlorine residual drops below recommended levels for any length of time, bacteria, unsightly algae patches and bad tastes and odors are certain to appear. Two powerful weapons that can be used to combat these problems are superchlorination and shock treatment.

Superchlorination is an extra heavy dose of chlorine—roughly 1 oz. of dry chlorine (65 or 70-percent available chlorine) added to 1000 gallons of water. Shock treatment is a dosage that is twice as powerful—1 oz. of dry chlorine (65 or 70-percent available chlorine) added to 500 gallons of water.

You should superchlorinate when a pool is opened for the season, when a pool is refilled, after a long period of sunny and hot weather, after heavy use, after severe rain or windstorms, or whenever unpleasant tastes and odors are present in pool water. A shock treatment should be used if algae patches appear on pool walls or submerged fixtures, or if the water gives off an objectionable odor.

7. *Keep your filter clean.* The two most commonly used filters are sand filters and diatomaceous-earth filters. Pool water is recirculated through the filter under pressure created by a pump. Increased pressure is usually an indication of ineffective filtration.

A pressure buildup across the filter occurs when the filter is clogged with sediment and dirt from the pool. Best cure is to backwash it (reverse the flow of water) according to the manufacturer's instructions.

8. *Use vacuuming equipment.* Swimming-pool vacuum cleaners operate on the same principle as ordinary home vacuum cleaners except that water is drawn through the machine instead of air. Sediment and dirt drawn from the pool floor and sides are carried through the cleaner's piping for removal through the filter.

9. *Don't forget the skimmer.* Practically all pools have an automatic surface skimmer built directly into the pool or attached to the filtering system to remove leaves, bugs and other floating objects from the water. During filtration, surface water is drawn through the skimmer and into the filter, carrying off dust, oil film and other inert matter before it can settle to the pool floor.

10. *Handle dry chlorine with care. Never* mix calcium hypochlorite with anything but water. It should not be mixed or contaminated with any foreign substances, including household products, soap or paint products, solvents, acids, pool chemicals, vinegar, garbage, beverages, oils, pine oil or dirty rags. Always keep burning material such as a lighted cigaret away from any container of dry chlorine.

A swimming pool filter you can make

By JAMES M. MILLER

■ I RIGGED A FILTER for my 15-ft. above-ground pool from an old lawn-mower engine, a 30-gpm centrifugal pump from Sears, some 1-in. plastic pipe and two canvas bags, as shown in photo A.

To use the filter, you first prime the pump by running a garden hose in the intake pipe. Next you place diatomaceous earth in a bucket and mix with water until you have a thick slurry. (Use ½ lb. of earth for each filter bag.) Submerge the bucket in the pool under the intake pipe (photo D), and with the pump running, suck the slurry into the canvas bags. The earth, coating sides of the bags, does the filtering. It takes about six hours a day to filter my pool.

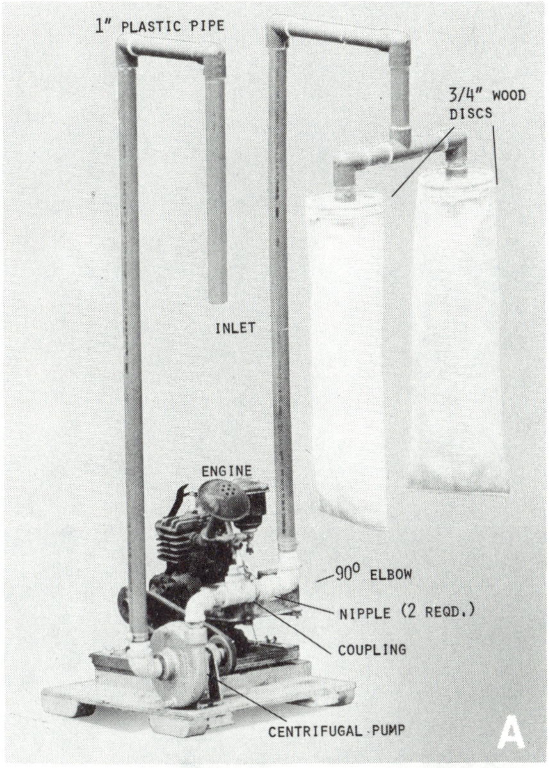

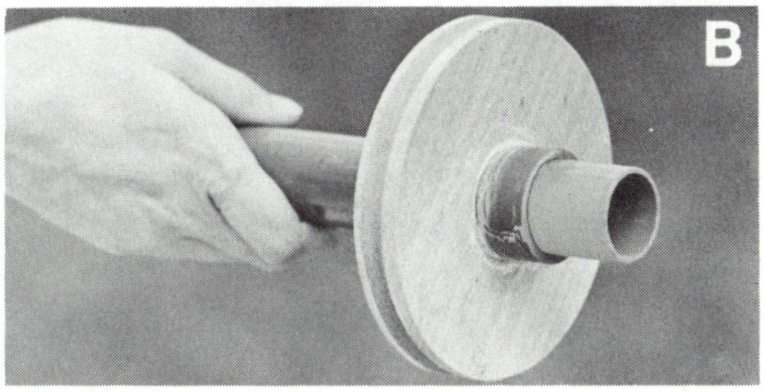

THE WOOD DISCS that hold the filter bags (photo B), are cut from ¾-in. solid wood, grooved around the edge for drawstrings, waterproofed with three coats of marine paint and cemented to the plastic pipe with epoxy. Use two bags for 15-ft. pool, three for 18-ft. Intake pipe should extend at least 8 in. in water to prevent pump cavitation (diagram C) and permit swimming while filter runs. Each supply pipe should be about 20 in. long. If near an outlet, electric motor can be used to drive the pump; I used a gas engine because my pool was too far from house.

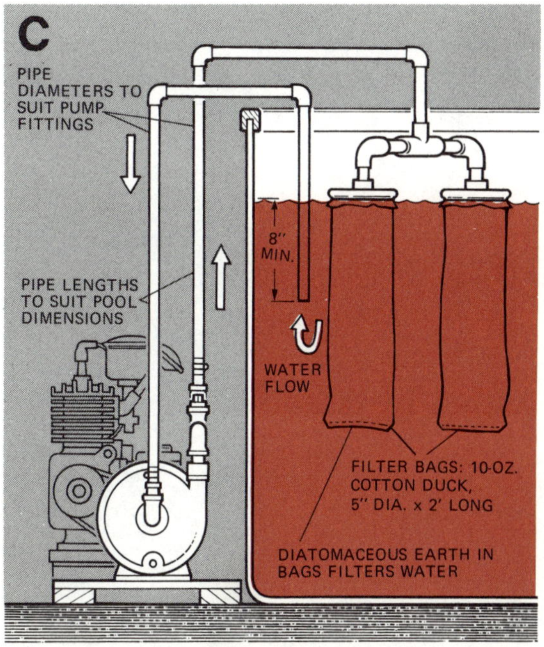

SEE ALSO

Cabanas . . . Carpeting, outdoor . . . Poolhouses . . . Yard lighting

A diving deck gives added storage

This structure solves two problems at once. It provides a diving deck for your above-ground pool and a place to store outdoor equipment and the pool filter

By HARRY WICKS

■ ABOVE-GROUND POOLS have become very popular. A common problem, however, is providing a diving arrangement as a "launching pad" for the kids. In addition to being unsafe, a diving board is just too hard to rig in an elevated position.

We were determined to solve this problem, and the diving deck shown here is the result. Our main goal was to provide a safe diving platform. But, in addition, since footage would be taken from the yard, we wanted the space beneath the deck to serve as seasonal storage as well as to house the pool filter system. It was also decided to place the stairs behind the door to protect young ones. Extras that "make" the structure include a foot bath, indoor/outdoor carpeting and nautical rope for the railing.

construction is easy

Design is basic; there are no fancy, frilly construction techniques. Tried construction methods were used to insure maximum sturdiness, yet details were kept simple to keep costs down to a minimum. For example, careful layout permitted cutting the deck from just two 4x8-ft. sheets of exterior plywood with practically no waste.

Overall dimensions of the deck can be varied to suit the size of your family. The version shown provides ample room for sunbathing as well as diving. One critical measurement to keep in mind—when laying out your structure—is the portion of the deck that overhangs the pool. This can be altered to suit without any problems.

The four-by-four posts are anchored to footings which should be below your area frostline. Once the four-bys are in place, and the concrete has set, the post-holes can be backfilled and cutoff marks at the top located. To do this, determine desired height on one corner post and mark off the other posts using a mason's line and line-level.

Top and bottom rails are simply spiked to the posts and framing is completed with joists and bridging installed. The rails and posts are fitted with cleats positioned to give a setback (architectural shadowline) when the exterior plywood panels are in place. (In place of cleats, the 2x4 rails can be edge-rabbeted on a table saw.)

Doors to the storage area and stairs are simply plywood panels framed with rails and stiles fastened to the structure with strap hinges. Catches to hold them closed and vertical half-round moldings complete their construction.

the stairs

A limited run made a steep riser-to-tread ratio a must. But, unlike conventional stairs, it is not a drawback. Actually, their "marine-ladder" steepness adds to the nautical design.

AN ABOVE-GROUND POOL mandates a structure alongside for diving fun. This one has steps inside (upper right) that are inaccessible when the door is locked. Space behind the doors (upper left) is ample for year-round storage of bike and yard equipment plus the pool filter.

SEE ALSO
Benches, deck . . . Cabanas . . . Carpeting, outdoor . . . Decks . . . Poolhouses . . . Yard lighting

INDOOR-OUTDOOR carpeting insures skidproof footing. It is laid over 15-lb. felt and 6-mil polyethylene.

THE PLATFORM overhangs the pool slightly. Measurements might vary from the drawing to suit your pool.

The deck can be finished using an exterior latex paint with some fine masonry sand mixed in for skidproofing. (Or, you can purchase a ready-mix sand paint.) But our suggestion is to cover the plywood with 15-lb. felt, followed by 6-mil polyethylene and Ozite outdoor carpeting. (The felt waterproofs the storage area while the polyethylene prevents any possible stains from the felt rising to the carpet.) Either way the finished surface is an effective safeguard against accidental skids and falls. The latter method is just more comfortable underfoot.
bath at bottom is optional (it's an inexpensive plastic baby bathtub from Sears, Roebuck), but it does decrease the mud tracked up to the deck carpet by overzealous youngsters.

Since a slab wasn't used here, you'll notice in the photos that the structure walls leave space at the bottom to permit rainwater runoff. If you prefer slab construction, you are well advised to install a block wall or form the slab to create a curb. A standard soleplate can then be installed, with posts toenailed to the plates, and conventional wall framing used. But remember that a slab would require the addition of a pitched apron in front of the doors to provide positive water runoff. The apron will also make it easier to roll bikes and other wheeled vehicles in and out of the storage area.

To finish, the entire structure was primed and painted (inside and out) with a high-quality, latex house paint. (For additional safety, the stair treads could also be carpeted or coated with a sandmix paint to make them skidproof.)

The prototype project shown took the owner four weekends to complete. He started it late in April, and by the time the thermometer climbed to swimming temperatures he was happily spending his vacation atop his "Slip-Proof Diving Deck" in his own back yard.

THE STORAGE DOORS are built with one-by stock and ¼-in. plywood. Half-round moldings are added to give a decorative touch. As shown at right, the prebuilt stairs are lowered into position after frame is complete.

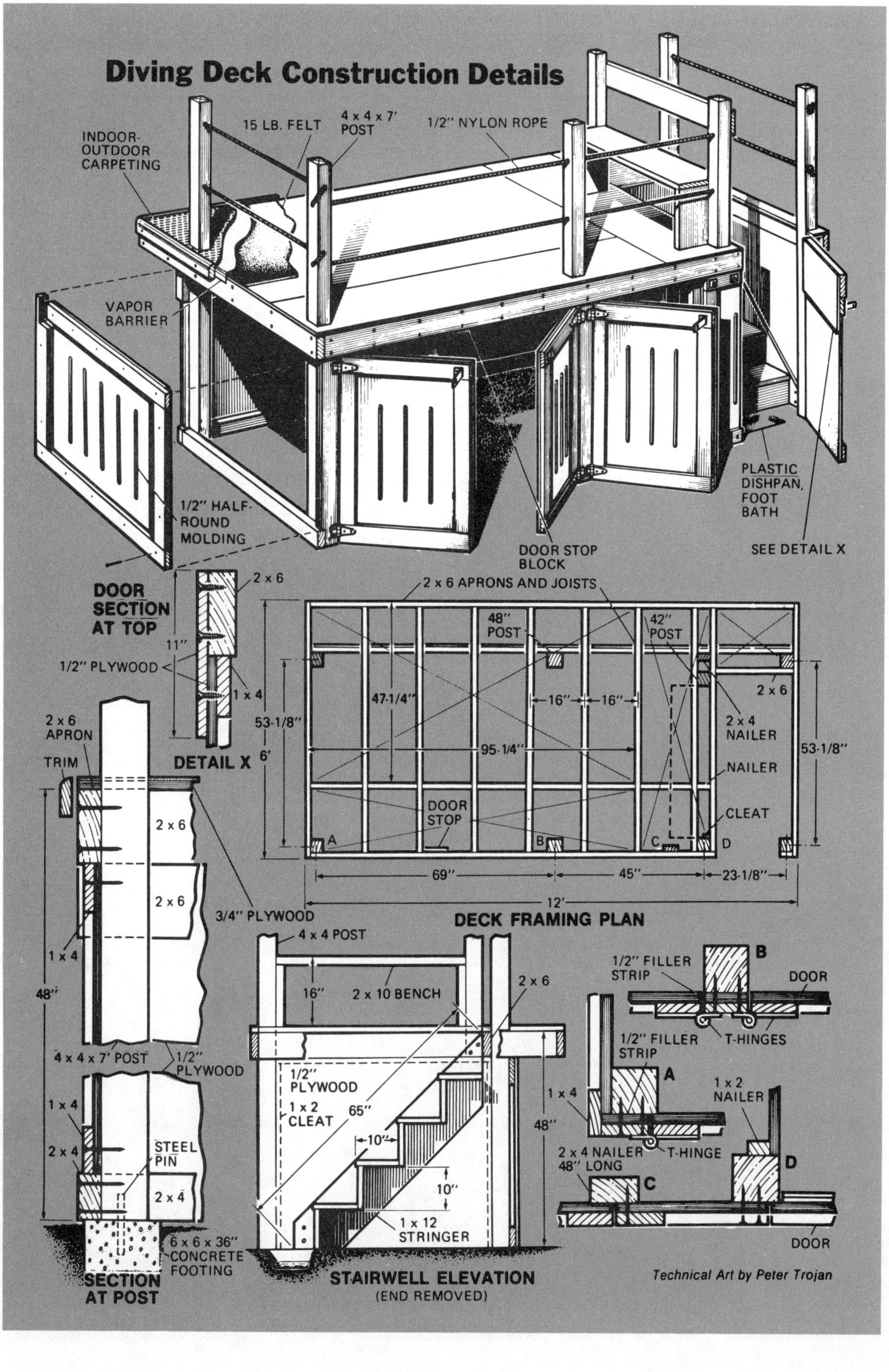
Diving Deck Construction Details
INDOOR-OUTDOOR CARPETING
15 LB. FELT
4 x 4 x 7' POST
1/2" NYLON ROPE
VAPOR BARRIER
1/2" HALF-ROUND MOLDING
DOOR STOP BLOCK
PLASTIC DISHPAN, FOOT BATH
SEE DETAIL X
DOOR SECTION AT TOP
2 x 6
11"
1/2" PLYWOOD
1 x 4
DETAIL X
2 x 6 APRONS AND JOISTS
48" POST
42" POST
47-1/4"
16"
53-1/8"
6'
95-1/4"
2 x 4 NAILER
NAILER
CLEAT
DOOR STOP
A
B
C
D
69"
45"
23-1/8"
12'
DECK FRAMING PLAN
2 x 6 APRON
TRIM
3/4" PLYWOOD
48"
4 x 4 x 7' POST
1/2" PLYWOOD
2 x 4
STEEL PIN
6 x 6 x 36" CONCRETE FOOTING
SECTION AT POST
4 x 4 POST
2 x 10 BENCH
1/2" PLYWOOD
1 x 2 CLEAT
65"
10"
1 x 12 STRINGER
STAIRWELL ELEVATION
(END REMOVED)
1/2" FILLER STRIP
DOOR
T-HINGES
T-HINGE
1 x 2 NAILER
2 x 4 NAILER 48" LONG
Technical Art by Peter Trojan

Build this old-time yard swing

By WAYNE C. LECKEY

This two-seater is not only a reminder of yesterday, but a challenge for any craftsman

■ THE TWO-SEAT LAWN SWING of yesteryear is making a comeback. Once a familiar sight in everyone's yard, this old-time favorite is finding new life even in this modern age of air-conditioning. The spot where you'd once go to seek cool breezes on a hot summer's night, such a swing has become a welcome place to get away from teen-age din, to relax and unwind—or occasionally just to sit and think.

My folks had one when I was a boy and I can remember what fun it was to stand up and pump, making believe the swing was a train. Later I found it to be one of the more favored spots to watch the moon with my best girl.

You can bring back a bit of the good old days by copying this old-time swing, setting it up in your yard and becoming a real "swinger" once again to the envy of your neighbors.

The whole thing is made from standard lumberyard materials, which means that all the members are already the right thickness and width when you get them. For the most part you simply cut the pieces to length and bolt or screw them together. The exceptions are the four curved seat rails. Many of the members are alike, with two or more of each required.

Start with the swing-supporting framework detailed in the drawings. Here 8-ft. 1x4s are used for the legs and braced with 1x3s and 2x2s. Notice that the 1x3 side braces lap the legs, one inside and the other outside, and are filled where they cross each other with a ¾-in.-thick spacer block. Notice, too, that the legs spread out at the bottom in both directions for better rigidity and overall strength.

The conduit rods from which the swing seats hang are tightened securely between the legs by nuts and washers as shown in detail A. Standard ⅜-in. Redibolt rod is used inside the conduit. Carriage bolts are used to secure the braces.

THE CROSS BRACES for the supporting framework are bolted securely to the four legs.

EACH SWING ASSEMBLY is hung from conduit hanger rods which fit between supporting legs.

SEE ALSO

Landscaping . . . Lawns . . . Paths, garden . . . Patios . . . Playgrounds

yard swing, continued

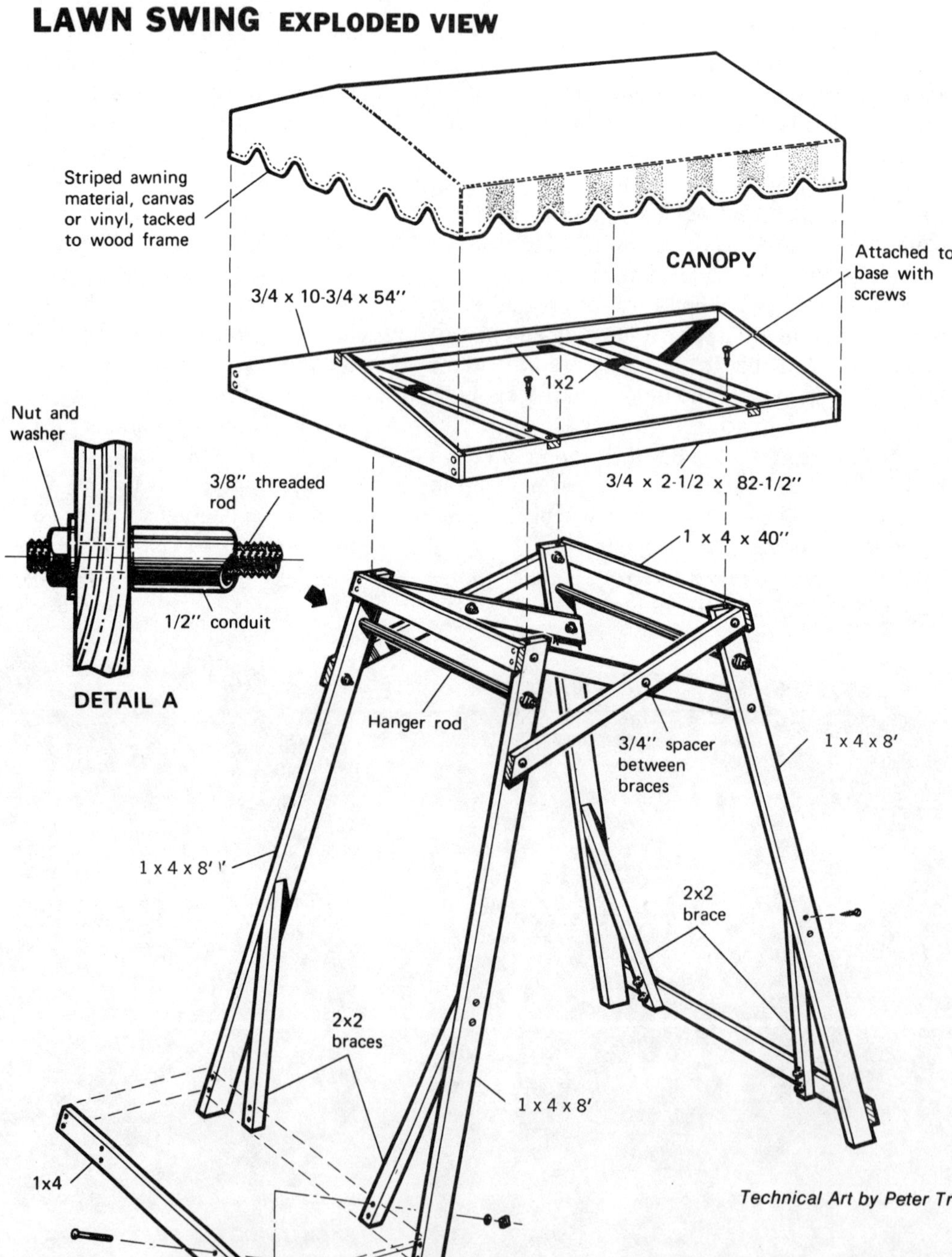

Technical Art by Peter Trojan

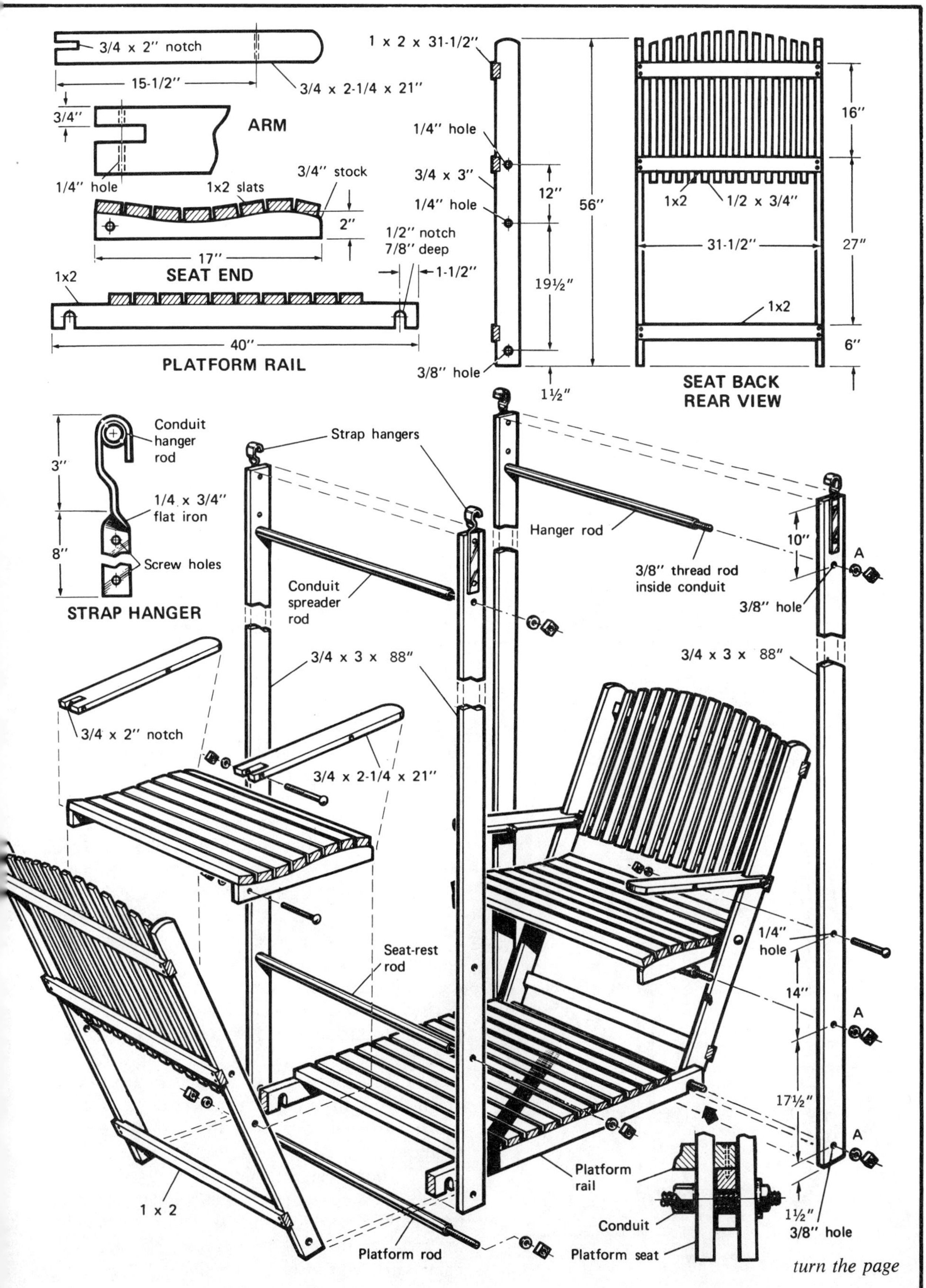

turn the page

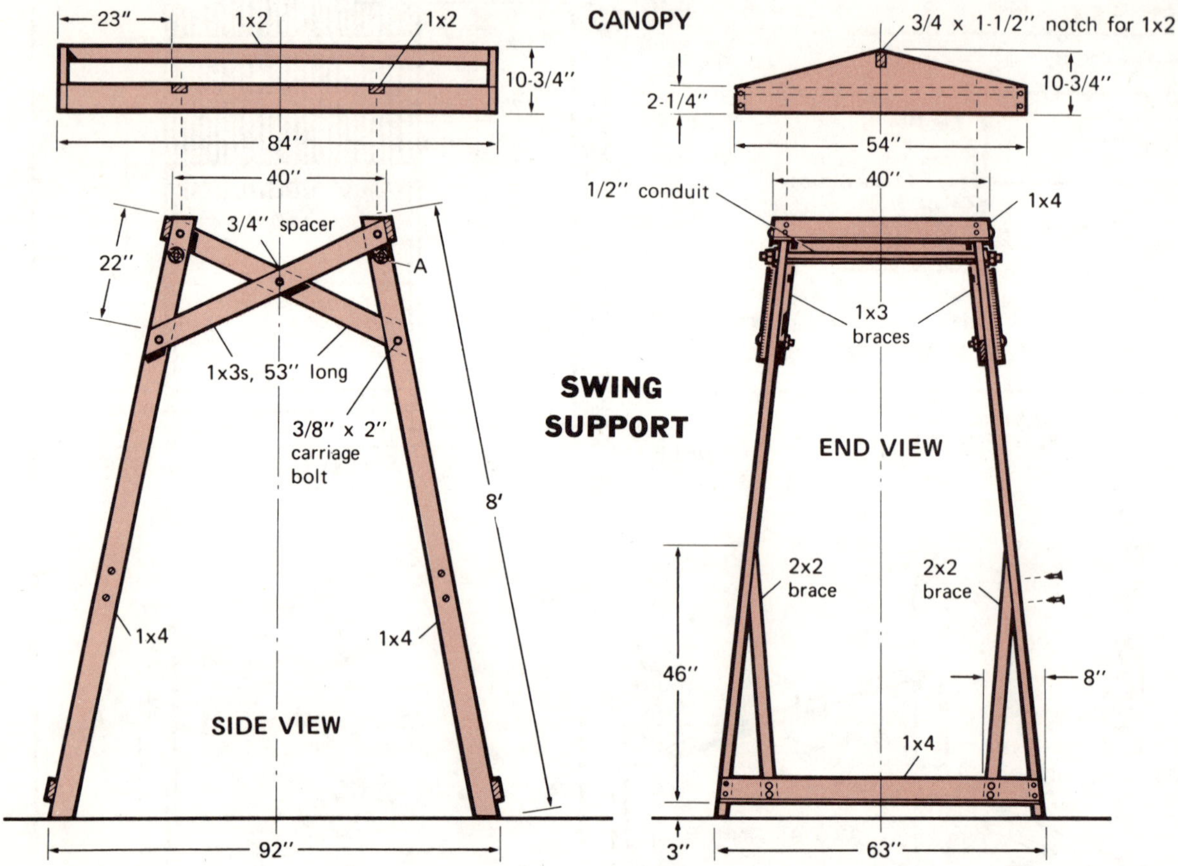

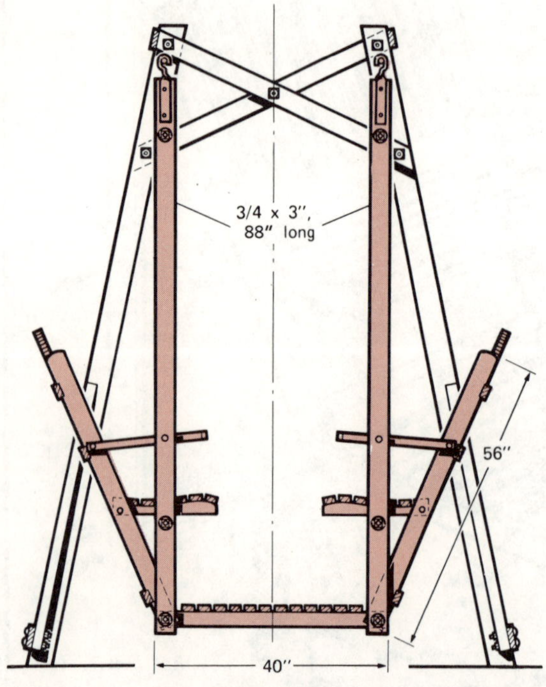

SIDE VIEW

The swings are made alike, so you can save time by cutting duplicate parts. Start with the backs, then go on to the seats. You'll notice that three conduit rods are used for each swing-seat assembly which serve primarily as spreaders. The separate platform assembly hooks over the bottom one and the seat rests on the middle one. The notched ends of the platform actually insert between the uprights and the seatback members. Each swing is suspended by two straps that are bent from flat iron. A little grease on the conduit rods will keep the straps from squeaking.

The canopy is optional, although it does provide shade and adds a colorful touch. You make the supporting wood framework as shown and then tailor a canvas cover to fit it. Four screws down through the cross members of the wood frame are used to anchor the canopy to the swing.

Give your swing a couple of coats of good-quality exterior paint to help it stand up against the weather. You can paint the platform to match the strips in the canopy if you wish. Once the paint is dry, you are ready to relive the "good old days."

Two extensions for a table saw

By ROSARIO CAPOTOSTO

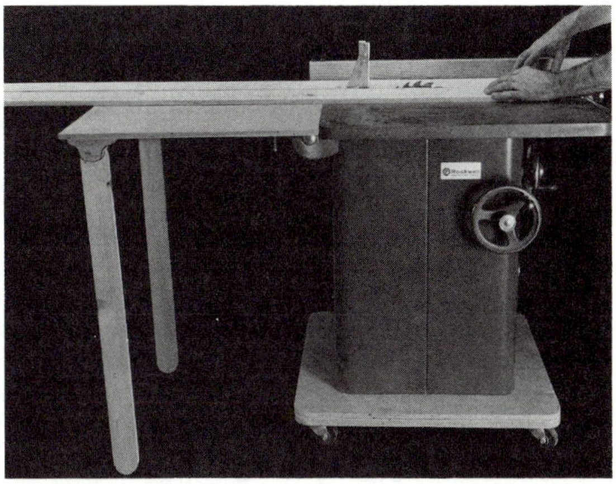

IF YOUR SAW has a rear rip-fence guide bar which is below table level, as on this Rockwell, attach a pair of pivoting legs to the rear edge of a plywood top and drive a row of 6d nails along the other to serve as hooks for attaching the unit.

THIS ROLLER support can be made of scrap, but does require a sawhorse and C-clamps. A 1-in.-dia. dowel is supported by blocks glued to 1x4 posts which are clamped to the horse so they're level crosswise and even with the saw table. Dowel is sanded down at ends.

■ STRUGGLING TO HOLD a long board single-handed when you rip it on a table saw is not the best practice for either safety or ease of handling. Either of these "helping hands" will prove a valuable aid.

One is a roller affair attached to a sawhorse with C-clamps and the other is a two-legged plywood table that hooks over the saw's rear rip-fence guide bar. The friction-fit legs swing to bring the top even with the saw table, and to adjust to an uneven floor. Pick a straight dowel for the roller support, and sand and wax the ends so it turns freely as it supports the work.

Both take little space to store.

SEE ALSO
Bench saws . . . Motors, shop . . . Power-tool stands . . . Workbenches . . . Workshops

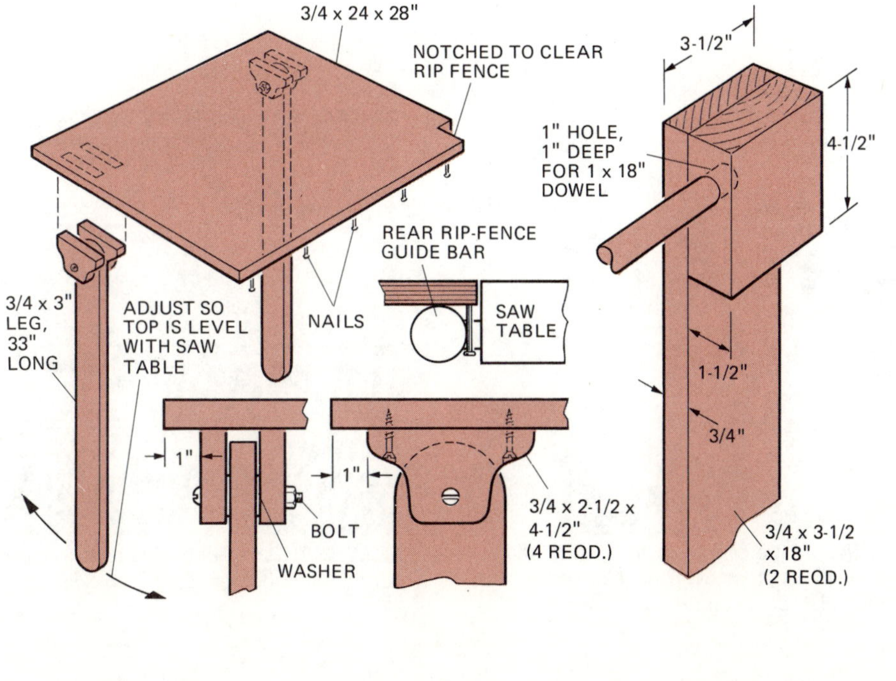

Tape up your repair problems

By PENELOPE ANGELL

Think you know tapes? Here are some with new or unexpected uses you'll find helpful around the house. Give them a try the next time you have a "sticky" problem. They are easy-to-use and require no messy cleanup

■ AS NEW TAPES ARE DEVELOPED and new applications for existing ones found, more and more homeowners are turning to tapes to solve their repair problems. And for good reasons: Tapes are handy, easy to apply, do a remarkable number of jobs, present no messy cleanup problems and are generally inexpensive.

There are the old reliable standbys—plastic electrical tape, medical adhesive tape and cellophane (Scotch) tape—that are probably used more around the house than any other types. But there are also a lot of less familiar, more specialized tapes that have many important household uses. Here's a rundown on some of the most versatile with suggestions for some useful applications you may not have thought of.

special drywall type

Flex Corner drywall tape helps make clean inside or outside corners. The tape has two ½-in. galvanized-steel reinforcing strips that are placed on either side of the corner to form and reinforce the angle. Flex Corner can be cut to length and applied with a standard three-coat, cement compound process (metal strips facing toward the wall), the same as with perforated tape. However, Flex Corner has the strength to prevent the seam from opening.

Drywall tape can also be used to reinforce joints, finish curved surfaces and arches, join drywall partitions to plastered walls and repair chipped or cracked plaster walls. Goldblatt Tool Co., 511 Osage, Kansas City, KS 66110.

aluminum-faced tape

Flashband, an aluminum-faced tape with a layer of self-adhesive asphalt, helps seal and waterproof your home. It is flexible enough to

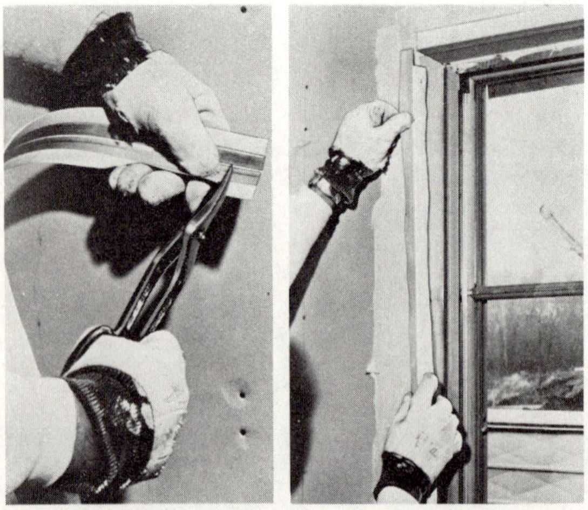

CUT THE DRYWALL tape or score with a knife and bend, fold it in half and press over the joint cement. Later, apply the finish coats and feather the edges.

FLASHBAND self-adhesive tape is a permanent sealer for this airconditioner.

seal gutters, downspouts, irregular-shaped metal flashing, airconditioners, heating ducts and the like. Flashband is also available with a gray vinyl coating over the aluminum for situations where the aluminum might corrode (such as in a cabin at the seashore). Both types can be painted with water-base paint and can be purchased in 20-ft. rolls, ranging from 2 to 9-in. widths. The aluminum-faced type also comes in a patch pack.

Flashband was developed for use by professional roofers and has many roofing applications, but can also be used to repair swimming-pool covers, garden equipment, awnings and aluminum siding. Evode, Inc., 401 Kennedy Blvd., Somerdale, NJ 08083.

fiberglass repair patch

A fiberglass cloth patch that cures in the sunlight or when exposed to an ultraviolet lamp has many applications around the home. The

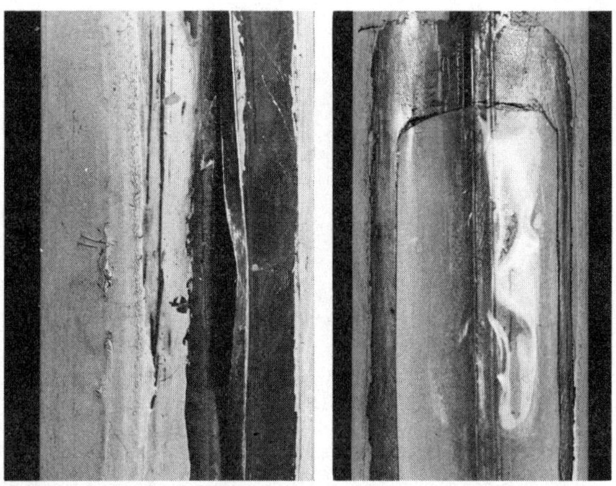

THIS DOWNSPOUT damaged by expanding ice was repaired with an "Auto-Pak" fiberglass patch which cures in the sun. It is invisible when painted.

"Auto-Pak" lay-it-on body patch is made by 3M. A patch cut to cover the damaged area adheres on contact and hardens to make a permanent, waterproof repair when subjected to the proper light. The top covering is peeled away and the patch can be sanded and painted to match the color and finish of the surrounding surface. The patch repairs metal, wood or fiberglass surfaces.

As its name implies, the "Auto-Pak" patch was designed to be used on cars—to repair rust-outs. But it is also helpful in repairing cracked fiberglass shower stalls and laundry sinks, wood or metal gutters and downspouts, plus many other damaged wood, metal or fiberglass surfaces.

keep pipes from freezing

This "Heater Tape" from Smith-Gates is used to eliminate frozen water pipes. It is a heating wire wrapped around a glass-fiber core and encased in a vinyl jacket. The tape can be equipped with an automatic "Press-to-Test" thermostat as shown and a pilot lamp that lights when the tape is heating. The length of Heater Tape needed depends on the pipe size, length and lowest temperature expected. For example, according to the Heater Tape chart a 1-in.-diameter pipe 10 ft. long would need 15 feet of tape (wrapped three times per foot around the pipe) to keep it from freezing at 11° below zero. An additional fiberglass blanket with outer wrap for extra protection is available. A waterproof cover can also be purchased. Smith-Gates Corp., Farmington, CT 06032.

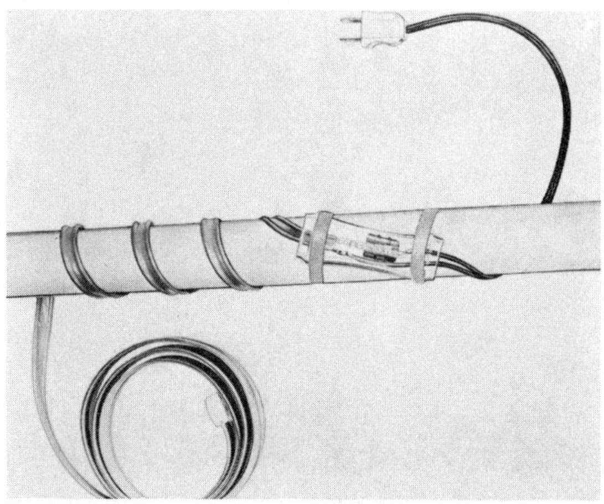

FLEXIBLE Heater Tape is wrapped around a pipe to prevent it from freezing in winter.

seal threaded pipe joints

Wrap Chemplast Ready-Seal Thread Tape around threaded pipe to insure a leaktight joint. It is made of soft, pliable Teflon that conforms to any type or size of thread. It also seals hose fittings, sprinklers, nozzles and fire extinguishers. Chemplast, Inc., 150 Day Rd., Wayne, NJ 07470.

THE TEFLON TAPE is wrapped around male pipe threads to lubricate and seal the joint.

experimental concrete patch

A wide range of concrete repairs will be possible for the homeowner with Rok-Rap, a tapelike material still in the experimental stages. Manufacturers propose that it can be used to patch concrete basement leaks, protect pipework and posts from corrosion both above and below the ground, repair spalled concrete, join and repair concrete pipes, face concrete structures and solve other problems. The tape is activated by wetting with a special activator or cold water. After drying out, the tape forms a dry, rugged rocklike, but, resilient, protective covering. Evode, Inc., 401 Kennedy Blvd., Somerdale, NJ 08083.

ROK-RAP is used to patch a basement crack where water had been seeping in as shown above.

tape 'staples' with many uses

Saw duplicate shapes in one operation. Join two pieces of wood together with Mystik masking tape. Then saw the pattern marked on the top piece through both pieces. Also use masking tape to cover trim while you're painting around it, and to wrap around plumbing fixtures to protect them from wrench marks.

With masking tape you can also keep small parts in order and in sight when assembling kits and complex units. Placed sticky side up on your worktable, the tape keeps easy-to-lose items from straying. Masking tape also helps to keep glued parts together until the glue has had a chance to set.

MASKING TAPE is wrapped securely around boards at right angles to stop them from shifting while being cut.

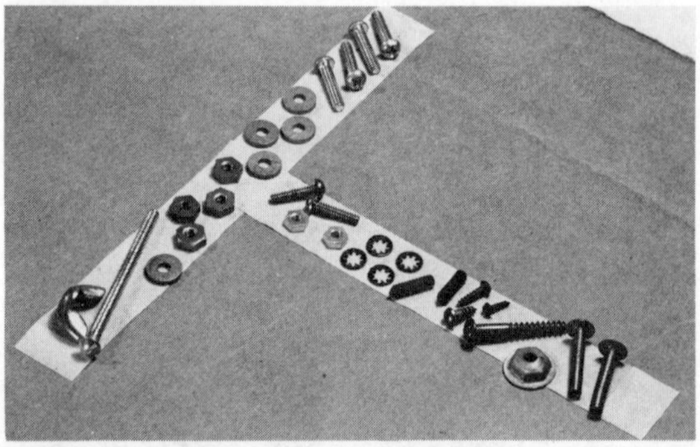

MASKING TAPE used sticky side up holds small parts in place until they are needed.

protective sponge tape

With Mystik Sponge Tape you can protect fine wood and other delicate surfaces in your home from heavy or rough objects. Just cushion the bottom of such objects with strips of the tape. This tape can also be used as an insulator around windows and doors.

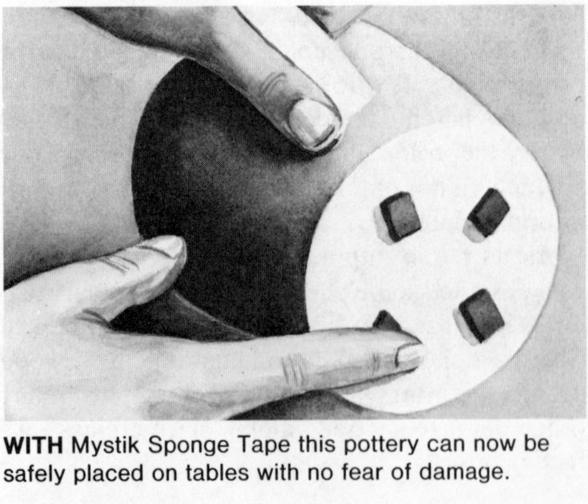

WITH Mystik Sponge Tape this pottery can now be safely placed on tables with no fear of damage.

Removing creosote stains

Creosote from the flue of my wood-burning stove has leaked onto the stove hearth. The stone is unpainted. How can I remove the stains?—Robert Posner, Monticello, N.Y.

First, call in a reliable chimney sweep to check your stove and metal flue. Contrary to popular belief, the male end of a flue pipe should point down. In a proper installation, any dripping creosote will then remain in the pipe.

As for removing the stain on your hearth, any cleaner containing phosphoric acid should do the job. One product is No Soot, a fireplace brick cleaner made by Chattahoochee Research Co., Box 12141, Atlanta, Ga. 30355. Another is Cam-Kleen, a heavy-duty ceramic tile and grout cleaner made by Woodhill Permatex. Both cleaners are sold in hardware and houseware stores.

Be sure to follow the manufacturer's directions. Wear gloves, goggles and a long-sleeve shirt.

House too tight?

My husband and I bought a 20-year-old, Cape Cod-style house. In the last five years, to help conserve energy, we've added insulation, storm windows and doors, and caulked the exterior. We now have black mold appearing on walls and ceilings and condensation on the windows. If we can't control it, we'll be replacing windows again, this time because they'll have rotted. We run two dehumidifiers in the basement in the summer. My washing machine in the basement drains into a French drain, which carries the water to a drain field.

My husband says the mold is due to the fact that our house is now too tight. If that's the case, why aren't some of the newer, insulated houses I've seen affected by the mold, too?—Danielle Bloomberg, Northampton, Pa.

Mr. B is correct. Your house is now too tight. Before you did such a fine job of combating heat loss, cool, dry air could infiltrate under doors, windows and uncaulked gaps in the walls. This dryer air would offset the moisture in the air caused by normal, daily activities such as showers, baths and cooking.

You have to introduce cooler, dry air into your system and eliminate the moist air from your house. Start by getting rid of the French drain in the basement. Add exhaust fans in the kitchen and baths. Once a day, open a window slightly while you run these fans for 10 or 15 minutes. Also keep your dehumidifiers running in the winter. Opening the house will negate some of the good you've done conserving energy.

If you have a warm-air system, it is possible to duct fresh, outside air into your plenum. This should be dampered and connected to a humidistat to go on when your furnace motor starts. It is possible to preheat this air also, but if you do, you should consult a licensed mechanical engineer.

Another alternative is to run more dehumidifiers on the first floor.

I doubt if the newer houses are tightened to the extent that yours is. Also consider lifestyle: Doors are constantly opened and closed in a house with children and pets. This seemingly short exposure to fresh, dry air, when multiplied 20 times per day, adds up.

Homeowner bug equipment

We seem to get all the bugs: ants, roaches, you name it. We also have problems with professional exterminators who forget their monthly visits. Is there equipment available for the homeowner to do the job himself?—E.D. Unger, Spencer, W. Va.

When it comes to debugging, there are myriad devices for a homeowner. A pump-action handle on a plastic bottle will cost about $1.50. For $25 or so, you can buy a galvanized pump-up pressure tank with a spray nozzle. Supermarkets sell spray cans of bug repellent; this with termite treatment is my choice.

A reliable exterminator will know the most bug-prone areas of your house. However, if you do your own spraying, read all instructions. Also, wear goggles and gloves.

Flexible filler

A professional plasterer is coming to my 100-year-old house to patch the hairline cracks in my living-room walls and ceiling. He said that after he does the job, the cracks will probably reappear. Are there flexible fillers or paints that will continue to seal the cracks?—Mark Lisowski, Rosendale, N.Y.

If I were a plasterer, I'd tell you the same thing. Not knowing the original makeup of your plaster with regard to scratch coat, thickness and other characteristics, a plasterer can't guarantee his work. Your walls are most likely on wood lath, which moves slightly with changes in climate and humidity. A pliable filler wouldn't work, as even it would show as a bulge or crevice.

One way to correct the situation is to install ⅜-in. drywall over the existing walls and ceilings. You also may want to try paneling. An older house might lend itself to a paneled wainscot and heavy vinyl wall covering from the wainscot to the ceiling.

Turn your camera lens into a telescope

By WALTER GOTTLIEB

You can convert your powerful photographic lenses for use as a telescope without damaging their function as camera lenses. All you do is combine them with a small eyepiece lens

■ PHOTOGRAPHERS use nonphotographic gadgets all the time. But you can also use your photo gear for nonphotographic purposes. Your camera's interchangeable lenses, for example, can be turned into compact, highly corrected telescopes at hardly any cost, with no more labor than drilling two holes—and no impairment of their photographic usefulness.

A telescope is merely a comparatively long focal length lens (the objective) that aims at the object to be viewed and a shorter focal length lens (the eyepiece) that magnifies the image formed by the objective lens and presents it to the viewer's eye. The longer the focal length of the objective and the shorter that of the eyepiece, the greater the magnification of the telescope. So if you couple a short-focus lens from your movie camera to a telephoto from a 35-mm or larger camera, you can assemble a telescope that's powerful indeed. (The actual power of the telescope can be found by dividing the objective's focal length by the eyepiece's.)

If you don't shoot movies or if your movie camera, like most current models, does not have a removable lens, you can pick up a lens for your eyepiece dirt-cheap at a used camera counter. The least expensive way is to buy an obsolete, inoperative regular-eight camera, unscrew the lens and throw the camera away.

Now drill a well-centered hole in the larger lens's rear cap, just wide enough to clear the movie lens's threads (⅝ inch for lenses from 8-mm cameras, one inch for 16-mm-camera lenses). Then drill out the movie lens's rear cap as wide as you can without damaging its screw threads, or grind the cap's bottom off just below the threads. (This cap must be metal, though the larger lens's cap can be either metal or plastic.)

Centering the hole in the larger lens cap is important for good optical performance. One way to center it precisely is to coat the cap with white tempera paint, then scribe a series of straight lines in the paint with a marking gauge set at approximately the lens cap's radius, turning the cap slightly for each line. The intersections of the scribed lines will form a polygon small enough for you to judge its center with as much accuracy as you need to center-punch the hole before drilling it.

To assemble, insert the threaded end of the movie lens into the hole in the larger lens cap and fasten it in place by screwing on the drilled-out movie lens cap. Screw the telephoto cap onto the back of its lens, and there it is—a high-power

A LITTLE WORK and an old movie camera lens made this powerful telescope from a telephoto lens.

INTERCHANGEABLE movie lens, mounted through a hole in telephoto's rear lens cap, serves as eyepiece.

SEE ALSO

Binoculars . . . Camera accessories . . . Outdoor photography . . . Photography

telescope! If you can't bring a distant object into focus using the telephoto's focusing ring, insert one or two extension tubes between the lenses to bring the eyepiece to the proper focal point. You can estimate the amount of extension necessary by looking through the two lenses, both hand-held, and varying the separation between them until a distant object looks sharp.

With a 300-mm telephoto and the 5.5-mm wide angle from my 8-mm camera, I get over 50-power magnification. For less power and wider viewing angle I use the 12.5-mm normal lens or the 25-mm movie tele as eyepiece. If you have a telephoto lens converter, its use will increase the power of the 'scope by its usual conversion factor. Naturally no matter how many lenses you use in your combinations, you need make only one coupler.

While these telescope combinations are powerful, they have a disadvantage common to all celestial telescopes: The view is reversed, upside-down and backwards. For looking at things down here on earth, you'll find it convenient to have a negative-focus eyepiece (one that makes things look smaller to the eye) that keeps things right-side up. For this I use the negative front element of an inexpensive lens salvaged from an old 8-mm camera (practically all normal focal length lenses use a negative first element). Unscrewing and discarding the rear element, I mounted the remainder of the lens in the eyepiece coupler as before. This eyepiece needs less extension behind the objective lens than the other eyepieces; it may even have to be mounted on the *inside* of the telephoto's cap to obtain the proper focus.

mounting your telescope

In use, mount your telescope on your tripod by means of the socket built into your long lenses for clearer, less tiring viewing. Telephotos without built-in tripod sockets will usually yield low enough magnification so that they can be used hand-held.

The telephoto lens cap which has been converted into the eyepiece coupler can still be used for lens protection when not being used in telescopes by plugging the hole with a movie camera body cap or turret plug, held in place by the drilled-out movie lens cap.

Now, just by reaching into your gadget bag for a combination of lenses that you're not using on your cameras at the moment, you're ready for a close-up look at anything on land, sea, sky or beach.

THE MOVIE LENS'S own rear cap, drilled out, serves as its retaining ring (see text).

HOLE IN LARGER lens cap must be centered carefully and be wide enough to clear movie lens's threads.

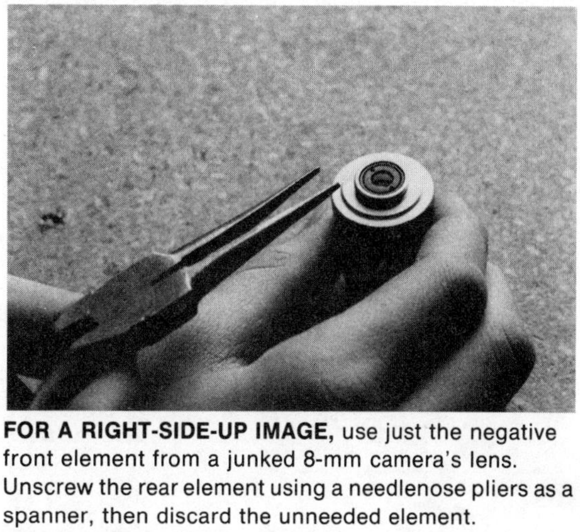

FOR A RIGHT-SIDE-UP IMAGE, use just the negative front element from a junked 8-mm camera's lens. Unscrew the rear element using a needlenose pliers as a spanner, then discard the unneeded element.

Restore your TV antenna

No matter what kind of antenna you own—TV, CB or ham—it can literally fall apart. Here's how to put it back together

By GEORGE X. SAND

FRUSTRATED TV viewers, CBers and ham operators often blame their receivers and transmitters when it's their antenna systems that are at fault. There is seldom a quick way for an owner to measure the efficiency of a faulty antenna. Thus, the difficulty may remain overlooked and steadily worsen.

check for clues

Antennas suffer most from exposure to the elements. Close-up inspection is necessary. Antennas are usually located as high as possible. So exercise caution against falling when making your inspection!

A poor connection is the most common antenna difficulty. When necessary, remove and clean (sandpaper or scrape) the connectors where the twin wire or the coaxial lead-in cable attaches the antenna to the TV or other set. Then restore the connectors and tighten each securely. Apply a weatherproof, nonhardening sealing compound over the cable terminals.

Inspect each element of an antenna array. Make certain that corrosion or rust has not formed to break the electrical contact at the supporting end of the element. In the case of TV

SEE ALSO
Antennas, TV . . . Interference, TV . . . Masts

beams, this contact is usually riveted fast. If necessary, grind or file off the head of the rivet. Clean the contact surfaces and use a small bolt and nut to restore the element to its original position. Apply weather seal compound over the new joint.

Replace *any* missing elements of a TV antenna. These elements are made of ultralight, thin-wall metal tubing, usually anodized. Make sure that each new element is the same length and approximately the same diameter as the old one (usually it will be identical to the one on the opposite side of a damaged array).

Light metal tubing suitable for TV element replacement can sometimes be purchased at hardware stores and lumberyards. Junk dealers frequently have available discarded TV beams from which some of the elements can be pirated as needed. In some cases, a short length of metal rod or tubing of slightly smaller diameter can be used as a dowel to reattach a broken-off element to its original support.

Make an electrical check to see if a lead-in wire has broken somewhere along its length. This can be done by twisting together the two conductors *at the antenna,* then measuring for continuity at the two bottom wires of the lead-in. (If an ohmmeter is not available for this check, a battery and bulb connected together in series with the lead-in wire can be used. The bulb will light if the wires are not broken.)

restoring masts and towers

Rust is the tireless enemy of antenna masts and towers, as well as guy wires and other supporting fixtures used for roof, chimney, eave and wall-mounted antennas. Sometimes the offending rust can be cleaned away, down to the bare metal,

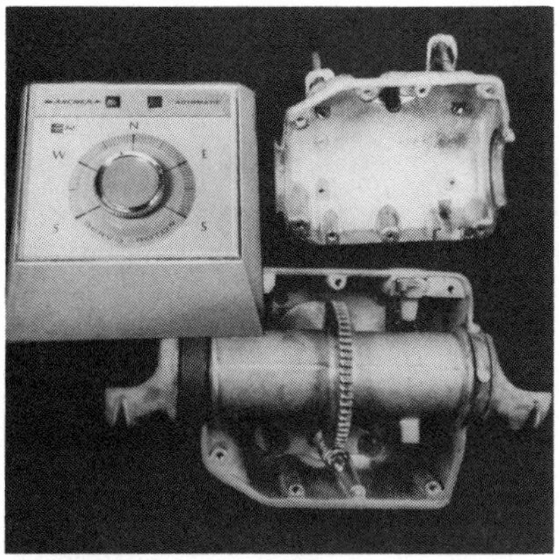

ANTENNA ROTATORS are often the cause of antenna woes, and most people think they are unfixable. Not true; follow these steps for successful repair.

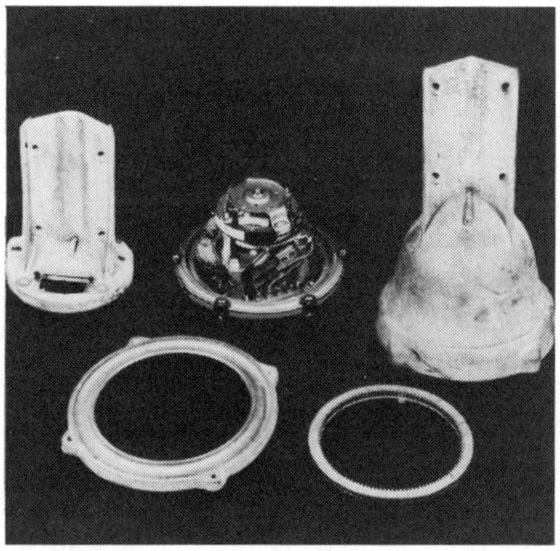

ONCE THE HOUSING of an antenna rotator is opened, it becomes clear that there really are many user-serviceable parts inside.

IT'S ALWAYS possible that the ball bearings and races may have become misaligned, especially if the case has been jarred or previously opened.

ONE of an antenna rotator's most frequently called-upon parts is the pulsing switch. Check carefully to be certain that the switch's contacts are clean.

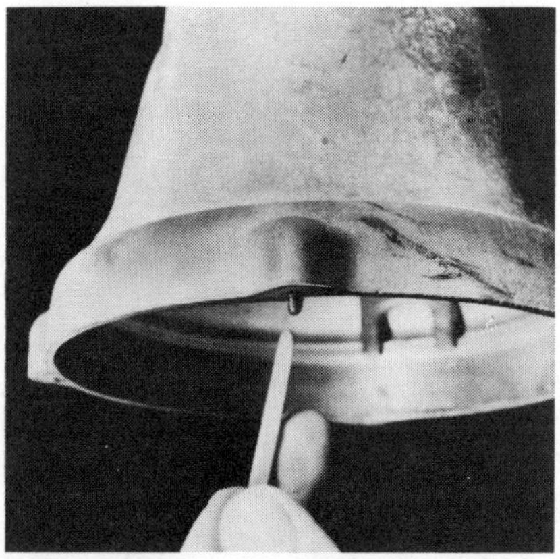

OXIDIZED housing bolts can break right off. To remove the stub, weld on a nut. Apply heat from a torch. Then carefully turn the nut with a wrench.

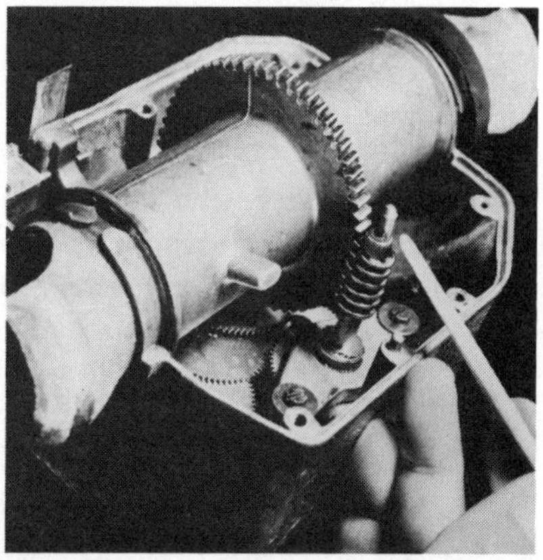

ONCE THE ROTATOR is open, clean all gears thoroughly. Use a good grade of medium-weight grease to assure that operation will remain smooth.

after which the surface is painted. Often it is easier (and safer) to replace weather-weakened U-bolts, chimney straps or whatever.

Most telescoping antenna masts are made of galvanized steel that will eventually rust. Steel towers will do likewise, even though they may be made of hot-dipped galvanized metal. When this happens, you have no choice but to remove the rust and apply a good grade of rust-inhibiting paint. After that, a sprayed-on finish coat of chrome-aluminum paint will enhance the appearance of the reclaimed mast or tower.

Towers usually come in bolted-together sections, each about 10 feet long. Sometimes rust, corrosion, wind or other damage makes it necessary to replace one or more of these sections. This work can be facilitated by the use of a gin pole. Such a pole can be purchased.

The gin pole shown on page 2848 is homemade from a 12-foot length of cast (for strength) square aluminum channel, 1⅝-inch outside measurement on each side. A metal pulley, secured with an eyebolt at the top of the pole, accommodates a ½-inch rope used to lift clear (for lowering) the mast sections, one at a time, if the tower is being disassembled. This is done while a helper pulls on the rope from below. The procedure is reversed to replace the sections.

C-clamps can be used to hold a gin pole securely against a tower. To minimize weight and provide easier handling, the gin pole should have thin walls, be it made of metal pipe or channel. (Caution: crimped-together, screen-enclosure-type channel may lack the strength needed to erect a heavy tower section or antenna array.) Should you prefer, the control rope may be operated inside the hollow gin pole.

antenna rotators

Movable antennas are driven by remote-control motors that vary considerably in size, shape and power. Some operate satisfactorily for long periods. Others become balky and even stop completely. The rotator must then be disassembled for inspection. If there are broken parts, these must be replaced. Often, all that is needed is a cleaning and lubrication.

Frequently, the motor will not operate because of a break somewhere in the multiwire cable connecting it to the directional control box below. So check these wires for continuity as explained previously.

When removing the protective housing from the rotator, be careful not to break off the heads of the steel bolts that hold it together. The housing is nearly always made of aluminum, to make it lightweight, and this metal will oxidize to steel bolts, freezing them tight.

The rotator's moving parts and motor bearings are factory-lubricated. In time, however—especially if a faulty weather seal should develop—the rotator's ball bearings and associated race may become gummy from grit and hardened grease. Clean with mineral spirits and relubricate with good-quality, medium-weight bearing grease.

Check the rotator's interior for loose or broken wires. There will likely be a relay pulsing switch present. Make sure the contacts are clean.

Restore the rotor housing. *While the unit is still at ground level,* operate the control box to check for proper forward and reverse rotation. Should there still be problems, more extensive inspection will be necessary. Check for both continuity and unwanted grounding of the rotator's motor windings. Make a similar check of the transformer in the control box.

Depending on the type of rotator being serviced, you may find a faulty thermal overload switch, perhaps a faulty motor reversing switch, or a bad relay pulsing switch, solenoid or capacitor.

Before returning a serviced rotator to the mast or tower, adjust the control box so the rotator moves to its "end" position. (It is assumed that the rotator has been properly synchronized with its control box according to the manufacturer's instruction sheet.) Install the rotator while it is still in this position, making sure that two antenna down-lead stand-off insulators are properly positioned 180° apart, one immediately above the rotator, the other immediately below. Such positioning provides for sufficient slack in the down-lead to prevent binding during maximum rotation.

lightning protection

Since antennas are customarily mounted higher than surrounding objects, they become prime targets for lightning bolts. A lightning arrestor should always be used between the antenna and the equipment it feeds!

When restoring antennas, it is *most* important to make sure that a snapped guy wire, falling mast or damaged antenna element has not made contact with adjacent power lines. Workers have been electrocuted when this happened. So plan your antenna restoration work carefully beforehand. Always remember—safety first, even before good reception!

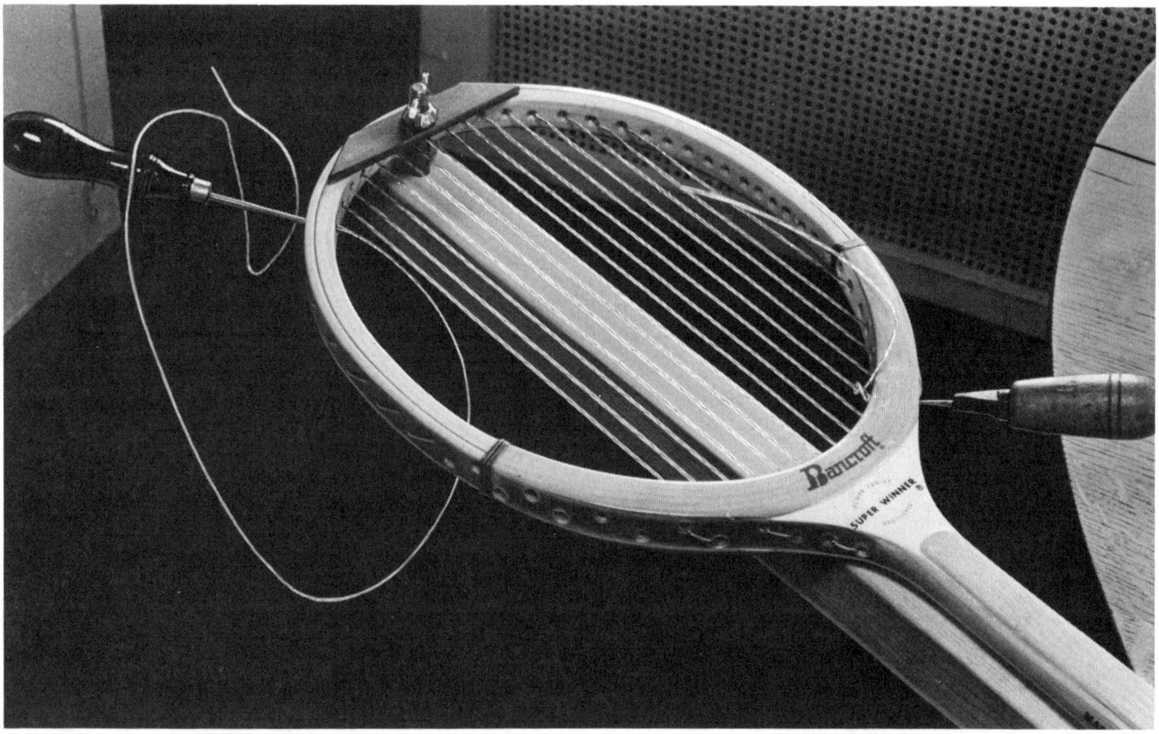

SIMPLE JIG for holding racket is length of wood and clamps, turns table into rig for racket repairs.

Restring your own tennis racket

By ELMER K. NORTON

Using these simple techniques and tips, and a little practice, you can save playing time—and money. You'll be pleased at what surprisingly good results this system gives. Use it on badminton rackets, too

■ IT'S SATURDAY MORNING and during a warm-up rally you pop a string on your favorite racket. No need to give up the weekend matches or play with an uncomfortable borrowed racket. If your restringing and repair shop is closed or miles away, try some of these simple shortcuts I've developed over 25 years.

Less than $12 can provide you with a jig to hold the racket and materials for restringing and replacing your grip as well. Sending your racket out for restringing alone might cost you $10 to $13 in nylon, $20 to $24 in gut. A professional restringing machine can cost over $400.

Materials you will need for the method shown here are simply a three-foot length of 1½x1½ stock, preferably hardwood, an eight-inch length of 1½-inch dowel (like that on which rugs are sometimes delivered) that you will cushion with a wrap of leather or adhesive tape. Also two three-inch or four-inch "C" clamps to hold the wood base and your racket to your workbench or kitchen table plus a four-inch ⅜-16 NC hold-down bolt with wingnut to secure the head of the racket, and some scraps of hardwood so the clamps don't scratch your racket handle. A couple of awls from a hardware store will hold the string in place.

I recommend nylon string in a 35-foot length from your tennis shop or mail-order supplier, at about $4.50 or $5, for your 18 main and 20 cross strings. Nylon lasts several times longer than gut and is much easier to work with. Mail-order sources include The Tennis Center, 68 Harrison Ave., Congers, NY 10920, and Tennis Accessories, 616 Schreiber Ave., Coplay, PA 18037.

Clamp down your racket, as shown, with the

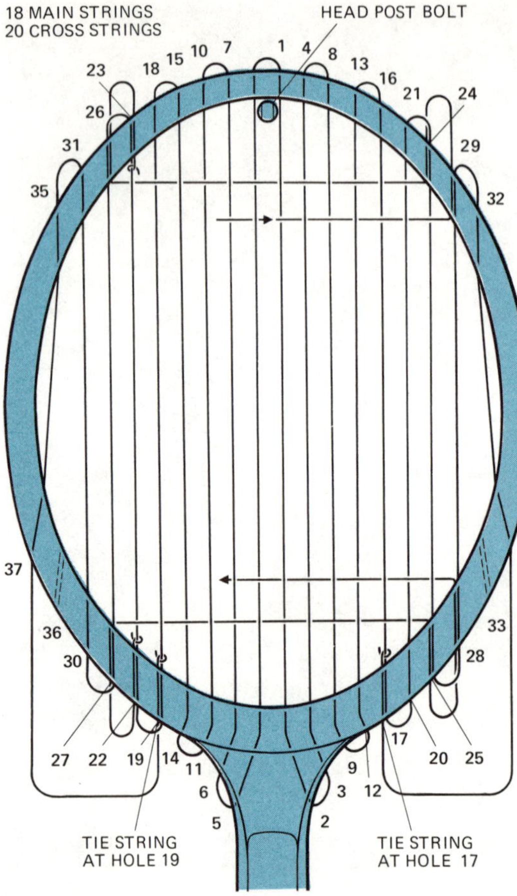

restring your racket, continued

side grooves slanting down and toward the head of the racket. All strings always go into the lower hole and out the upper hole of the groove. Starting with the main strings, the vertical ones, cut a 19-foot length of nylon and thread through the two top holes so that half (9½ feet) goes on each side of the center-post bolt holding the racket head. The bolt is filed flat on each side to protect strings from damage. Thread these main strings down through the first holes on each side of the neck.

Sight through these holes to see their direction and then carefully but firmly insert one awl into No. 1 to hold the string in place. Wrap the string coming out hole No. 2 one and a half turns around the string-tightening dowel handle and, using the frame for leverage, turn to tension the string. Be sure the string coming out is straight so you are not tightening against added friction. Insert the second awl in hole No. 2 and remove the tightening handle. Thread the string through holes 3 and 4, tighten, and insert the awl in hole 4. Repeat this procedure on the other side through holes 5, 6, 7. Awls are now in holes 4 and 7.

Continue this threading and tightening process alternately in numerical order, as shown, until there are 16 strings threaded and awls are in holes 29 and 31. Strumming each string as it is tightened will give you an indication of proper tension. Thread 32 and 34, then 35 and 37, being careful to skip holes 33 and 36. Pull strings extra tight, insert awls, rethread those loose ends through holes 17 and 19, and tie off each with a simple half hitch. If the nylon is slippery, add an extra half hitch; then cut off excess string ¼-inch from the knot.

threading the cross strings

Cross strings are threaded from the remaining 16-foot length. If hole 22 is a top hole, thread one end up through and half hitch to the main string there. If a bottom hole, No. 20 on the other side must be used instead. Thread the other end through hole 27 and weave under and over the main vertical strings over to and through hole 25 on the opposite side. Tighten, insert awl and continue weaving across and up the racket until 20 cross strings have been strung. The 20th string goes through hole 26, is tightened, threaded through hole 23 and then tied to the main string there and cut off. During cross-string threading when a main string already occupies a hole, it's helpful to sharpen the tip of the cross string; snip it off diagonally to a point.

Now go over the racket with a slim dowel or pencil (since your awl might cut into a string) and straighten those strings out of line so that they all cross at right angles and are parallel.

Grip replacement is also not too difficult—once you know how. A good quality leather grip, about 3½ feet long, is approximately $3 from a sporting goods store or tennis shop. Remove the old grip, and coat the handle with mucilage or shellac. Air until tacky. With a ⅜-inch flat-headed nail, secure the tapered end of the grip strip flush with the butt end of the handle, nailing through ¼ inch from the end of the leather. Hold the racket head between your legs and wrap the grip flush around the butt end and then on down the handle clockwise with the leather layers butting or slightly overlapping, if so designed. Tack the finished end with a ⅜-inch nail, trim off excess leather with a razor, and cover the nail and edge with two or three turns of ½-inch plastic tape.

Gut restringing can be attempted after you have become proficient with nylon. Because of gut's reaction to moisture (a rain shower can ruin its tension), it should be treated with preservative after stringing and occasionally during active use after exposure to damp conditions or when the strings are becoming slightly frayed.

Mix one part of white three-pound cut absolute shellac with five parts of water-free ethanol in an 8-ounce salad dressing jar with screw top. Store a ¾-inch brush with cutdown handle inside the jar. When strings are frayed or damp, first dry with talc or a fluffy towel, then paint on a light coat. Thin mixture with alcohol from time to time. Too thick a coat or too frequent use makes gut strings lose resiliency. Never use it on any type of nylon strings.

The stringing method outlined here can also be used with all metal rackets except the Wilson Steel and Seamco Aluminum. The rig works as well with squash, paddle and badminton rackets, although badminton strings are 19-gauge and much thinner.

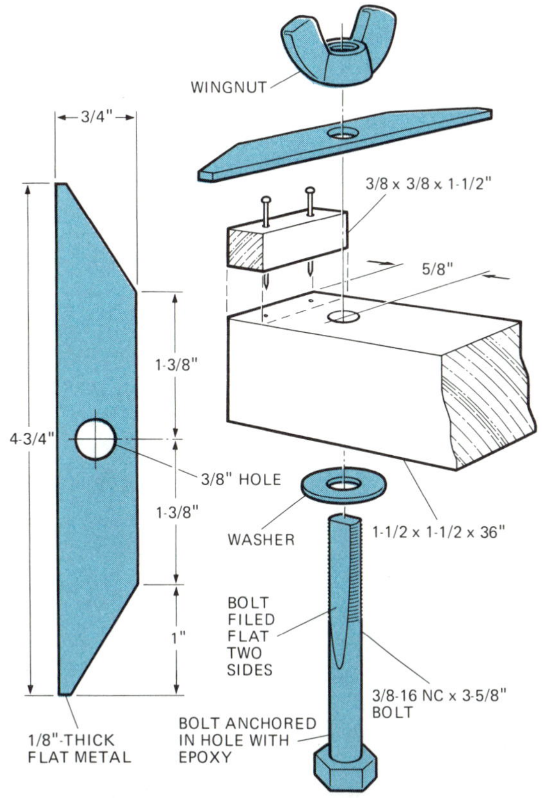

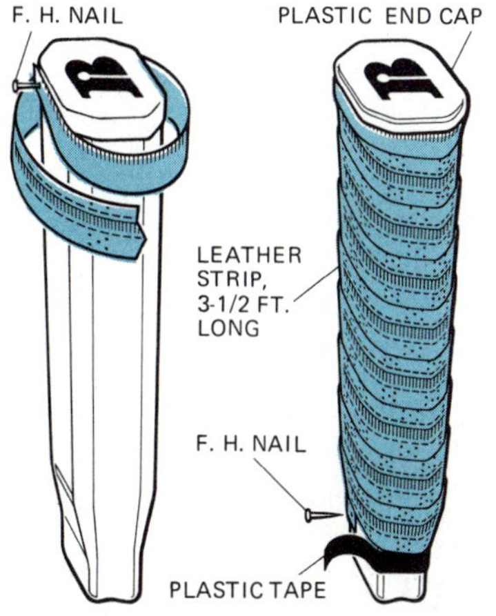

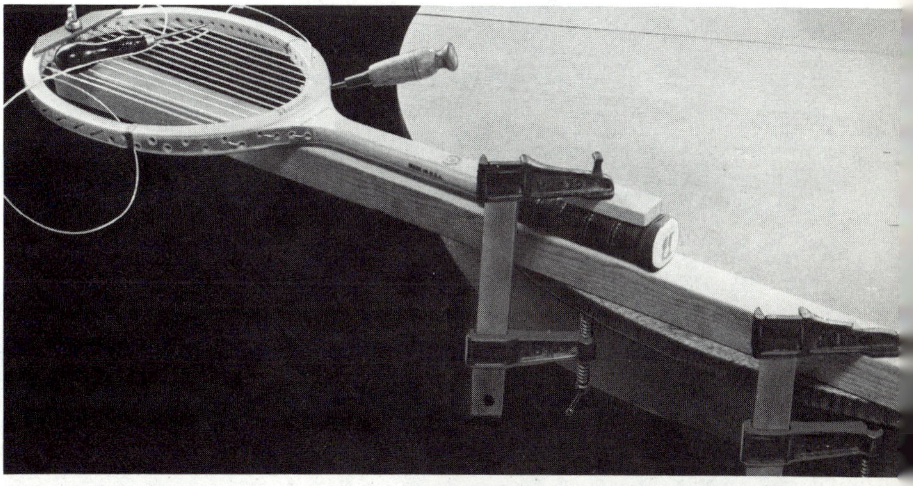

RACKET JIG uses bolt cap (at upper right) to hold the head of racket plus C-clamps to secure a brace to the table. Renewing grip (above) starts with a leather strip 3½ feet long which is stretch-wrapped down the handle and finally secured with a nail and a plastic tape ring.

TENSIONING OF NEW STRINGS (right) is done with a 1½-inch-thick dowel with leather or adhesive wrap. The string is looped around the handle and is turned to tighten, held with an awl while the next length is laced in place. Cross strings weave under and over the main strings.

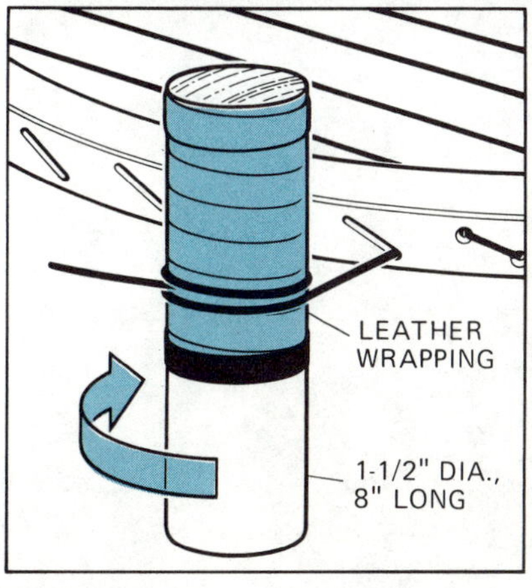

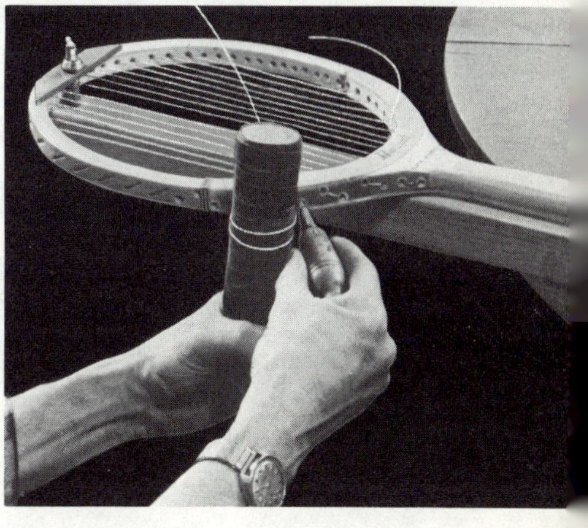

What to do about termites

By ED KERR

■ WHAT'S THE USUAL reaction when a homeowner discovers termites in his house? Sheer panic.

Actually the discovery of termites is *not* an occasion for panic because time is on the homeowner's side. Even a mature, well established colony of 60,000 workers eats only ⅕ ounce of wood a day. There's plenty of time to approach the problem rationally and get bids on a termite control job.

In his booklet, *You Can Protect Your Home from Termites,* Dr. Michael I. Haverty of the Forest Service points out that most Americans need worry about only two types of termites. The drywood termite is important mainly to homeowners along the southern rim of the United States, especially in Florida, California and Hawaii. Where they do occur, drywood termites pose a serious problem because they need no contact with the soil. They can enter the house under shingles, through cracks in windows and

SEE ALSO

Concrete . . . Home improvement . . . Planters . . . Plumbing . . . Steps

TERMITES AT WORK—here they are nibbling away in one of the galleries they love to create.

eaves or through screened vents in the attic, and if they become well established, the house must be fumigated.

The subterranean termite is more common. Found in every state except Alaska, this one must have warm air and moisture. To stay moist, he builds tubes made of soil as he goes. Of course he won't need to build tubes if wood is already touching the soil. Cut off his contact with moisture, whether it's direct contact with soil or through mud tubes, and you can solve practically any termite problem.

The eight major danger areas for termite entry are:

■ *Cracks in concrete.* Because termites eat only wood, people have a false sense of security about concrete-slab foundations. They don't realize that slabs often develop cracks that allow termites hidden access to the house framing. Wood posts provide an access route when the post goes all the way through the concrete and contacts soil underneath. For protection, the soil beneath slabs and footings should be treated with a termite insecticide.

■ *Earth fill under porches.* Here, again, concrete may give false security. If the concrete porch has earth fill underneath it, soil may be in contact with framing members. To be safe, make certain

CRACK IN concrete slab (below left) can give termites an entry into your house.

SCRAP LUMBER in earth-floored basement (below) invites termite infestation.

TERMITES, with access to wood from soil that is completely unchecked, can do this kind of damage.

RAIL-SUPPORT POSTS in contact with soil provide another excellent opportunity for termites.

soil is at least 8 in. below the lowest wooden member.

■ *Buried wood.* Too often, wood scraps left over from construction are buried near the house or forms are left in place after pouring the foundation.

■ *Leaking pipes and faucets.* These can provide all the moisture needed for a thriving termite colony. The same holds true for gutter downspouts that fail to carry water away from the building.

■ *Poor ventilation.* When air doesn't circulate, moisture forms. This is a special hazard in crawlspaces, so adequate venting should be installed to assure good cross-ventilation. Be sure that shrubbery doesn't block vent openings.

■ *Flower planters.* Planters built near the house should be waterproofed below soil level. An air space between planter and house is an added safeguard.

■ *Porch steps.* If in contact with soil, wood porch steps offer termites their own stairway to your home. Steps should rest on a concrete apron and soil below should be protected.

■ *Wood trellises.* A common mistake—often after taking other precautions against termites—is to build a wood trellis that provides a direct link from soil to house.

The best time to think about termites, of course, is *before* your house or addition is built. It's easy—just make certain that your builder's contract calls for soil pretreatment with a termite insecticide.

Soil pretreatment includes spraying of all the soil that will be underneath or around the outside edge of the house with a chemical. It's done after the foundation footing trenches, plumbing and electrical conduits are in place—just before laying the vapor barrier and pouring the slab. Extra chemicals should be poured in those areas adjacent to foundation walls and interior walls, and around sewer and utility openings. When buying a termite-control job for an existing house, be sure to check the operator's references.

More information on protection against termites is in Dr. Haverty's booklet, available from Superintendent of Documents, U.S. Government Printing Office, Washington, DC 20403. (Stock No. 001-001-00420-1.)

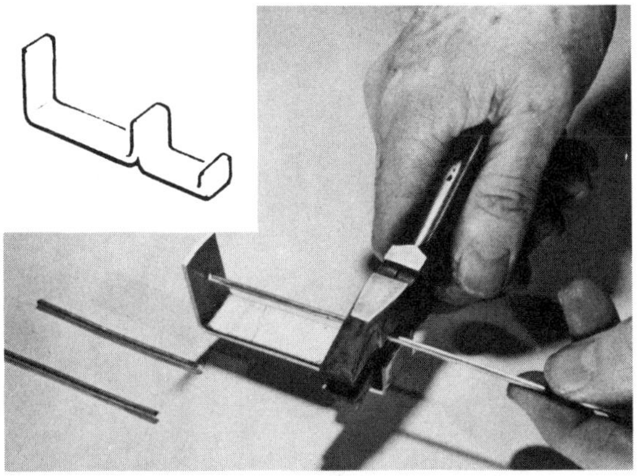

WHEN A JOB requires several short, uniform lengths of wire, this simple gauge for use with your wire-cutting pliers will enable you to cut them to identical lengths. Make it by bending a strip of sheet metal to form two troughs—a narrow one for the pliers and a wider one to match the wire length. The narrow one should be a press fit over the pliers.

USING ONE JAW of a pair of pliers, you can easily turn a monkey wrench into a pipe wrench. Place the plier jaw between the wrench jaws and tighten it against the pipe in the usual way. This will allow you to turn the pipe in one direction. By reversing the position of the plier jaw, you can turn the pipe in the opposite direction. Naturally, the thicker the jaws of the pliers, the more teeth area to grip the pipe—so use as large a pair of pliers as possible.

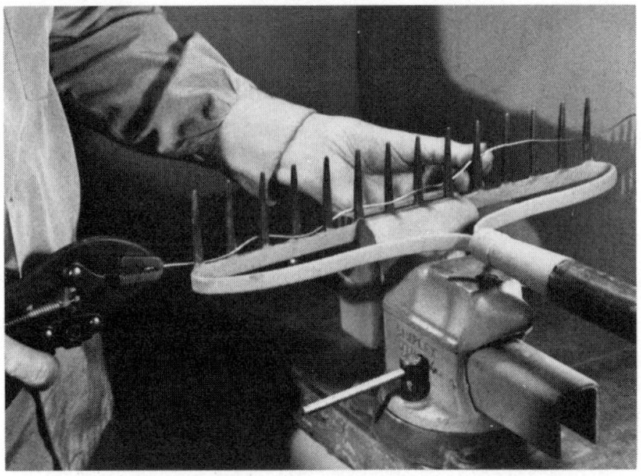

IF YOU WANT to take the kinks out of a length of small or medium-gauge wire, try drawing it through the tines of a garden rake. Just clamp the head of the rake in your vise, propping up the handle so as not to put an undue strain on the ferrule. Weave the wire between the tines, the spacing depending on the size of the wire and the amount of resistance needed to straighten it. Then grip the end with a pair of pliers and pull it through the tines.

SAVE THE PLASTIC CAPS from toothpaste tubes or similar containers, and you can use them in making jumbo pushpins for your bulletin board. Just fill them with any material that will harden (i.e., plastic auto-body filler or plaster of paris) and embed a pin headfirst in each so that it projects about ¾ inch. If the pins are too long, cut off enough from the head end to make them the right length and bend this end to a right angle for better anchoring.

Make a Tiffany-style terrarium

Create this miniature oasis using the same method Lewis C. Tiffany used for his famous lampshades

By PHIL and LORETTA HERMANN

■ MAKE THIS jewel-like "birdhouse" terrarium and fill it with your favorite ferns, mosses, African violets or other suitable house plants.

To begin, cut full-size paper patterns of the front and back sections. Secure them to glass using double-faced tape. Next, score the glass along the patterns' edges. The square sections can be marked on the glass with a grease pencil and scored with the aid of a straightedge.

For best results, hold the cutter as shown on the opposite page. The cutter's tip should be dipped in fine lubricating oil prior to making each cut. Draw the cutter toward you in one smooth and even stroke. Retrace only spots that the cutter skips. Avoid excessive pressure; it will leave small chips on the scored line and may cause erratic breaks. Curved sections of glass may be parted by tapping with the knob end of the cutter *under* the score. Pliers are also useful in forming the breaks (wear safety goggles).

Next, cut lengths of ⅜-in. copper foil tape long enough to encircle each cut piece, plus ¼ in. for overlap. Peel only a few inches of paper backing at a time. Center and apply the foil tape to the perimeters of the glass sections as shown. Rub tape on edges and sides with a burnishing stick to remove air bubbles.

To tin the foil, brush a thin coat of tinner's flux on the copper. (Try not to get flux on the glass because it may stain.) Then touch a small amount of 50/50 solid-core solder to a hot iron and quickly draw the molten solder along the foil.

Assemble the terrarium by arranging the front pieces on a flat surface and tacking them together. Center the front and back walls on the floor section and tack in place. Set each sidepiece on the same foundation and tack at the corners. Then tack roof sections in position.

making beaded joints

To obtain beaded joints, touch the solder wire to the hot iron and move them along the seams without touching the foil. After soldering, wash the terrarium thoroughly with detergent to remove any acid.

For a bronzed, antique finish on the beading, brush a solution of copper sulfate and water onto the soldered edges. *Caution:* Copper sulfate is toxic, so wear rubber gloves. Give the terrarium a final scrubbing. Before planting, run a bead of silicone sealer around the lower seams.

After you've mastered Tiffany's technique, you may want to experiment with colored glass or mirror for other creations.

SEE ALSO
Benches, potting . . . Dry sinks . . . House plants . . . Planters . . . Plexiglass projects

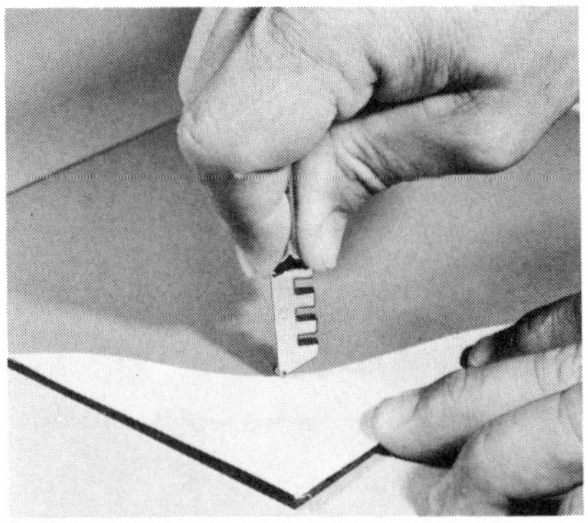

FULL-SIZE stencil cutouts give visual guide for scoring nonsquare sections.

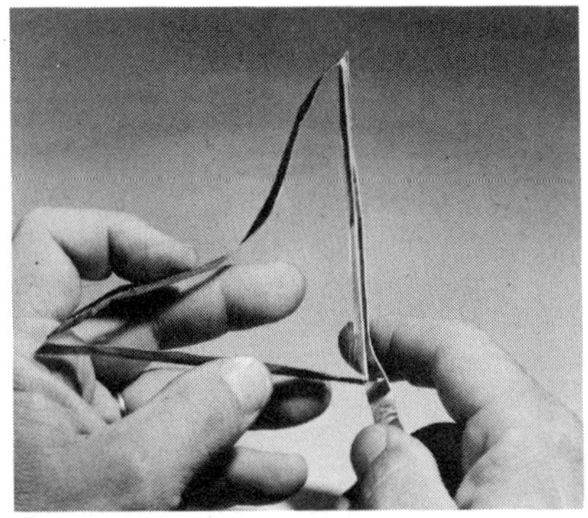

CUT COPPER foil strips long enough to wrap glass edges, adding ¼ in. overlap.

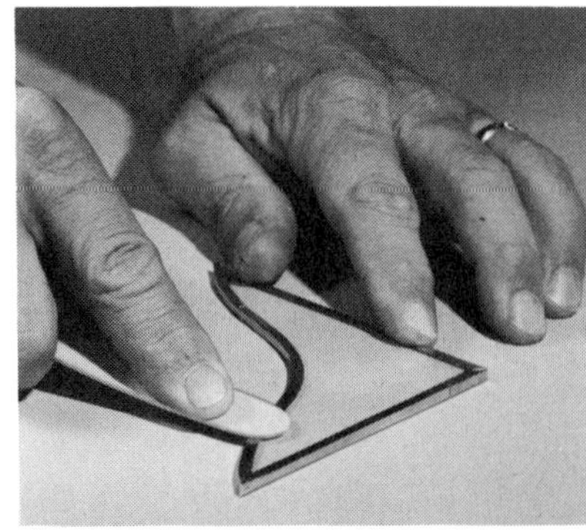

RUB ALL SURFACES of the foil with burnishing stick to remove air pockets.

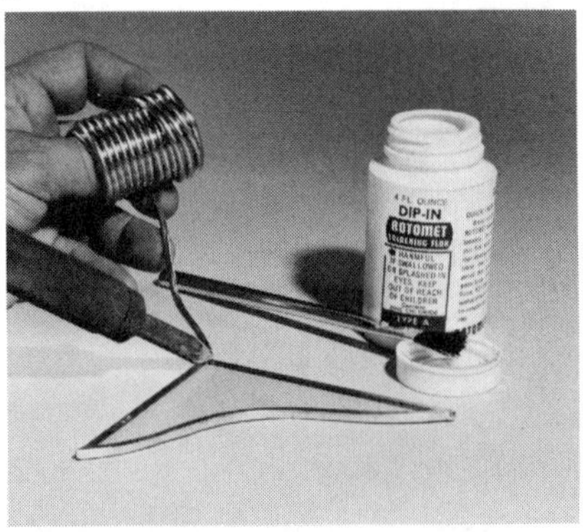

APPLY THIN COAT of flux with acid brush. Then draw solder along foil.

LIGHTLY TACK corners until all pieces are in place.

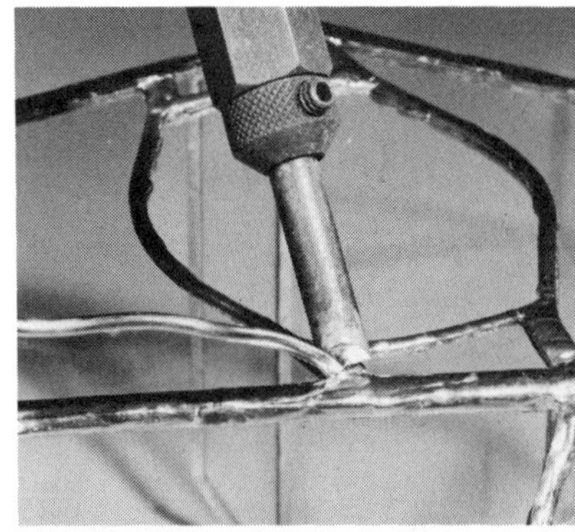

HOLD IRON'S TIP ⅛ in. above horizontal joint to form rounded edge bead.

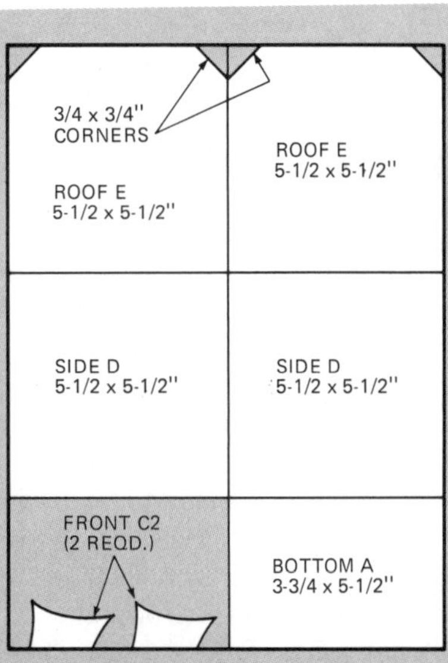

1 PIECE 11 x 14-3/4" DOUBLE-STRENGTH GLASS

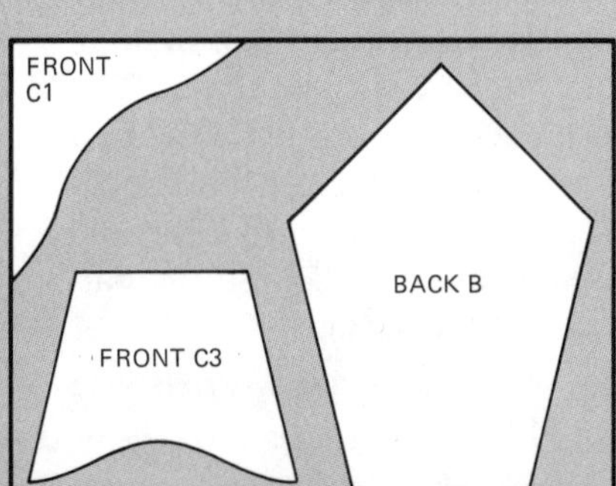

1 PIECE 9 x 12" DOUBLE-STRENGTH GLASS

GLASS CUTTING PATTERN

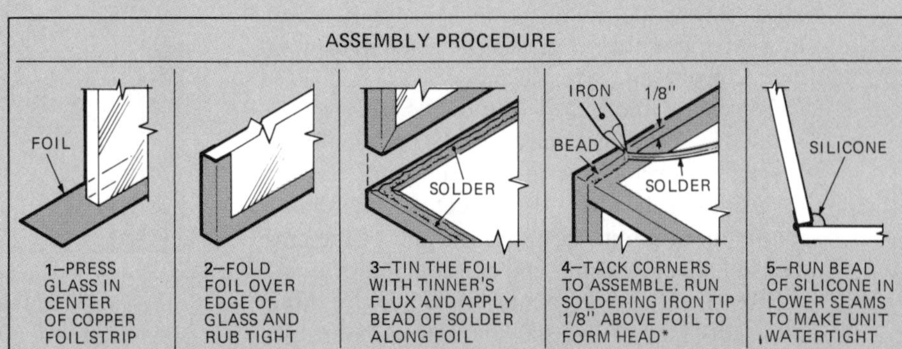

* SEE TEXT FOR ANTIQUE FINISH FOR SOLDER

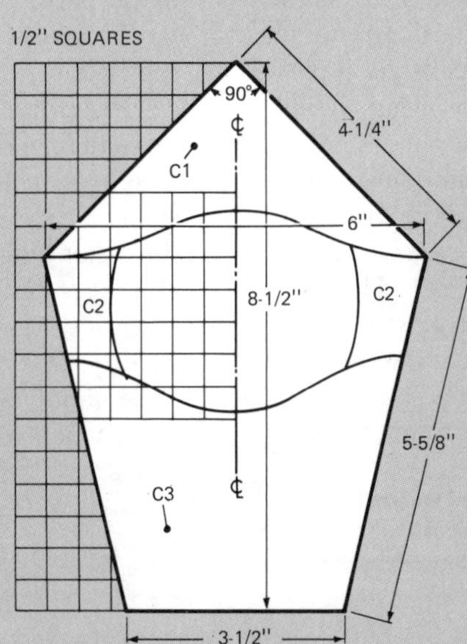

FRONT AND BACK PATTERNS

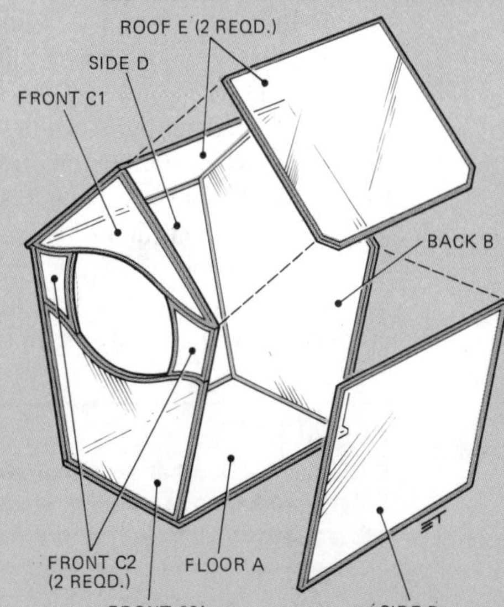

TERRARIUM ASSEMBLY

Put a tester in your screwdriver

By RAY SHOBERG

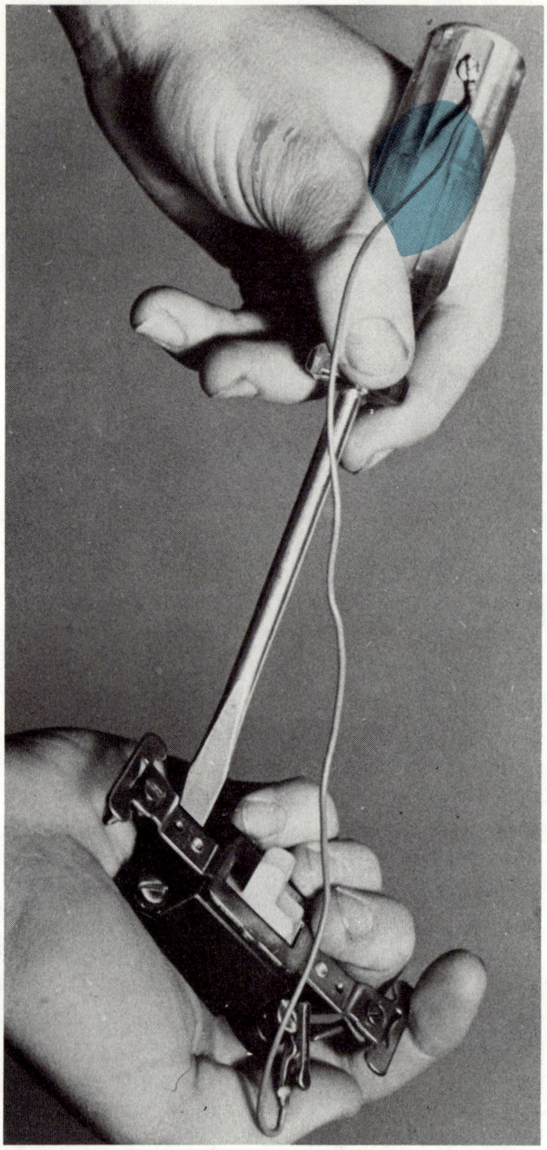

■ LIKE HAVING A COMB on the end of a brush, a continuity tester in the handle of a screwdriver is a natural when it comes to electrical troubleshooting.

A continuity tester consists of a battery and a bulb arranged in series with a pair of test leads. Any device placed in series across these leads, which completes the circuit, will light the bulb. Conversely, if the circuit being tested is "open" or incomplete, the bulb will not light. Suppose, for example, you have a fuse that is questionable. Connect it across the tester. If the bulb lights, the fuse is good.

In addition to fuses you can trace circuit continuity of motors, coils, switches and other devices. You can also check for grounded circuits or apparatus by inserting the tester between the suspected terminals and "ground"; in most cases this is the metal frame. Always be sure, however, that the circuit being tested is disconnected from any external power.

To make such a two-in-one tool, pick a screwdriver that has a clear plastic handle. Since you will be drilling a ⅝-in. hole, buy one that has a 1¼-in.-dia. handle. Also select one that has a minimum of 2½ in. between the end of the embedded shank and the end of the handle.

The handle is counterbored with three different-sized drills, starting with a ⅝-in. bit, then a ⅜-in. one and finally a 1/16-in. drill. As the detail shows, the ⅝-in. hole is made deep enough to hold two mercury hearing-aid cells and a plastic plug. The ⅜-in. hole is for a spring and a bulb from a two-cell penlight, while the 1/16-in. hole is for a wire which makes electrical contact with the shank. Where a regular tester has two test leads, this combination screwdriver-tester makes use of the blade for one lead. The deep 1/16-in. hole is drilled in the soft plastic with a homemade drill made from a piece of wire. Two sides are filed flat for a distance from the end and then sharpened like the end of a conventional metal-cutting drill. This will do the trick but you'll have to back it out often in order to keep the hole cleared of chips.

The spring is made of light wire (about .025-in.) and formed around a ¼-in. dowel so only the nose part of the bulb can enter. One end of the spring gets soldered to the shell of the bulb, while the other end is inserted into the 1/16-in. hole to make contact with the screwdriver shank. The batteries are inserted with the button of the first battery in contact with the bulb. Here you should have about ⅛ in. of extra space so that the end plug, when pressed in place, will push the batteries and bulb against the spring.

Next a 3/16-in. hole is drilled crosswise through the plug and handle for a plastic rod or

SEE ALSO
Batteries . . . Doorbells . . . Electrical wiring . . . Safety, workshop . . . Wiring, electrical

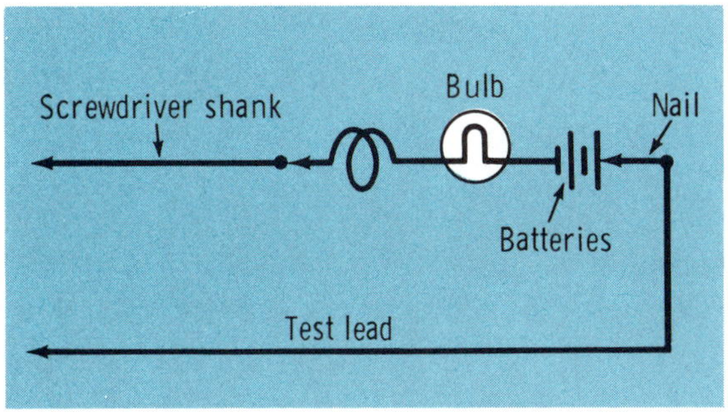

wooden dowel. The purpose of the plug is to make certain that, should the screwdriver contact a live electrical circuit during use, the voltage potential available through the spring, bulb and batteries will not come in direct contact with the hand. A rubber crutch tip pressed over the end of the handle will provide additional insulation and safety.

At the point where the plug contacts the batteries, drill a ⅛-in. hole for the test-lead tip which is a 7d box nail. Since the hole becomes more of a V-groove across the end of the plug, you'll do best to remove the plug and form the groove with a small round file. A length of stranded wire (18 or 20-ga.) is soldered to the cutoff nail and to an alligator clip. When inserted, the pointed nail contacts the batteries, readying the tester for use.

When it's not in use, keep the test tip out of the handle. This will conserve the batteries. With the test lead removed and the crutch tip in place, contact of the blade with high voltage will not damage either the bulb or batteries because the circuit is no longer complete.

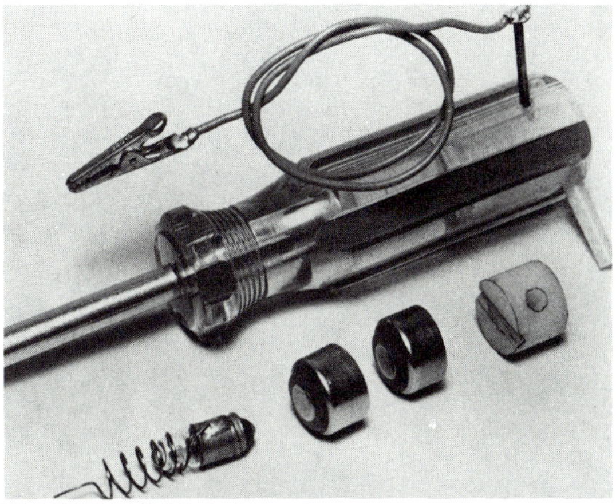

PLASTIC PLUG is held in place by dowel or plastic rod. Slit in plug is a keyway for nail contact.

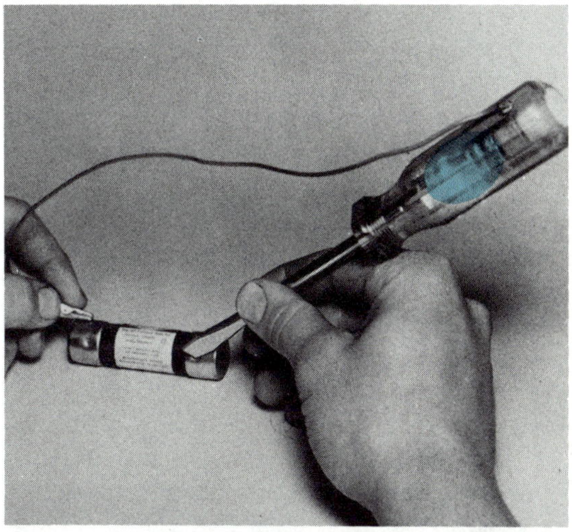

THE SCREWDRIVER SHANK is one probe, the wire with the alligator clip is the other. The glowing light means that the fuse being tested is good.

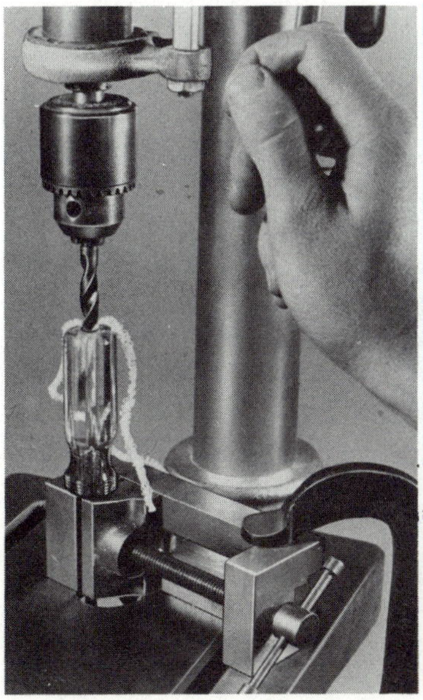

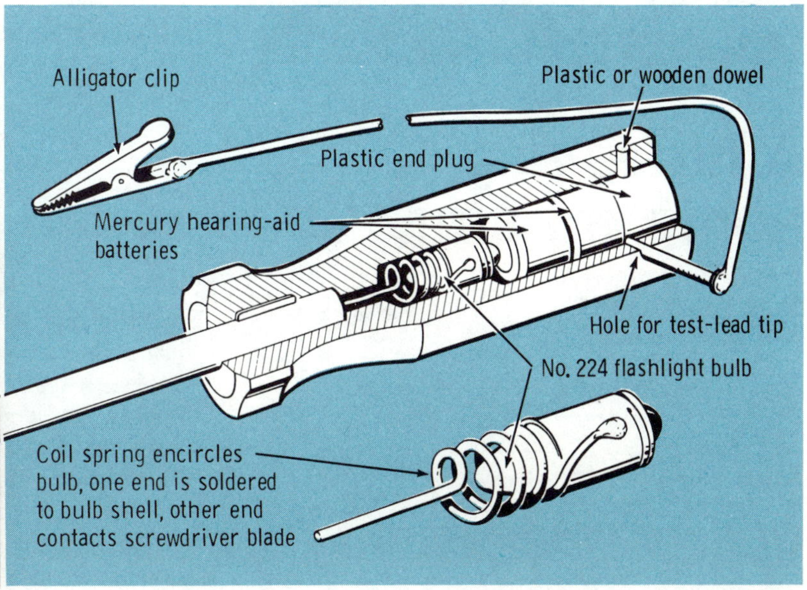

WITH THE SCREEN RETRACTED (left), the unit looks like an ordinary wall cabinet with storage cupboards and knickknack shelves. Conversion to home theater (above) takes only seconds, makes showing slides or movies fun instead of a nuisance. The unit can be anchored to wall or suspended on shelf brackets.

A hideaway home theater

By SHELDON M. GALLAGER

SEE ALSO

Family rooms . . . Hi-fi centers . . . Illuminators, slide-copy . . . Photography . . . Projector stands . . . Remodeling ideas . . . Slides, photo

■ BY THE TIME you haul out all the gear required to put on a slide or movie show, a lot of the fun has gone for you and your guests. This hideaway wall unit is designed to end the fuss and put the fun back into showing slides and movies. There's no screen to get out and set up because it's already built into the unit—you just pull it down and slip the projector out of one of the side cabinets.

When the screen is not in use, it disappears up into a recess at the top and is completely hidden from view. In its place are shelves for displaying decorative objects, giving the unit an attractive appearance when it's not serving as an instant home theater. The cabinets, besides storing photographic gear, can also house hi-fi equipment, making the unit an all-around home entertainment center. The cabinets are spaced apart just right for good stereo listening from small bookshelf-type speakers placed inside the cupboards. The doors have mesh-covered openings designed to let sound through.

If you go in for sound movies or sound-synced slide shows, the setup is ideal because the accompanying sound, filtering out through the mesh doors, will appear to come right from the projection screen. For added convenience, you can install one of NuTone's flush-mounting music/intercom systems, as shown in the photos below. These systems come in a variety of types and price ranges and offer a complete home communication center in a single, smartly styled unit with built-in radio, speaker and intercom controls.

The wall unit is built around a 40x40-inch pull-down screen made by Da-Lite. This type is designed expressly for wall or ceiling mounting and has brackets on the case that permit the screen to be hung from hooks or attached with screws. Such screens cost about the same as the regular floor-stand type.

Dimensions of the unit can be altered as desired, but the 10-inch depth was chosen because it enables all parts except the back panels to be ripped from stock 1x12-inch lumber with little waste. The unit can be screwed directly to the wall, just as you would mount a kitchen cabinet, or it can be supported on metal shelf brackets of the type that hook into slotted wall standards. The 10-inch depth enables the unit to fit perfectly on standard 10-inch-long shelf brackets.

If you decide on wall brackets, one construction pointer is important. The unit should be supported on no fewer than *three* brackets—one at each end and one at the middle. The center bracket can't extend the full cabinet depth, however, or it would obviously block the screen from coming down. The answer here is to build up a small supporting framework at the center of the span just behind the screen. This framework is 6 inches deep and rests on a 6-inch shelf bracket, supporting the middle of the unit without interfering with the operation of the screen. The knickknack shelves also rest on 6-inch brackets,

UNDERSIDE VIEW with fascia board removed shows how the screen mounts at top of the unit between cabinets. With fascia board in place, the screen is hidden from view. Screen shown here is a 40 x 40-inch model made by Da-Lite. Two-way end brackets permit it to be hung from hooks or attached with screws.

HANGING SIDE CABINETS can house various pieces of equipment depending on your needs. Here, one is fitted with NuTone's in-a-wall music/intercom system designed to mount in shallow spaces. Upper unit (left, below) is AM/FM radio with 10-station intercom. Lower unit is fold-up record changer that swings out horizontally for use (center). Opposite cabinet (right) holds a Kodak Super-8 movie projector, film reels and a Model AS-18 Heathkit speaker.

providing sufficient clearance for the screen to pull down in front.

For maximum strength, the main strut running across the back at the top should extend the full 80-inch width—behind the cabinets as well as the screen—since it supports the entire weight of the unit where hung on shelf brackets. If you plan to mount the unit directly on the wall, you can, of course, eliminate the strut and center supporting framework.

Other options and variations are possible, too. As shown here, the unit incorporates a recess at the top for installing fluorescent lighting fixtures. These provide a soft, pleasing cove lighting effect. You can also build just the screen enclosure without the hanging side cabinets. Several alternate versions of this type are shown. Further information on screens can be obtained from Da-Lite Screen Co., Warsaw, Ind. 46580. For more details on Nu-Tone's in-a-wall music/intercom systems, write to NuTone Div., Madison and Red Bank Rds., Cincinnati, Ohio 45227.

home theater, continued

Technical art by Peter Trojan

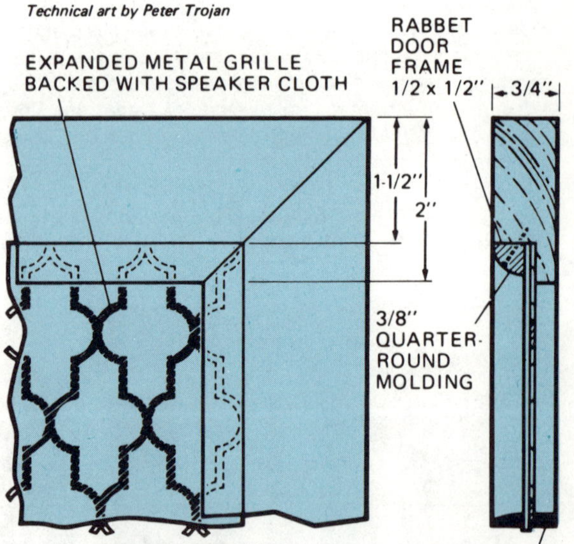

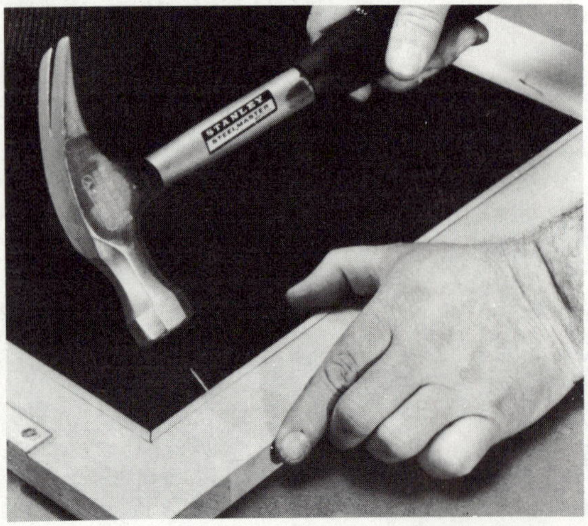

GRILLE-COVERED OPENINGS in doors are designed to let sound through even when the doors are closed. Door rails are rabbeted to form recess on back side, then decorative Reynolds brass mesh is trimmed with tin snips to fit inside (top photo at left). The mesh is backed with black speaker cloth, and both are held in place with ⅜-inch quarter-round molding strips tacked in with small brads.

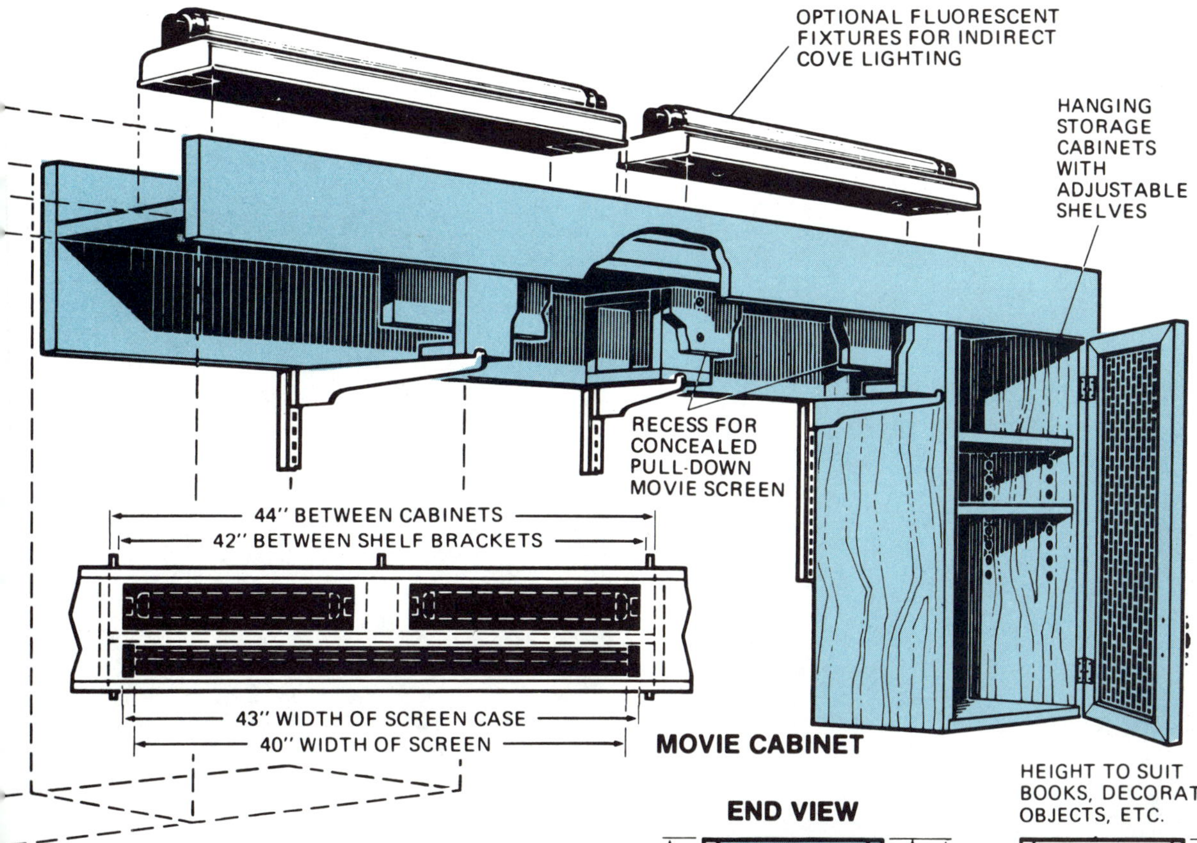

MOVIE CABINET

END VIEW

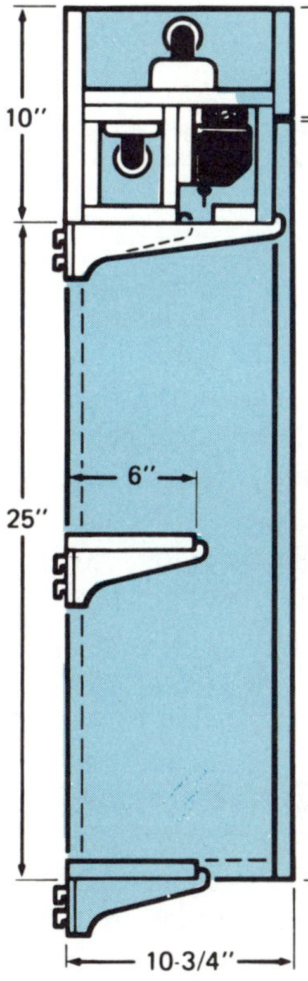

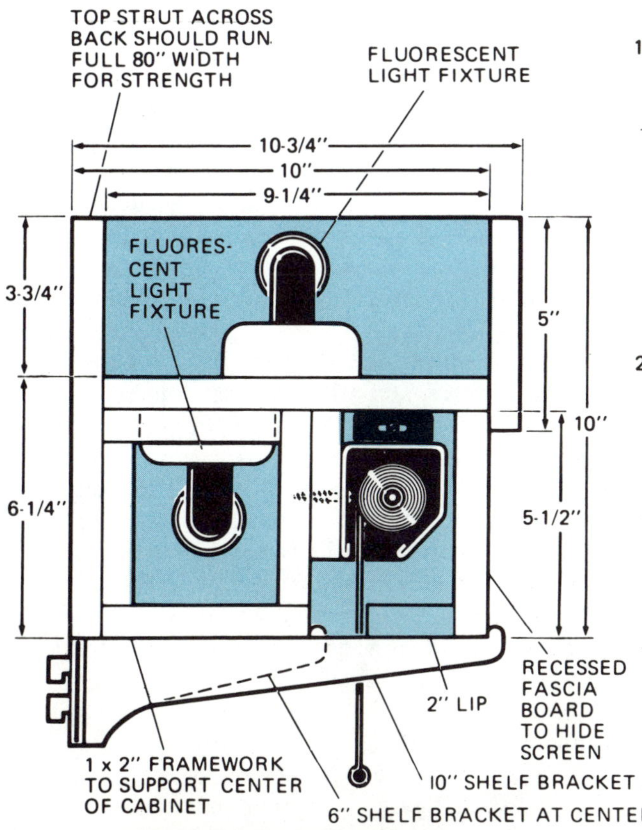

CROSS SECTION DETAIL THROUGH CENTER

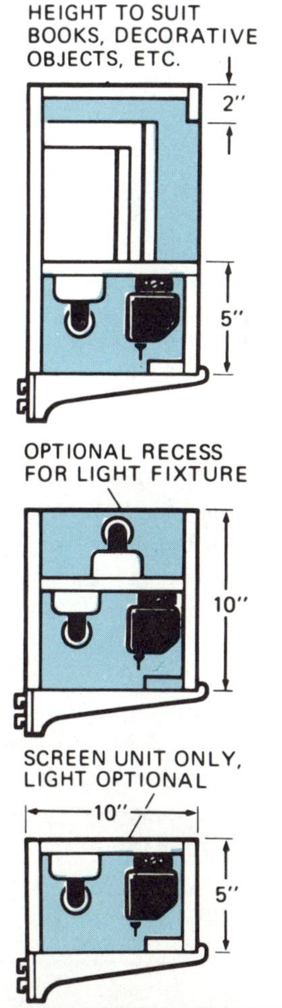

THREE ALTERNATE VERSIONS WITHOUT HANGING CABINETS

VINYL FLOOR TILES faithfully simulate brick, wood and other surfaces yet are easier to maintain.

ANYTHING BUT DRAB, vinyl floor patterns can accent the motif of any room.

How to tile a floor

By LEN HILTS

■ THE MOST DIFFICULT part of laying a new tile floor is deciding which tile pattern you like best. The stores and home centers which sell vinyl flooring have such a wide range of colors and designs that you'll probably need several hours for browsing and choosing.

Vinyl and vinyl-asbestos tiles are the most popular types of do-it-yourself floors. Most rooms can be floored with them in a day, or at most a weekend. Best of all, vinyls offer no-wax finishes so you can put down a floor that is both beautiful and free of upkeep.

You'll find two basic varieties of resilient tiles: self-adhesive and dry-back. With the self-adhesive, just peel off a backing paper, place the tile in position on the floor, and press it down. With the dry-backs, you first apply an adhesive to the floor.

SEE ALSO
Bathrooms . . . Floors . . . Kitchens . . . Quarry tile . . . Tile, wall . . . Wall tile

Selecting the tile. Which kind to use? Because they are easier to use, most people now prefer the self-adhesive vinyl tiles. But your choice may be determined by other factors, such as pattern or price.

All-vinyl tiles are relatively soft, have embossed surfaces, and are offered in an incredible selection of designs. Vinyl-asbestos tiles are harder, a little thicker, have smooth surfaces, and are not available in as many designs. The design goes clear through the tile so that wear doesn't show for a long time. Vinyls may have a no-wax finish, while vinyl-asbestos tiles need an occasional waxing.

If you need long service in a high traffic area, opt for the vinyl-asbestos. It often is used in stores and offices. You may find some with self-adhesive backs, though most are dry.

If you want a wide selection of patterns, a no-wax finish and easy installation, then choose the embossed vinyl styles. You may have to replace them sooner than vinyl-asbestos but they are easy to take up and replace.

Preparation. Good preparation is the secret of laying any floor covering. The basic rules are these:

1. The subfloor must be level and smooth. Any bump in the subfloor soon will show up as a bump in the tile, and that bump will wear rapidly.

Some homeowners lay new tiles directly on existing tile floors. If the old tile is sound and smooth, this is all right, but examine the old floor before you do it. Wear may have made it uneven. Any imperfections in the old floor will quickly appear in the new floor. If in doubt, take up the old tiles.

2. The subfloor must be dry and free of dust. Dust interferes with any adhesive but especially the adhesive on self-sticking tiles. Vacuum the floor just before you lay new tiles.

3. Plan your layout with care so that the tiles align properly.

4. With concrete floors, notably basement floors below grade, you not only may have dust, but often a moisture problem as well. Moisture may seep slowly up through the slab. In past years, asphalt cement adhesive was used to lay tiles below grade, and only asphalt tiles were used. Now a vinyl floor sealer can be brushed on to provide a thick coating which seals out both moisture and dust. This permits the use of most types of floor tile below grade.

Removing the old floor. When taking up an old tile floor, remove all traces of tile, old lining felt and adhesive. *Do not sand old flooring materials to remove them.* Many were made with asbestos fibers; the dust may contain asbestos particles and be very hazardous to your health. Remove old tiles by pulling up and scraping. Dispose of the old material in heavy-duty plastic bags, tied shut and marked, "Caution—contains asbestos. Dispose in an approved landfill only."

If the felt sticks to the subfloor, remove it by wetting—not soaking—and then scraping. Scrubbing the dampened felt with a stiff brush helps in difficult cases. Asphalt solvent will remove any old adhesive.

Once all the old stuff is off the floor, check the surface. If it isn't flat and smooth, take the time to level it now. You'll get a much better final result.

Leveling the subfloor. If you are tiling a wood floor, the best way to achieve a smooth subfloor is to nail underlayment over the surface. You can buy hardboard sheets made for this purpose at your home center. All nailheads must be flush with the surface.

You can fill low spots in concrete floors with leveling compounds available at tile stores (usually latex cement mixtures), taking care to bring the low spot just up to the level of the rest of the floor and to feather the edges of the patch.

To level slight depressions in a concrete floor or to smooth out rough surfaces, you can brush several coats of the vinyl sealer on low areas. This seals the floor against moisture and dust and provides a level, smooth surface for both dry-backed and adhesive-backed tiles.

Finally, pry away any molding at the walls. This molding should be replaced after the new floor is down.

Floor layout. Mark your floor with guidelines before cementing tiles down. To do this, find the center points on two opposite walls and strike a chalk line across the floor from one to the other. Measure this line and place a tile at the midpoint, as shown in the drawing, to establish a perpendicular line.

Extend this line to both walls, thus dividing the room into quarters. Next, place tiles temporarily along these lines from the center of the room to the side walls. At this point you may want to move one or both lines slightly to avoid cutting narrow strips along the walls.

Placing the tiles. If installing self-adhesive tiles, strip the release paper from one tile and place the tile at the point where the lines cross in the center of the room. Before putting the tile down, turn it over. Some brands, notably Armstrong, have arrows printed on the back. Install all tiles with the arrows running in the same direction. Be sure to align the sides of the tile with the chalk lines. Strip a second tile and butt it against the first, and also align it with the chalk line.

The placement of these first tiles is vitally important because if they don't line up, all others also will be misaligned. After positioning a tile, press it firmly in place. Continue putting tiles down until the floor is covered. The final job is to cut tiles to fit the spaces at the base of the walls.

If you are installing dry-backed tiles, you will use a canned adhesive. Read the instructions on the label before applying it, and follow them exactly. Adhesives differ; instructions vary from brand to brand. Most call for application with a notched adhesive spreader, but some adhesives are brushed on. Most are applied to a section of floor at a time, and require a short drying time before the tile is applied.

When the adhesive has set, place a tile at the point where the chalk lines cross. Don't slide the tile into place. Instead, place one side accurately on the chalk line and snap the other side down. You can slide the tile a little for accurate placement, but if you move it too much, you may disturb the adhesive. Place a second tile against the first and snap it into place. Be certain the tiles butt accurately. Continue until the floor is finished except for the areas at the base of the wall.

Cutting tiles. Soft vinyl tiles can be cut with a utility knife or heavy scissors. Harder vinyl asbestos tiles are scored deeply with a utility knife, then snapped along the score line. Place the tile on a table with the score line along the table edge, then snap sharply down on the part of the tile extending beyond the table.

To cut tiles to fit at the base of the wall, place a loose tile over the last full tile in a row. Place another tile on top of this and slide this tile toward the wall until it touches the wall. Use the edge of this tile as a guide and draw a line on the tile beneath it, as shown in the drawing. When you cut along this line, the cut tile will fit exactly into the space at the base of the wall.

To make irregular cutouts to fit around pipes and other obstructions, draw a paper pattern of the cutout. Trace this on the tile and cut it out with a utility knife.

With the last tile installed, just move the furniture back into place and start enjoying your new floor.

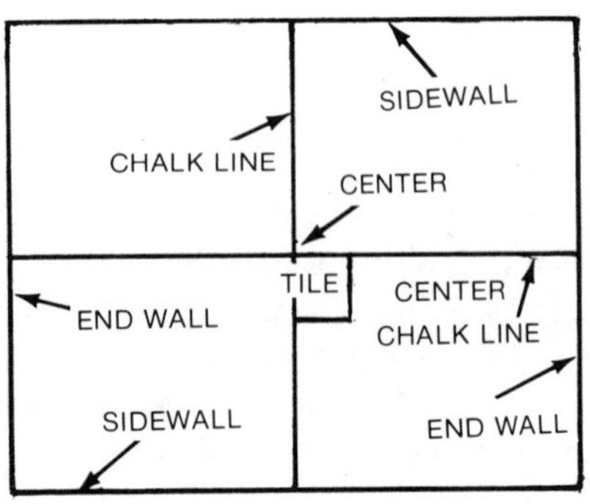

1

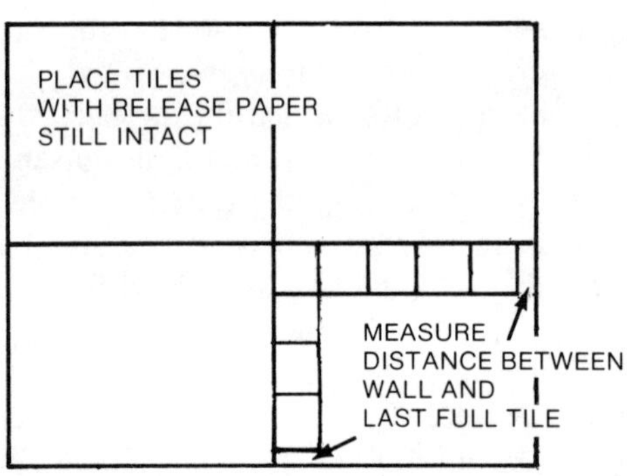

2

1. To begin floor layout, find the center between opposite walls, and strike a chalk line across the room. This is the "center chalk line." Next, locate the center of this line. Place a tile, as shown, at the center point and use it to draw a chalk line perpendicular to the first line. The floor is now divided into quarters.

2. Place a row of tiles along the perpendicular chalk line from the center of the room to the sidewall. Do not remove release paper. Measure distance from last tile to wall.

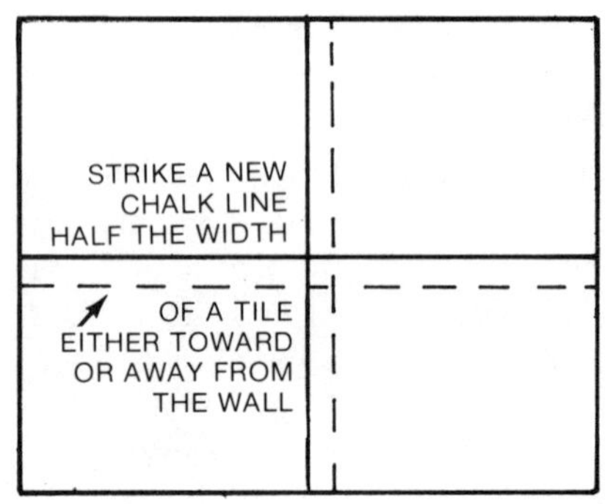

3

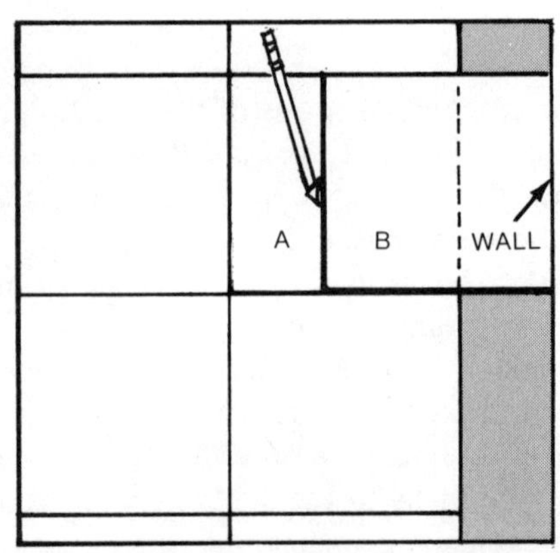

4

3. If space from last tile to the wall is less than half the width of a tile, strike a new chalk line beside old center line. Make it half the width of a tile on either side (your choice) of old center line. This provides even borders on both sides of the room.

4. To measure tile to fit space at base of wall, place a loose tile exactly on top of last full tile in any row. Place third tile on top of this and slide it until it contacts wall. Use edge of tile as a guide to mark the tile under it with a pencil. Cut along this line with heavy duty scissors or utility knife.

What you should know about tiling walls

By LEN HILTS

You can put plastic, metal, ceramic, and even marble tiling on one or several walls in your home. Today's materials make the job easy

■ NO DOUBT ABOUT IT, tile adds the finishing touch to a house. It is both pleasing to the eye and practical in bathrooms, kitchens and even as a part of the decorative motif in living rooms. Add to that the fact that you can now tile any area yourself, and tile becomes an important material for the homeowner to know about.

Here are some of the ways you can use tile in your home to increase its livability and, incidentally, to increase its sale value:

1. *Bathrooms.* Tile the tub enclosure all the way to the ceiling. Tile the area above and back of the sink as a backsplash. Tile all the walls to chair-rail height, or tile the entire wall area. Tile the floor. Whether you do a lot or a little, new tile will make the bathroom easier to care for and better to look at,

2. *Powder rooms.* As a rule, powder rooms (half baths) have less tiled area than bathrooms, with the majority of the wall area painted or wallpapered. However, if you choose, you can tile the whole thing, including the floor. At a minimum, you can install a tile backsplash for the sink.

3. *Laundry room.* Tile behind the laundry machines and the laundry sink can really add a touch of class to the usually plebian laundry room. If your laundry area is in the basement, tile on those gray concrete walls will dramatically elevate the appearance of the place.

4. *Kitchen.* You can tile your counters here if you choose, but the usual use of tile in the kitchen is on the walls between the cabinet bottoms and the countertops, and as a backsplash for the sink. You can, of course, tile the floor but keep in mind that tile when wet can be slippery. Vinyl floor tiles with a nonslip surface would probably be more practical here than ceramic tiles.

5. *Living areas.* If you are looking for a way to create a distinctive living area, think about using tile, especially small mosaic tile, on one wall. There is a wide array of colors in a variety of shapes available, so you can really employ your imagination in designing this wall. Obviously, you can do too much tiling, too. Think about doing one wall or even a section of one wall. If

SEE ALSO
Bathrooms . . . Kitchens . . . Tile, floor . . . Wallpaper

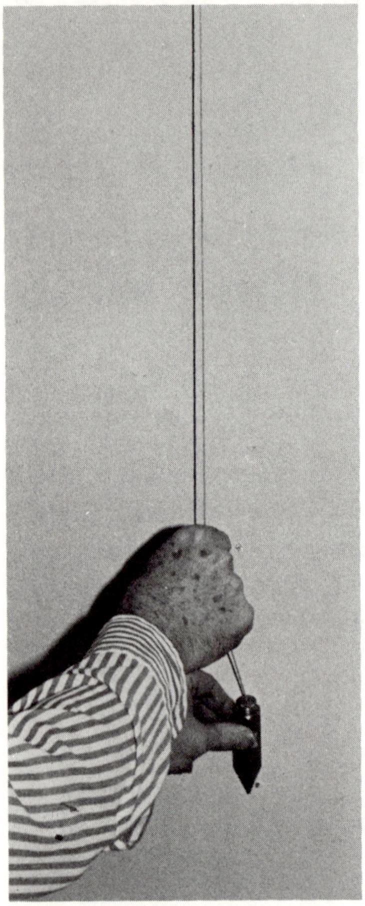

DROP a chalked plumb line and snap it to make a vertical guide.

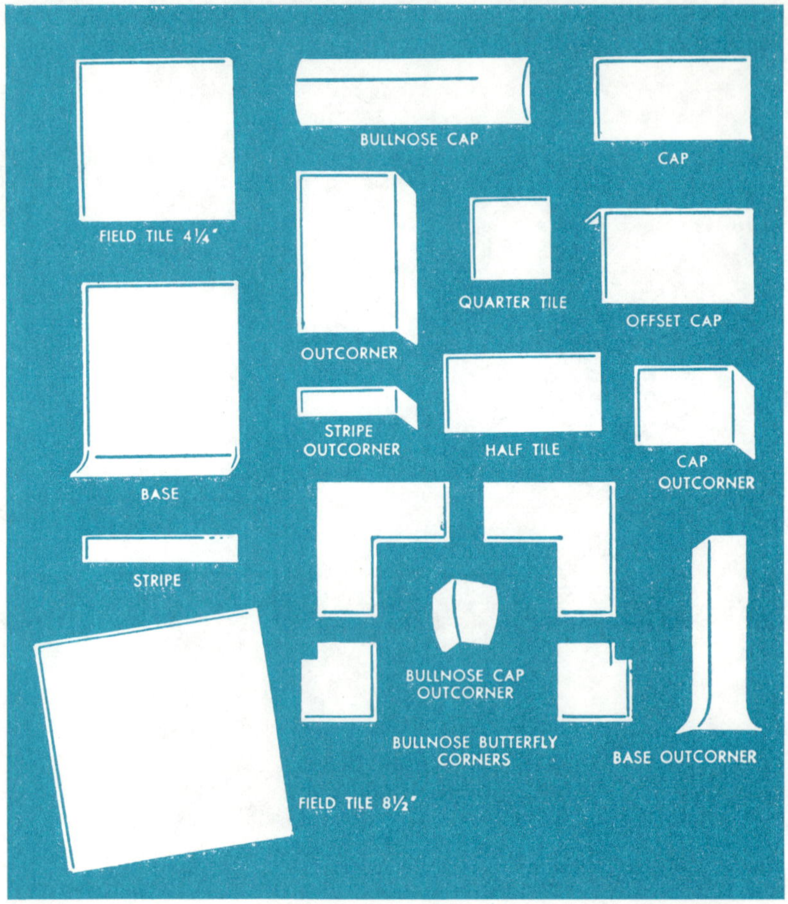

MATCHING ACCESSORIES are available with all types of tile. These include bases, caps, soap dishes, glass holders, towel bars and tissue holders.

you have a fireplace that seems a bit humdrum, you might tile the wall above or around it for a new effect.

6. *Much-used areas.* Take a tip from the people who design public buildings if you have an area such as a long hall which is constantly in need of painting or washing because of fingerprints. You can cut the maintenance of such areas by tiling the lower, most-soiled portion. Don't use stark white bathroom tiles for this. Achieve a decorative effect by using colorful, small mosaic tiles.

types of tile

There are three basic types of wall tile—ceramic, metal and plastic. Plastic tile is considerably less expensive than ceramic tile, and is easier to install because cutting the plastic is easier than cutting the ceramic. But you pay a penalty because plastic tile tends to scratch easily in areas of heavy use. When scratched, it loses its luster. Also, some of the colored plastic fades with age. Metal tile is enameled, and its colors also tend to fade.

TILES ALSO COME in a variety of novelty shapes and sizes, including the small mosaic variety. You can use these for both walls and floors.

Ceramic tile, on the other hand, maintains its appearance under very heavy wear and does not fade. Its hard surface resists penetration of all types of dirt and grime. The surface of the grout between the tiles can get dirty and can become mildewed, however, so you need a regular cleaning program to keep the tile looking good.

Realtors tend to put a higher value on homes with ceramic tile baths, so keep this in mind as you make your decision. A larger expenditure now may mean a better price later.

The basic tile size is 4¼ x 4¼-in. Both plastic and ceramic tile are produced in this size. You can also find tiles up to 8½ x 8½-in. sq., but these usually are special-order items, while the standard sizes can now be purchased at most home center stores and from major mail-order houses.

In addition to the square field tiles, you can purchase a number of special shapes, including several different shapes of base and cap pieces. See the accompanying illustration. When planning your tiling job, make a list of the number of field tiles and of special shapes you will need. In addition to the shapes shown, you can also buy tile towel bars, toilet tissue holders, and soap dishes, all of which attach directly to the wall with tile mastic.

Tiles in decorative shapes have become available, too. With these, you can get away from the "standard" tile look and create exceptionally attractive tiled areas. Lozenge shapes, for example, provide a very Spanish look. These unusual tiles are no more difficult to install than the square units.

You can also buy small tiles, down to as small as half an inch square. These smaller tiles, called mosaics, come in square-foot sheets, with the tiles cemented to a mesh backing. Thus, you don't have to lay each tiny tile individually, but can put the tile up a square foot at a time. You'll find these mosaic tiles available in many colors, in sheets with multicolors on them, and even sheets with special designs already created.

If you are thinking about tiling any area in your home, the best way to start is to visit a couple of local home centers to see which types are readily available. Just looking at the tile displays will give you some ideas on how to use these fine home additions.

the mastic

Tiles are glued in place with a special mastic which you buy in large cans. The mastic is applied to the wall with a toothed spreader which leaves tiny ridges of mastic of just the right height. This prevents you from putting too much mastic on, and makes for a neat final job. If you apply too much mastic it will squeeze out between the tiles and mar the new surface.

Modern square tiles have another built-in solution to an old problem. Each tile has small spacers on all four edges. Thus, when you put the tile in place on the wall, you butt it up against its neighbor without worrying about how much space to leave between the two. The spacers on the tiles automatically provide the correct spacing.

cutting tile to fit

Many people have shied away from putting up their own tile, especially ceramic tile, because they have heard that cutting and trimming tile is difficult—a job for a professional. This isn't true. Cutting tile is similar to, but easier than, cutting glass.

Plastic tile is easy to cut with a coping saw or sharp knife of the wallboard type. To cut a piece of tile to fit around a pipe, for example, all you need do is draw or trace the cutout on the surface of the tile, then lay the tile on a wooden cutting surface (a piece of 1 x 10 lumber is fine), and follow the drawn line with the knife or saw. You can make good, smooth cuts this way.

Cutting ceramic tile is more difficult. To make straight cuts—for example, to cut a field tile in half—you place the tile in a tile cutter (which a majority of stores that sell ceramic tile will either loan or rent to you), draw the stylus of the cutter across the tile at the point where you want the cut. You then tap the tile along the line drawn by the stylus, and it breaks cleanly. To finish the cut, you smooth it by sanding the raw edge a little with an emery cloth.

Other cuts—curved, for example—can be made by using an ordinary glass cutter instead of the tile cutter. You can also make some types of cuts with a tile nibbler, which is a type of pliers with cutting edges on its jaws. To use a nibbler, you make a series of tiny nibbles, beginning at one edge, cutting away a small portion of tile with each nibble. You continue cutting until you have formed the cutout shape needed.

If you have a jigsaw, you can also use it to make cutouts in both plastic and ceramic tile. Use a fine-toothed blade of the type used to cut metal for this work. When making such cuts, be sure to wear safety glasses to protect your eyes.

The easiest way to plan a tile job is to make a sketch of the area or areas to be tiled on graph paper. Make the sketch in scale, with four

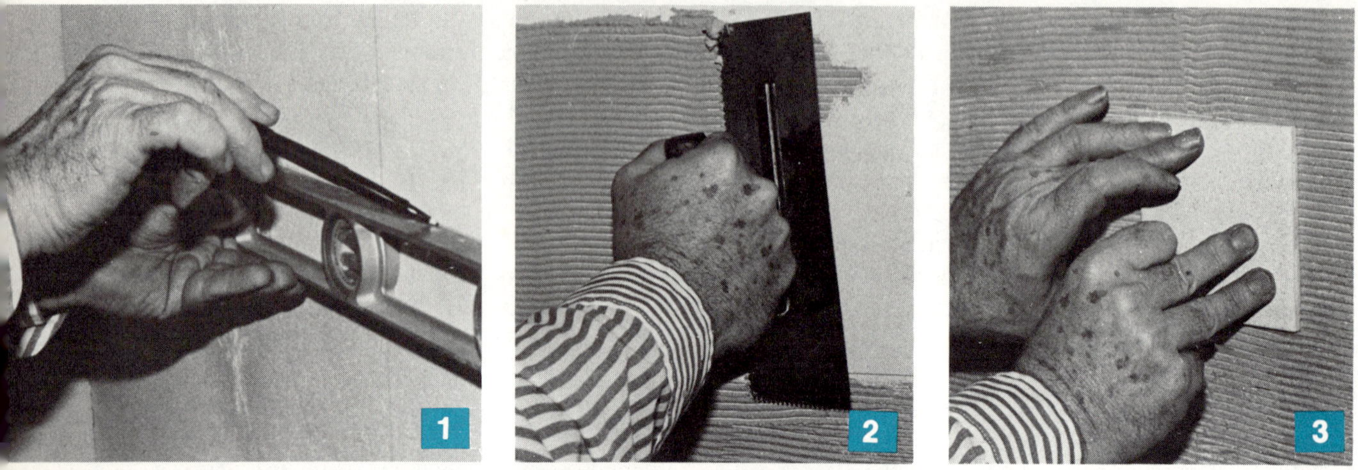

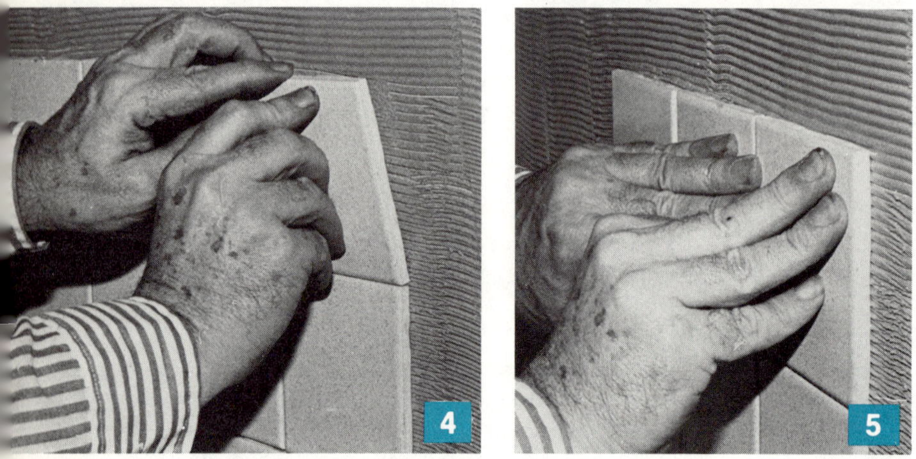

USE A SPIRIT level to make a horizontal guide line, then apply the tile mastic with a toothed trowel. Press hard on the trowel and spread the mastic thinly and evenly. Position the first tile at the intersection of the vertical and horizontal guide lines, which you should be able to see through the coat of mastic. Apply the second tile next to the first, snapping it into place. Slide it carefully so that it butts against the first tile. Take care to see that the mastic doesn't ooze out between the tiles. Be sure to align the tiles while the mastic is still pliable.

squares of the graph paper representing each square foot on the wall. Find out at your tile store what sizes the tile (and its accessory pieces) comes in. Then, working with these sizes, determine how many field tiles you'll need for the open areas of the wall, and how many accessory pieces, such as bases and caps, you'll need. If you plan carefully, you should be able to compute exactly how many tiles you'll need for the job, right there on the paper.

When you order the tile, it is a good idea to order somewhat more than the plan calls for. For one thing, if you haven't cut tile before, it is worthwhile to waste a couple of pieces in order

A RENTED TILE CUTTER is used to score a tile for cutting. You also can use a glass cutter.

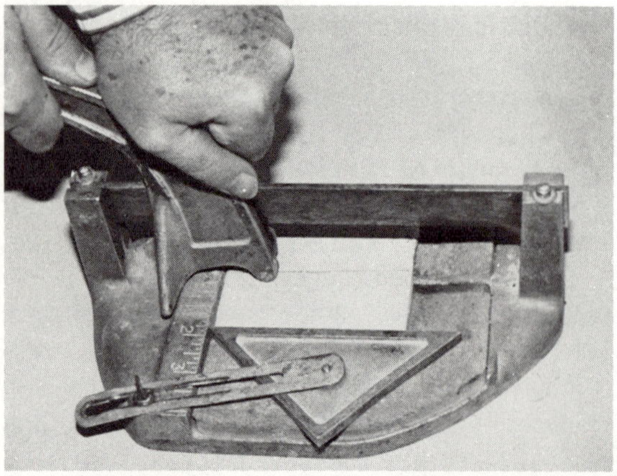

THE SCORED TILE can be snapped easily by placing it on a pencil and applying pressure.

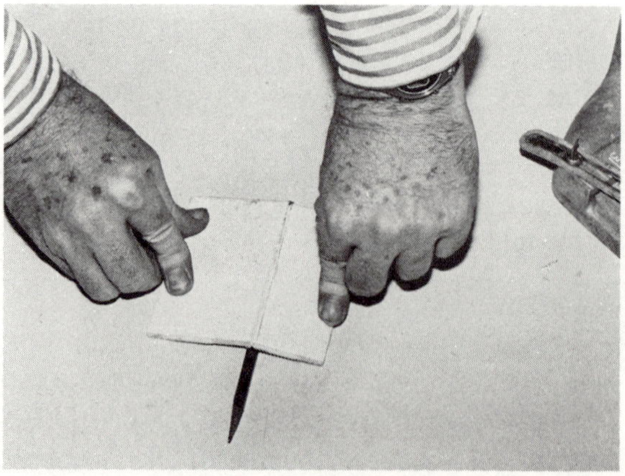

to practice cutting. You'll find you become proficient quite quickly—and it helps to know during this practice that it doesn't make any difference if you mess up a couple of cuts.

If you are using the small mosaic tile, you won't have to do much cutting. When you have to cut a larger tile, you'll find it easiest to do the job on tile cutter, a jigsaw, or with a coping saw. The nibbler, when used right, does a nice job on small tiles.

It is best to order all of the tile you need at one time. The reason is that the color may vary slightly from batch to batch. By getting it all at once, you are more likely to get tile in which there is no color variation. Usually you can get a refund on leftover tiles.

lining up the job

The first thing to remember when you begin to measure the wall for the tile is: no wall is ever true. Even walls which look perfectly square usually are not. For that reason, don't depend on the corner of the wall to provide a perfectly vertical line against which you can align your tiles. Instead, drop a plumb bob with a chalk line from the ceiling, and snap a vertical line on the wall. Use this line as your guide in placing the tiles.

Also, don't assume that the floor or the top of a bathtub is perfectly level. Use a good carpenter's level and draw a horizontal guide line across the vertical line drawn earlier. These two lines, if carefully made, will enable you to set your tile square.

In planning the layout of the tiles on the wall, you find that very often the last column of tiles, at the corner or edge of the wall, requires less than a full-width tile. The tile in this last column, for example, may be only 2 in. wide, so you must cut each tile to fit.

For the most professional looking job, however, center the tile pattern so that you don't have a full tile at the left side, for example, and 2-in. tiles at the right. Instead, cut 1 in. from the tiles at the left and 1 in. from the tiles at the right. While this means more cutting for you, it results in a better looking job.

The next step after establishing your horizontal and vertical guide lines is to put the mastic on the wall. Before you open the can of mastic, read the label; then follow the instructions exactly. You probably will be told to apply the mastic with a toothed applicator and cover 3 or 4 sq. ft. at a time. Then allow the mastic to set for 20 minutes before applying the tile. Do exactly what the label says. You'll get better results.

After the mastic has set the required time, press the first tile in place. Align it carefully with your guidelines, which you should be able to see through the mastic. Begin at the bottom of the area to be tiled, and at one corner. Lay in the entire bottom row, one tile after another.

When placing a tile on the mastic, put the bottom edge into the mastic just touching the tile beneath it and very near the tile to its right. Then sort of "snap" the tile onto the wall. Now press it into its final position, sliding it against its neighbors and seating it firmly in the mastic. Do not slide the tile more than a small fraction of an inch or you may force mastic up between the tiles. However, be certain that each tile is butted firmly against its neighbors, and that the tiles all appear straight and true. You can make adjustments now, while the mastic is still soft.

SAND THE EDGES of the cut tile smooth, using emery cloth or abrasive paper.

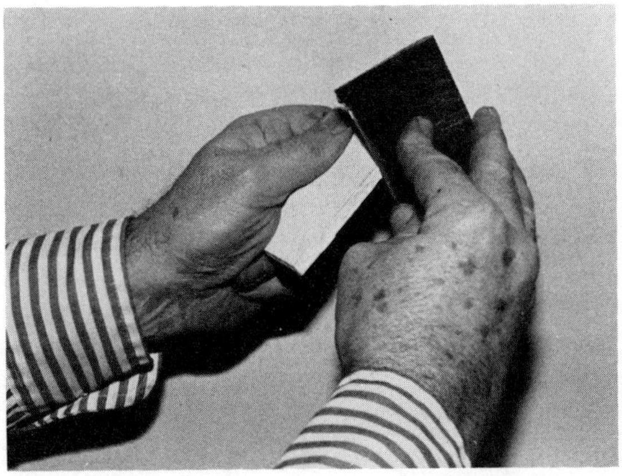

TILE NIPPERS are used to nibble away bits of the tile until you have cut to the mark.

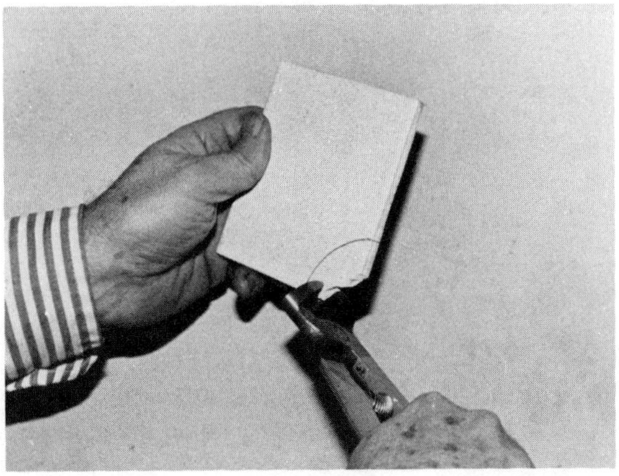

MIX THE GROUT to a creamy paste and apply it to the wall after the mastic has set for at least 24 hours. A rubber-faced grout float is used.

YOU ALSO CAN USE a cellulose sponge instead of a grout float to apply the grout. Be sure to work grout into all of the grooves.

AFTER THE GROUT has set for about 10 minutes, use the rounded end of a toothbrush handle to scrape away any excess in each of the grooves.

When all the tiles have been laid, allow the mastic to set according to the instructions. Usually, you are told not to apply the grout for at least 24 hours.

Mix the grout by adding water to make a thick, creamy mixture. Apply this mixture to the spaces between the tiles, using either a small cellulose sponge or a grout float. Work the grout down into the grooves; keep checking as you work to see that there are no unfilled spaces.

As the grout begins to harden, use the rounded end of a toothbrush handle to scrape away excess grout in each groove. The handle provides the proper concave surface to smooth the grout in each groove. After the grout has set hard, brush the entire wall with a medium-stiff brush to clean away all excess grout. Finally, spray the new grout with a silicone sealer.

In addition to the tiles already described, you can now buy real marble tiles. Made in Italy, these tiles are 6 x 6-in. slabs of genuine marble, ¼-in. thick. They come in several colors and are applied in the same way as ceramic tiles. Decorators use them for window sills, backsplashes for sinks, decoration around fireplaces, fireplace aprons, and as countertops.

Marble may stain or scratch in use, but if it does, you can restore its original beauty by polishing it. You can buy marble cleaners which remove most stains. To apply a new polished surface to scratched marble, buff the marble, using a soft polishing pad in your electric drill. Apply a paste of fine abrasive material first, then polish until the scratches disappear. For an abrasive, you can use an automobile rubbing compound, or a creamy mixture of water and pummice or rottenstone. A fine abrasive provides the brightest polish.

tile repairs

If you ever have a cracked ceramic tile—which could happen if something heavy falls against the tile sharply—you can remove the broken tile and replace it. To remove a broken tile, use a sharp-pointed tool such as an awl or ice pick to dig out the grout around it. Then insert the tool into the grout's groove and pry upward. The tile should pop off the wall without disturbing its neighbors.

Next, scrape all of the old mastic off the wall. Now apply a thin coat of mastic to the back of a new tile, no more than $^{1}/_{16}$-in. thick. Finally, press the tile in place to make good contact. After the mastic has set for at least 24 hours, apply new grout.

1 TO MANY PEOPLE this Stutz Bearcat is the symbol of the Roaring 20s. It's made of cracker tin and scraps.

2 A CANDLE in this lantern casts a playful light pattern. The lantern is two juice cans seamed together.

3 THREE-DIMENSIONAL metal plaques are easy to create and make interesting hangings.

Gems from junk

THE COUNTLESS tin cans we use each year can furnish you with an endless supply of useful metal. Here are three clever ways to recycle the empties. You should feel free to alter and embellish the designs to suit your tastes.

SEE ALSO

Candles . . . Candle stands . . . Gifts, Christmas . . . Modelmaking

Stutz Bearcat

The Stutz Bearcat is known as "The car that made good in a day." Enthusiasts say that it was

STUTZ BEARCAT

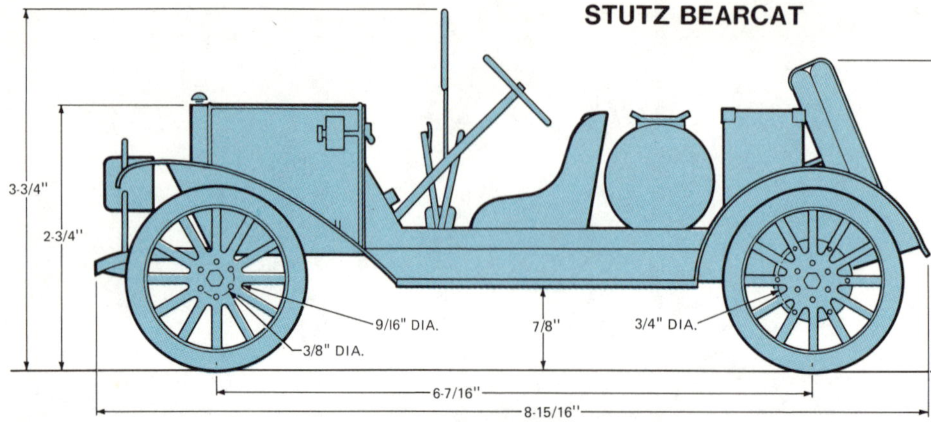

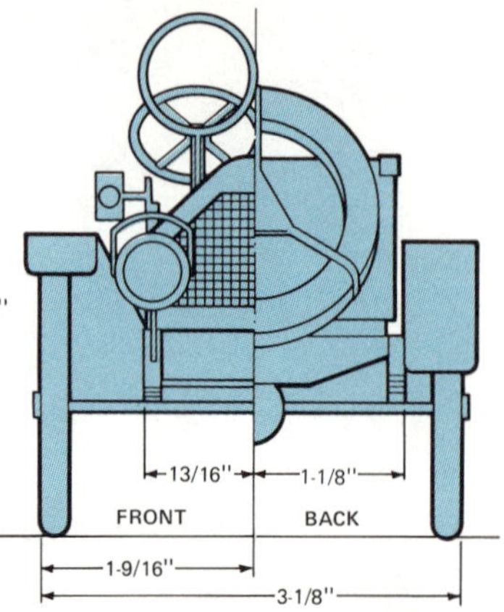

TIRES are copper tubing shaped around a dowel. Shape seven tires, keeping them tight against each other; cut and solder.

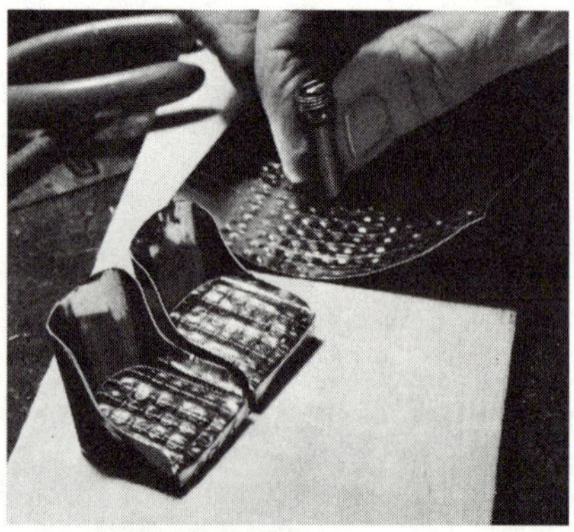

SEAT BOTTOMS and backs have textured upholstery made by scribing squares, then pressing with a punch or a stovebolt.

THE GAS TANK, tool/luggage chest and spare tires with spider are placed on the frame. The fenders are attached later.

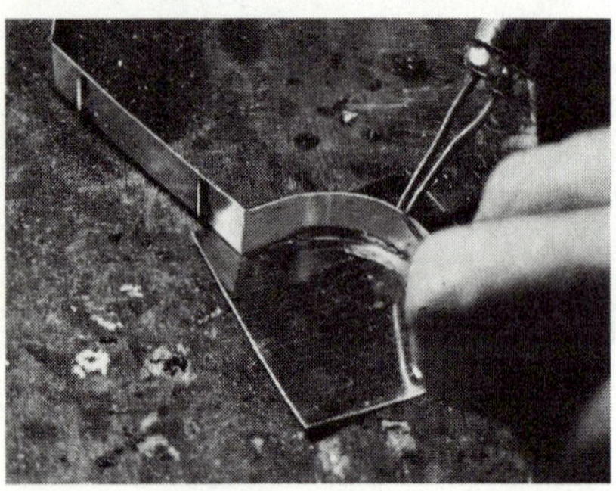

FENDER/RUNNING board is bent to shape, placed on edge and soldered to the inside mudguard. Guard will be trimmed to fit.

VIEW OF CAR'S underside shows tin transmission box and driveshaft (coat-hanger wire) soldered to the differential (a bolt).

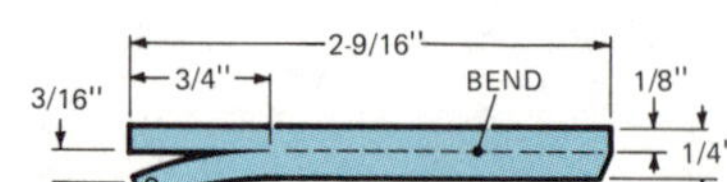

FIG. 7 – FRONT SPRING SUSPENDER (2 REQD.)

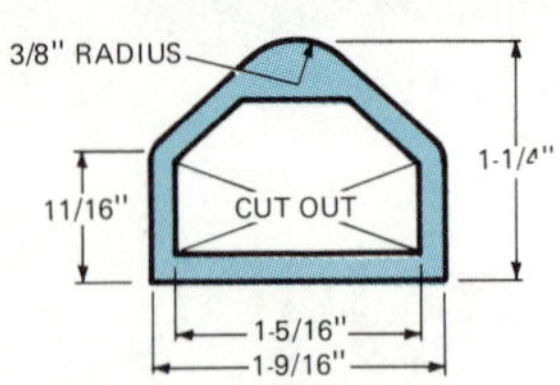

FIG. 4 – RADIATOR RIM

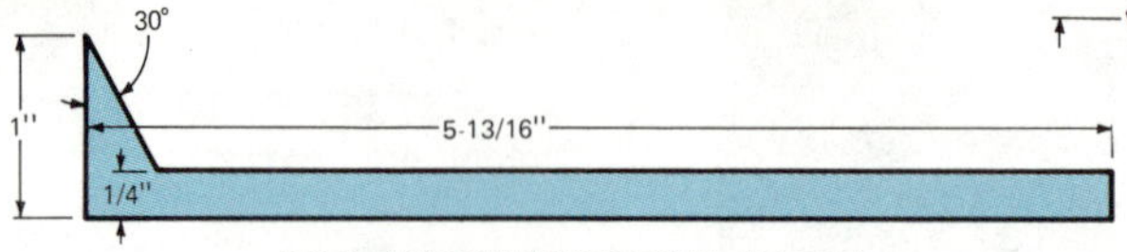

FIG. 6 – SEAT RUNNER BRACKET (2 REQD.)

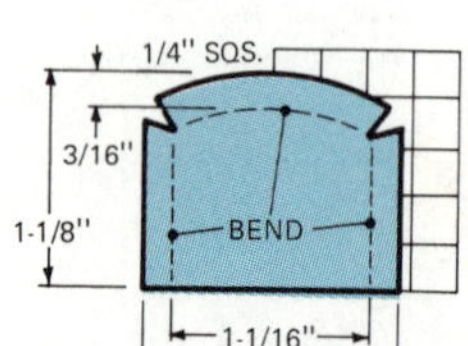

FIG. 10 – SEAT BACK CUSHION (2 REQD.)

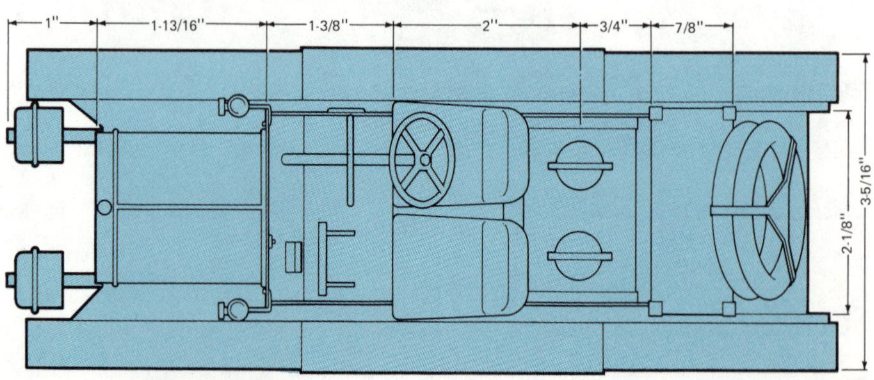

FIG. 2 – TOP VIEW

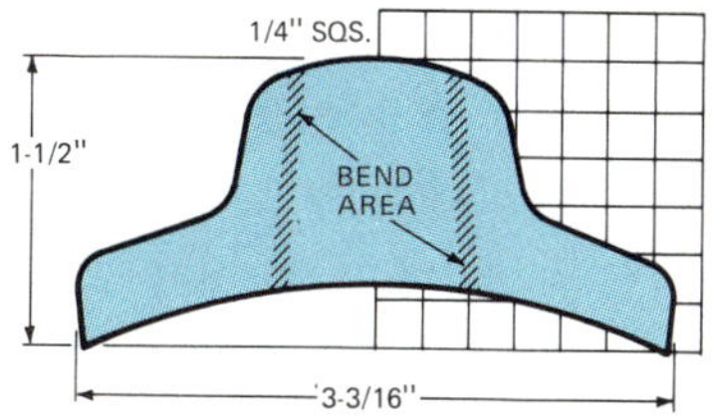

FIG. 8 – SEAT BACK AND SIDES (2 REQD.)

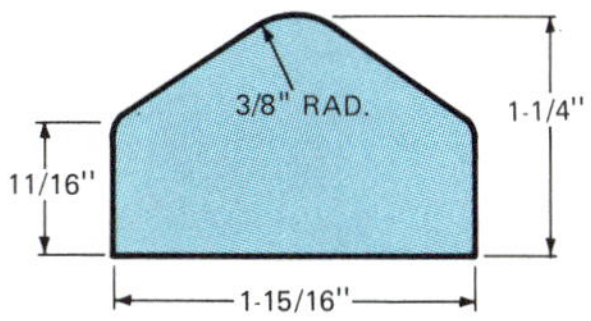

FIG. 5 – FIRE WALL

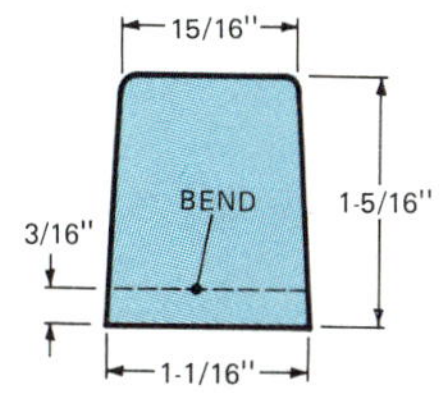

FIG. 9 – SEAT BOTTOM (2 REQD.)

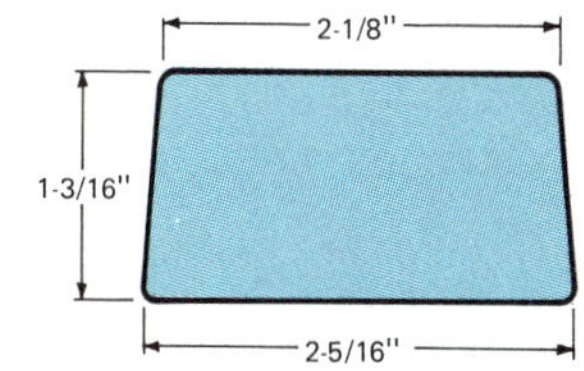

FIG. 11 – SEAT BASE FRAME

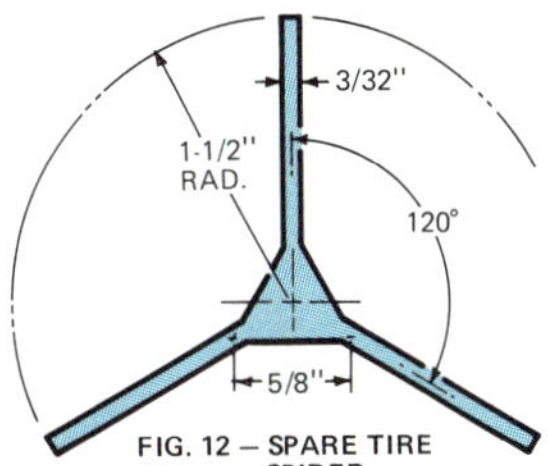

FIG. 12 – SPARE TIRE SPIDER

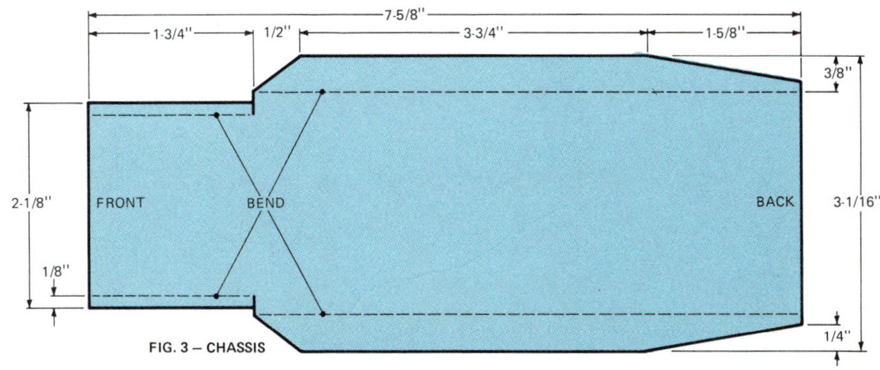

FIG. 3 – CHASSIS

and is America's greatest sports car.

This model of the 1912 Bearcat, designed by Ray Owen, is built from scraps found in your kitchen or workshop. The only special purchases we made were from the local trophy shop: small roundhead brads used as lug nuts and a scrap (2x3-in.) of 1-mm brass commonly used in making award plaques which we used to make the radiator and the gas tank caps.

Chassis and many other parts were made from a Ritz cracker tin. That particular type of tin is chosen because it's the right thickness and is already tinned inside. Seat bottoms and cushions are cut from a can of lighter metal (not aluminum) such as a soft drink can.

Other scrap materials you'll need are: 1-3/8-in.-dia. dowel to shape the tires: 3/16-in.-dia. copper gas-line tubing of the type used on power mowers for tires and parking lights; gas-line connectors for headlights; coathanger and stiff wire for attaching parts; 1/16-in.-dia. brass wire for steering wheel, wind screen, brake lever; metal window screen (not aluminum) for radiator; 1-1/8-in.-o.d. conduit for gas tank.

Decorative hardware needed includes: small hex nuts for axles, small screws for radiator cap and differential.

Tools needed are a small vise, clamps, tin snips, 250-watt (minimum) soldering iron, drill, hacksaw, hammer, small file, compass with scribe point, 3/16-in.-dia. punch or stovebolt and sandpaper.

Forming the wheels is the most complex part of the job. Secure a length of 1-3/8-in.-dia. dowel in a vise and carefully wrap seven turns of 3/16-in.-dia. copper gas-line tubing tightly around it to form the tires. Clamp the tubing in place and cut across the turns to form seven rings. Solder the ends of each together and set the six best ones aside.

Cut four strips of 1/8x4-1/2-in. cracker tin for tire rims. Insert them inside the tires, cut off the excess length and tack-solder.

With a compass, scribe only four wheels on cracker tin. (Spare tires on this model don't need wheels.) To do this, scribe concentric circles of 3/8 in., 9/16 in., 3/4 in. and 1-7/16 in. diameters for each wheel to locate, respectively, wheel lug nuts, hubs, rear lug nuts (that attach the rear-wheel brake drums) and overall spoke diameters.

Scribe the spokes by halving, quartering, then by eye-dividing each quarter into three parts. Using the 12 scribed lines as a center, mark each spoke 3/32-in. wide; cut out the wheels and spokes. Then cut the two 15/16-in.-dia. rear brake drums.

To assemble the wheels, first add the roundhead brads used as lug nuts. Clamp the brake drums on the rear wheels, bore holes as needed and solder the brads on the wheel backs. Then solder the assemblies inside the tires.

The axles are 3-5/16-in. lengths of coat-hanger wire. Remove paint from the ends with sandpaper. Bore holes in the wheel hubs; solder axles in place with hex nuts at ends.

the car body

Now the car begins to take shape. The chassis is one piece of cracker tin cut and bent as shown in Fig. 3.

To make the radiator (Fig. 4), use something thicker than cracker tin, such as a 22-ga. (about 1-mm thick) piece of brass. Cut a radiator backing of cracker tin with the same dimensions without a center cutout. Cut and sandwich screening (window screen, other than aluminum which

LANTERN

CANS are tack-welded in four spots to prevent warping, then seamed together by moving torch in small circles.

CUT SECOND of first pair of slits. Touch top rim with torch to mark slit location; turn 180° for next cuts.

AFTER SLITS are made, begin shaping cans. Position hand inside the cans and slightly push outward on struts.

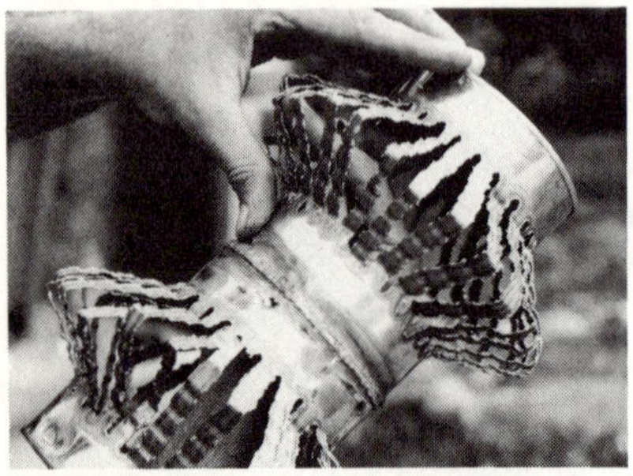

PLACE WORK on a table and bend struts farther outward; then place hand inside cylinder to finish shaping.

TOP DECORATIVE design is cut. A lighted candle under it will cast this pattern on the ceiling.

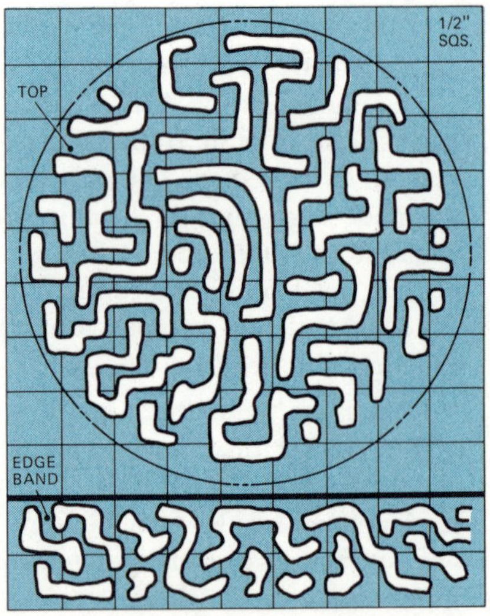

can't be soldered) in place and solder along the edges to join the pieces. Then file edges clean. Cut the firewall of cracker tin (Fig. 5).

The hood is a 1¾x3¾-in. piece of tin shaped around the radiator, trimmed and soldered to the radiator and firewall. Solder this in place, slightly overhanging the front edge of the chassis. The triangular ends of the tin seat runners (Fig. 6) are soldered against the firewall; their bottoms run along the chassis.

textured seat upholstery

Cut the seat back and sides (Fig. 8) out of cracker tin and shape the curve with your fingers.

Use thinner metal such a a soft-drink can (not aluminum) to make the seat bottoms and back (Figs. 9 and 10). Before you cut them, emboss the metal to give it an upholstery effect. Here's how: scribe ¼-in. squares, then tap the center of each square lightly with a punch. Then cut, trim and solder in place. Position on the seat base frame (Fig. 11) and solder to the chassis.

rear accessories

The big gas tank is a 1⅛-in.-o.d. conduit and the ends are tin. Filler caps are two thicknesses of brass with wire handles. Solder the tank in place (Fig. 2).

The luggage/tool chest is a simple 15/16x2-1/16-in. tin box soldered at the edges. Before you bend the tin, emboss the rivet lines. Don't forget to add corner reinforcements.

Next cut the spare tire spider (Fig. 12). Solder it to the two spare tires and position the assembly using a wire bracket.

Working on the underside of the car, cut and install the front spring suspenders (Fig. 7). Cut two front and two rear springs. To do this, cut 3/32x3-in. tin strips. Make four layers, cutting each a little shorter than the previous one and shackle together with small tin strips. Leave the top stringer long enough to make adjustments. Install the springs so the car is level.

The fender/running board is a 9/16x9½-in. tin strip. You may need another tall can to cut the pieces. Shape the two fenders (Fig. 1).

Place the strip on a piece of tin which will be a mudguard and solder. The front guards are angled to fill the space between the installed fender and the car frame. Trim to fit.

Make tin running-board reinforcements 1/8 in. wider than the fenders. Position and bend outside edges over to hide running-board hangers. These are of stiff wire that can be seen on the car's underside. Solder the hangers to the frame to align the running board and fenders. Then bend the inside mudguards over to meet the chassis piece and trim.

Attach the wheels by centering the axles on the springs and fastening them with a small shackle and solder. Axles shouldn't rotate. Add the tie rod between front wheels.

cockpit pieces

The footboard is a scrap of tin, soldered in the cockpit front along the seat bracket angle.

The big steering wheel, used before power steering, is a 1-1/16-in.-dia. circle shaped from brass wire. Cut a tin spider with four spokes; solder inside the wheel. Bore a center hole and add the steering column, a 3 1/8-in. piece of coat-hanger wire trimmed after installation. Locate the steering column position and bore a hole for it through the footboard and the chassis piece so you can insert the column; trim and solder underneath.

The windscreen is a 1-1/16-in.-dia. circle of brass wire with a piece soldered at the bottom and attached to the steering column.

The coil box is tin and the spark adjustment is a bent brad. The passenger footrest is wire.

The brake lever is brass wire and the shift lever is tin. Attach using a quadrant of wire for realism.

finishing touches

The parking lights are two 7/16-in. lengths of copper tubing with screws inserted. Attach them to the firewall with bits of brass wire.

The headlamps are gas-line fittings with wire handles. They rest on support brackets which attach through a small hole in the front spring suspender.

Add a small-screw radiator cap and wire hinges down the center of the hood. Wire also separates the hood and radiator and the hood and firewall. Add wire latches along the bottom on each side of the hood.

On the underside add a tin transmission box, a driveshaft made of coat-hanger wire, and a steering link of coat-hanger wire connected to the tie rod. The differential is a screw cut to length with the driveshaft soldered on one end and the axle soldered on the slotted head.

Spray the underside with dull black paint, then

SCULPUNCH DESIGNS

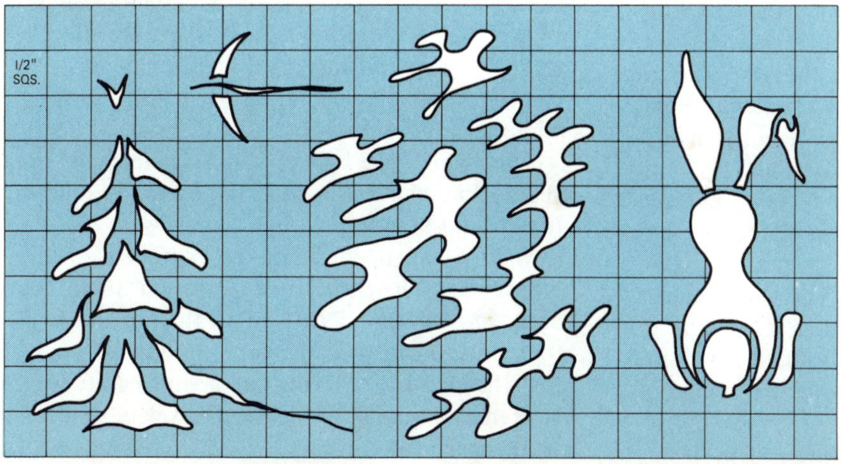

CUT RIMS from a can after slitting at the seam. Next, tack the can to plywood with the inside surface facing outward. Center and tape the pattern over the tin. Carefully outline it by punching holes with a nail or use a file ground to a point. Punch holes in background to apply texture. This also raises the figure to give it a slight three-dimensional effect.

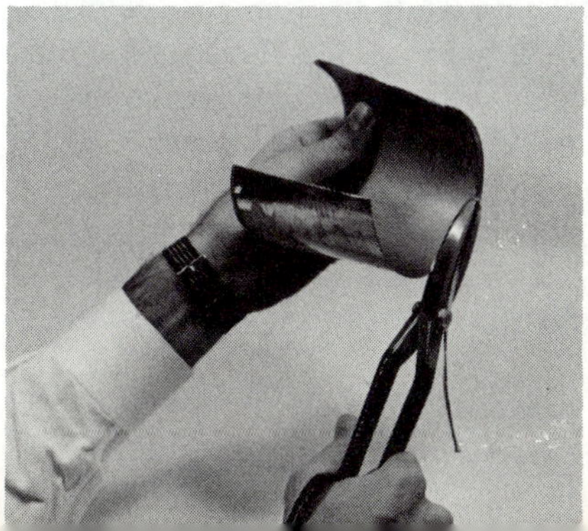

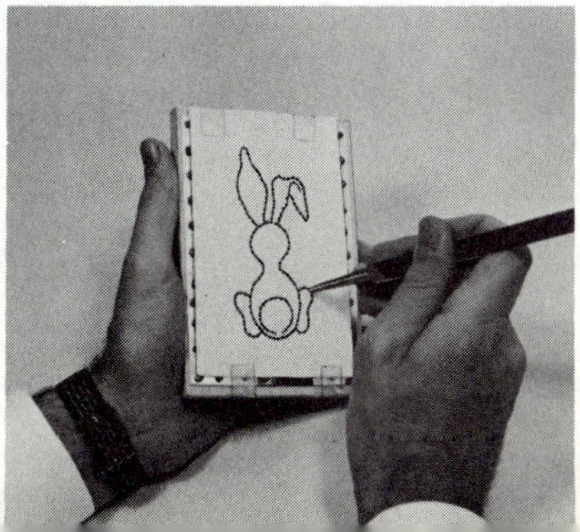

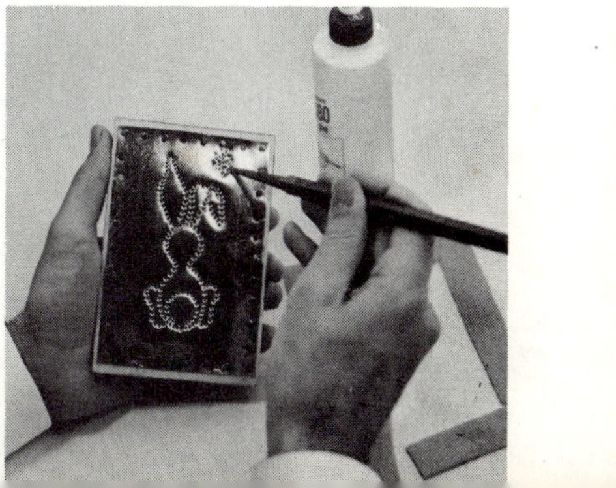

spray several coats of yellow or other color on the entire body. Barely highlight the radiator, steering wheel, seat, tank tops and tires with gold, and your model is complete.

Lantern

Two No. 5 juice cans are combined to make this lantern, designed by Charles A. Phillips. The small votive (church-type) candle placed inside it produces maximum light play on walls and ceiling.

To make the cutouts, you'll need a torch —preferably an oxygen-driven, acetylene type— which delivers enough pinpoint heat to cut a clean, thin kerf. Air-mix torches aren't hot enough. We use a No. 0 brazing tip and set both regulators at 5 lbs. The flame should have a pencil-point *sharp* blue tip, the clear part of the flame extending 6 to 8 in. Actual cutting is done about ½ in. below the blue point.

Goggles are a must for this work. A safe rule is: When the flame is on, the goggles are on. Also wear heavy shoes covered by cuffless pants, a long-sleeved shirt, hat, heavy gloves.

For maximum caution, it's best to play a fan on the cans as you work. Sometimes noxious gases are released around soldered seams and surfaces that have printing directly on them. Work outdoors or in a large, well-ventilated room.

preparing the cans

Remove any paper on the cans by cutting with one quick, vertical torch pass, and then peeling the paper off. Remove one end of each can by cutting as close as possible to the rim with a torch, or by using a can opener. If needed, shape the ends to return them to round, then place one on top of the other, open ends together.

First tack at the seam in four spots by putting the tip of the flame in between the rims and making a small circular motion to melt the material evenly so rims will fuse. If you get too near the rims, your torch will extinguish itself. Fill in between these tacks. A glove is useful here to turn and hold the hot welded can in the proper position.

Cut a slit on the top can beginning 1 in. from the top to about 1 in. from the seam between the two cans. The ridges around the can help you judge distance. On the bottom can cut a second similar slit directly below the first one, beginning 1 in. from the bottom can's top and ending 1 in. from its bottom. Then turn the cans 180° and cut similar slits. Before turning the cans, mark the slit position with a light brush of the torch on the can top directly above the top slit. After making the second pair of cuts, turn the cans 90° and make a third pair; make a fourth pair 180° from that point.

You'll have four equal sections of the cans left that you can slit as many times as you dare—but don't make slits on the vertical seams. Made six cuts between the original ones. You can also make slant cuts (not too severe or you'll have trouble flattening the cans later), wiggly lines and square or round cutouts. Then cut out the bottom.

To bend the cans, reach inside with one hand, being careful of any sharp edges. Supporting the outside with the other hand, push out each strut to slightly bend it. Then place the cans on a table and push down from the top until the struts are bowed as desired.

Draw, then cut the top and side bands in a design as shown in the plan. Cut angled slits in the middle, top and bottom bands.

Sculpunch designs

A sculpunch is a sculptured design that's made by punching tiny holes through a tin can that is flattened and nailed to a plywood backing. The designs here are by Larry Philpotts. Punching the holes creates a textured background and raises the image to give it a third dimension. Many cans have an attractive silver, gold or greenish inside surface which doesn't need a finish.

Materials you'll need include: a tin can that doesn't have ridges around its circumference; plywood of any thickness; tacks that are shorter than the plywood thickness—solid copper ones can be used as decoration—felt for framing; white glue; a hanger.

Tools you'll use include a can opener, saw, tin shears, hammer and a nail for a punch or an old file ground to a point.

With a can opener, cut the bottom from an empty can. Then use tin snips to cut along the can's vertical seam. Next cut off the top and bottom rims. Then tack the can to plywood backing—inside surface facing out—being careful not to mar its tin finish. If tacks will show in finished work, space them evenly.

To transfer the design to the tin, tape the plan, properly centered, over the tin. Then outline the design by punching through the paper. Pay special attention to subtle curves and corners.

Once the outline is completely punched, remove the paper and begin punching the background. The size of holes and distances between them are up to you.

METRIC CONVERSION

Conversion factors can be carried so far they become impractical. In cases below where an entry is exact it is followed by an asterisk (*). Where considerable rounding off has taken place, the entry is followed by a + or a - sign.

CUSTOMARY TO METRIC

Linear Measure

inches	millimeters
1/16	1.5875*
1/8	3.2
3/16	4.8
1/4	6.35*
5/16	7.9
3/8	9.5
7/16	11.1
1/2	12.7*
9/16	14.3
5/8	15.9
11/16	17.5
3/4	19.05*
13/16	20.6
7/8	22.2
15/16	23.8
1	25.4*

inches	centimeters
1	2.54*
2	5.1
3	7.6
4	10.2
5	12.7*
6	15.2
7	17.8
8	20.3
9	22.9
10	25.4*
11	27.9
12	30.5

feet	centimeters	meters
1	30.48*	.3048*
2	61	.61
3	91	.91
4	122	1.22
5	152	1.52
6	183	1.83
7	213	2.13
8	244	2.44
9	274	2.74
10	305	3.05
50	1524*	15.24*
100	3048*	30.48*

1 yard = .9144* meters
1 rod = 5.0292* meters
1 mile = 1.6 kilometers
1 nautical mile = 1.852* kilometers

Fluid Measure

(Milliliters [ml] and cubic centimeters [cc or cu cm] are equivalent, but it is customary to use milliliters for liquids.)

1 cu in = 16.39 ml
1 fl oz = 29.6 ml
1 cup = 237 ml
1 pint = 473 ml
1 quart = 946 ml
= .946 liters
1 gallon = 3785 ml
= 3.785 liters
Formula (exact):
fluid ounces × 29.573 529 562 5* = milliliters

Weights

ounces	grams
1	28.3
2	56.7
3	85
4	113
5	142
6	170
7	198
8	227
9	255
10	283
11	312
12	340
13	369
14	397
15	425
16	454

Formula (exact):
ounces × 28.349 523 125* = grams

pounds	kilograms
1	.45
2	.9
3	1.4
4	1.8
5	2.3
6	2.7
7	3.2
8	3.6
9	4.1
10	4.5

1 short ton (2000 lbs) = 907 kilograms (kg)
Formula (exact):
pounds × .453 592 37* = kilograms

Volume

1 cu in = 16.39 cubic centimeters (cc)
1 cu ft = 28 316.7 cc
1 bushel = 35 239.1 cc
1 peck = 8 809.8 cc

Area

1 sq in = 6.45 sq cm
1 sq ft = 929 sq cm
= .093 sq meters
1 sq yd = .84 sq meters
1 acre = 4 046.9 sq meters
= .404 7 hectares
1 sq mile = 2 589 988 sq meters
= 259 hectares
= 2.589 9 sq kilometers

Kitchen Measure

1 teaspoon = 4.93 milliliters (ml)
1 Tablespoon = 14.79 milliliters (ml)

Miscellaneous

1 British thermal unit (Btu) (mean) = 1 055.9 joules
1 calorie (mean) = 4.19 joules
1 horsepower = 745.7 watts
= .75 kilowatts
caliber (diameter of a firearm's bore in hundredths of an inch) = .254 millimeters (mm)
1 atmosphere pressure = 101 325* pascals (newtons per sq meter)
1 pound per square inch (psi) = 6 895 pascals
1 pound per square foot = 47.9 pascals
1 knot = 1.85 kilometers per hour
25 miles per hour = 40.2 kilometers per hour
50 miles per hour = 80.5 kilometers per hour
75 miles per hour = 120.7 kilometers per hour